MW00790344

SOLA:

*One Woman's Journey Alone
Across South America*

AMY FIELD

Copyright © 2015 by Amy Field.
All rights reserved.

WanderWomyn Publishing.
California, USA.

Cover design and map by Amy Field.

ISBN 978-0-9966264-0-8
ISBN 0996626409

For all the women who hold their breath,
dive in
and chase the unknown.

CONTENTS

PART I: COSTA RICA & PANAMA

PART II: CHILE & ARGENTINA

PART III: PARAGUAY & BRAZIL

PART IV: BOLIVIA, PERU & ECUADOR

PART V: THE RETURN TO MOONTIME

PANAMA
COSTA RICA
Quito
ECUADOR
PERU
Lima
Cusco
BOLIVIA
Lake Titicaca
La Paz
Ica
Nazca
Arequipa
Potosi
Salar de Uyuni
PARAGUAY
Asunción
Iguazu Falls
BRAZIL
Manaus
Salvador
Pantanal
Rio de Janeiro
CHILE
Valparaíso
ARGENTINA
Santiago
Buenos Aires
Pucón
Torres del Paine
Ushuaia

"Take off your watch," he said.
"We live on moontime here."

PRELUDE

That night I hardly slept. The walls dripped with perspiration while the ceiling fan pushed the warm night around on rusty blades. I lay there wondering… wondering what might happen if I did this, what might happen if I didn't, and at what specific moment over the last year I had lost all common sense.

The buzz of my travel alarm was barely distinguishable among the symphony of mosquitoes. 4 a.m. I looked out the window at last night's leftover traffic, the road in a dark world of puddle-filled stillness. And as I slid on my cargo pants and zipped up my pack, I focused on the gut feeling of yes, I gathered up what I'd never before considered courage, and I wondered what had happened over the last year to the girl who had submissively pulled on pantyhose every morning, who had had such a clear path laid out before her. And a great surge welled up inside me, and I knew there was no going back.

What had I done? What had I done…

NEW MOON...

Welcome to a place where time does not exist --
Where days melt into one another,
And every sunset is a work of art on a canvas
as big as the sky...
Where time is marked by high tide,
And every night you sit out on the beach and wonder how far
away
the stars are.
You eat when you're hungry.
You sleep when you're tired.
And you awaken to the soft sounds of the sea whispering
to the pastel dawn.

This is a place which lures people from all over the world,
Drawing souls magnetically to its core
Who belong exactly nowhere else.

This is a place where you can completely isolate yourself
in solitude from all other human beings,
Or where love affairs explode, and you can focus on no one
in the world but that person.
Where you can sit in a hammock for hours and read and
be completely inside yourself,

A place where you can begin asking the big questions in life...

This is a place where it is possible to enjoy every moment
        of every day,
To do whatever you want, as long as it makes you
        happy and healthy...
To stretch your mind and your body until they both ache.

Here, we live by the tides,
By the sunrise and sunset.
By the phases of the moon.

And somewhere
Deep in the dry jungles of the Guanacaste plains
Hidden within the boundaries of this marine reserve
Buried in the warm sands of Playa Grande,
Or far far out in the warm tropical sea
Bobbing and floating on the waves
Deep in the heart of Costa Rica's *pura vida*,
The layers fall away --
And all that is left
Is what is real,
What is essential,
What matters...

PART I:
COSTA RICA & PANAMA

THE LEAP AND THE LANDING PAD

"*Taxi, linda. Taxi?*" called the men holding paper signs, smiling sideways and guarding the airport exit to the street like gargoyles.

"I wonder who Linda is," I thought briefly as I emerged from San Jose airport, alone, dragging an army-green canvas suitcase which disobediently flopped at the end of its leash. The tropical air breathed warm and heavy with life, like a loved one bending down to softly wake me. My eyes searched anxiously, flitting from left to right and back again through the crowd. The Spanish immersion school, where I had signed up to take four weeks of classes as a gradual introduction to moving to Costa Rica, had said they would send their driver to pick me up at the airport and take me to my host family's home. And then I spotted it: "amiy Fild." A thin man with an easy smile held a hand-written paper sign, drooping at the corners from the humidity. *That must be me.*

His expectant eyes met my sigh of relief as he asked, "A-my?" the emphasis holding fast to the first syllable. He grabbed my luggage by the handle in a whir of momentum, and I was off behind him jogging toward his taxi, listening to the musical words roll from his mouth, inflection moving up and down like the wet green hills surrounding the city.

"*¿Hola, como esta usted?*" he began enunciating slowly.

"Hola," I ventured with a smile.

He hurled my bag into the trunk which compressed the car's shocks by a good two inches.

"Me llamo Lionel," he continued patiently.

Hmmm, I don't know any of those words. I'm not sure why I had been under the impression that despite having never spoken a word of Spanish in my life that I would be able to basically communicate and live in this new country based solely on two factors: 1) that I had been fluent in French a very long time ago, and 2) that I simply willed it -- I wanted it more than anything.

The driver rescued me with a resplendent display of charades, an index finger firmly poking himself in the chest.

"Lionel," he said.

I nodded in understanding and introduced myself in turn.

Lionel carried on in a mixture of Spanish and English for the next half hour as we swerved and dodged and passed other vehicles on our way toward the center of the city. The only Spanish word I understood within the soliloquy was *quiero,* as in *Yo quiero Taco Bell,* the immortal words of a well-marketed Chihuahua. I gazed out the window at the billboards whizzing by, trying not to think too hard, trying to calm the ever-growing anxiety that was climbing up from the pit of my stomach into my throat regarding the major life turn I had somewhat spontaneously made. And as we turned off the highway, the brightly-painted shops in reds and yellows sat side-by-side with homes surrounded by eight-foot-high iron fences and bars across the windows, and I wondered if my sense of foreboding was warranted.

Lionel opened my door for me and said that we had arrived at *la casa de la familia,* the Durante-Calvo home.

Then, in a final aside, he mentioned, "Daisy speaks no English."

Gulp. I reassured him that it was better this way, but I was relatively sure he saw the apprehension in my face. Well, I had signed on for immersion; now that I had taken the leap, all I had to do was keep from falling…

Lionel rang the doorbell as I hovered behind him, and a woman in her mid-fifties with fluffy brown hair opened the door and reached for me with soft hands and a kiss on the cheek. She motioned for us to come inside what was to be my home for the next month.   Her elderly husband, Pascual, purposefully massaged his twisted left hand from a threadbare green velvet armchair in the corner of the front room.   He greeted us cheerfully, explaining through Lionel that he had recently had a stroke and apologized for not being able to get up. And then, as quickly as he had appeared, I watched Lionel, my last thin strand of the English language, disappear into the bustling afternoon traffic. "I'll see you on Monday," he shouted from the car.   It was Friday afternoon.

***

My grand plan, when I'd arranged my immersion language school program, was to arrive in Costa Rica a few days early to get settled. Why it hadn't occurred to me that if I arrived on Friday and school didn't start until Monday that I couldn't communicate with a single soul, I do not know. I suppose I was so anxious to move beyond my carefully-planned-to-the-every-detail self, and I was so focused on getting on the plane before I could think myself out of it, that I had blocked out that set of normally-obvious details. But it was that kind of naiveté and disregard for possible consequence that got me through the first few months. *Don't think too hard, Amy. Just see what happens.*

On that first day, I still had the travel-weary in me, and as Daisy and I sat in silence, exchanging smiles atop the stiff couch decorated lovingly with doilies, interaction soon demanded too much energy.   I pressed my hands together and lifted them toward my tilted cheek. Daisy rose to lead me to my room where a single bed stood on a creaky antique frame below a window to the street trimmed with steel bars and lace curtains. She smiled and closed the door softly behind her, and I gratefully plunked down and laid my head atop an uneven pillow from which wafted a familiar homey smell: mildew.

The sneezing began immediately and with full force. One sneeze grew into two, grew into ten, grew into twenty by the time I was able to slide a T-shirt over the pillowcase. I braced myself for the next explosion, but the tension in my body dissipated as I fell into a snuggle of bed ruffles and drifted slowly into the solace of sleep, the newness and challenges of my uncharted world gradually fading away.

***

The sun was low in the sky when Daisy awakened me. *"Amy..."* came the familiar sound of my name as I swam up through the depths of dreams, taking a few perplexed moments to remember where I was. She asked if I'd like to go to the grocery store with her and offered me a glass of lemonade. My mind rewound to the warnings, the long list of *don't-s* that family and friends felt compelled to supply before my departure. *Don't drink the water.* But here I was, dehydrated from the plane ride and sauna-like climate, with no bottled water in sight. I had to drink *something.* So as Daisy led me to the kitchen, and I watched her cut a lemon in half and squeeze its juice into a tall glass of tap water adding a shovel of sugar, I smiled... And I prayed to my little travel god, and I crossed my sweaty fingers, and I hoped for best.

I found my way back to this three-step ritual again and again as I explored life on my own over the next few years, away from what I knew, and away from the illusion that life was under my control. Eventually, I loosened my stranglehold on believing that I could govern everything that went on around me, and the funny thing was that when I let go a little, things seemed to turn out better. It took a long time before I could let my journey steer me, rather than vice-versa, and look for opportunities rather than certainties. But on that first afternoon in Costa Rica, that first hope-for-the-best mantra was set in motion by a glass of lemonade made by a sweet little grandmother. Perhaps no gentler introduction exists.

As Daisy and I walked out the front gate down the wildly untamed sidewalk, Swiss-cheese with holes, covered in loose metal plates, and flanked by gutters nearly four-feet deep, I learned to look down while I walked, no matter what fascinating scenery I passed by. The sky hung low over the neighborhood of Vargas Araya, sun peeking through thick patchy storm clouds and creating humid-warm and crispy-winter all at once.

Daisy held my hand as we crossed the densely trafficked street, and although I felt vaguely like a five-year-old, I was grateful to have successfully reached the other side with the veteran's help. Despite having crossed in what appeared to me to resemble a crosswalk, we as pedestrians seemed little more than a nuisance for veering compact cars and the screeching brakes of buses.

As we turned corner after corner of unmarked streets, Daisy enthusiastically pointed out landmarks with the confidence that I would soon be able to return home on my own after I started school. Unfortunately, as a directionally-challenged American, the Costa Rican version of directions would prove particularly difficult. There were no street signs. There were no numbered addresses. Instead, directions are given based on landmarks. For example, something might be located 200 meters north of the hospital. Or 25 meters west of the university. Daisy lived at 50 meters east of the Tele-Video store. Years later when I wrote that address on an envelope to send her a birthday card or a photo, I still laughed at how strange it had all once seemed.

On that day, I was seeing the neighborhood of Vargas Araya for the first time. We passed every building ending in –ería. *Panadería. Carnecería. Ferretería. Peluqería.* And as we rounded another unmemorable corner, there towered a massive concrete building topped by four giant red letters. Palí. It was one of the biggest supermarkets in the area and reminded me a bit of a Costco warehouse with its high ceilings and unpainted walls of long shelves filled with large cardboard boxes. Women dragged whining children by their arms down the rows of merchandise and scolded them with "no" in the sweets aisle. By the end of the trip, we had oil, tomato sauce, sugar, meat, milk and a few sizable papayas. Although I had written on my language school application that I was a vegetarian, I had no way to explain this to Daisy now that I was here. *Hope for the best…*

Daisy muscled the heavy grocery bags toward home, and I trotted faithfully behind holding the ice cream cone she had bought me. Then I noticed it had stopped dripping. The air got very still, and the sky got very dark like someone had pulled down the window-shade and sucked away all the shadows. The wind came up, and then all at once, lightening cracked, thunder rumbled, and the sky opened. A torrential deluge fell out of what had only moments ago been a sunny sky, and although Daisy quickened her pace, she seemed unmoved by the apocalyptic event. In three minutes flat, the streets had been transformed into rushing rivers now overflowing their four-foot gutters, spilling over sidewalks and rising up driveways just short of residential living rooms. My mouth agape, I continued on at a canter, and although the outdoor crowd dwindled, they seemed mightily unimpressed. I guess it was just a regular day in the rainy season in San Jose.

***

That night, under the pitterpatter of jellybean-sized raindrops hitting the roof, Daisy made spaghetti. I wondered about the authenticity of my first Costa Rican meal until Daisy's son, Marco, arrived home to enlighten me. As a college graduate and union lawyer, Marco spoke excellent English and was my savior that night (although I had to remind myself not to become too dependent on him). And as we all sat down to dinner together, we talked and laughed and he told me the short version of the great love story of Daisy and Pascual.

Pascual, Marco's father, was actually Italian, and he had come to Costa Rica at the age of twenty-four, the same age I was now. Pascual met and fell madly in love with a beautiful Tica named Daisy and decided to stay. They started a life together, and a family. That was almost fifty years ago. And *that* is why the Durante-Calvo family ate so much spaghetti.

I wondered about Pascual's tale long after the animated narration had stopped. *What had made him come? What had drawn him here to Costa Rica from so many thousand miles away? What had he been looking for? Had he been scared? Had he been alone? Had he known on the day he left home that he would be changing his life forever?*

It was hard to see that sparkling young man in Pascual's tired eyes now. The seventy-two-year-old had lost most of the use of his left side of his body during a stroke, and he spoke in slow effortful slurs. But there was an intense unquestionable love and bond that he shared with the woman who sat across the table from him, the woman who cut his meat, and helped him with his physical therapy exercises, and helped him in and out of bed every night, and teased him, and laughed with him, and talked with him. And as Marco proudly retold his father's story that night over spaghetti dinner, I saw a dim flicker for the passion of his youth in Pascual's eyes, even if his wanderlust had long faded away.

A VERY LONG WEEKEND

"Without willing it, I had gone from being ignorant of being ignorant, to being aware of being aware. And the worst part of my awareness was that I didn't know what I was aware of. I knew I knew very little, but I was certain that the things I had yet to learn wouldn't be taught to me at George Washington High School." I Know Why the Caged Bird Sings, *by Maya Angelou*

The next morning was Saturday. My eyes still closed, I listened to the soft murmurs I couldn't understand and to the pots and pans clanking in the kitchen like the pancake mornings of my childhood. But when I opened my eyes, the morning light came flooding in, and I remembered.

I'm here. I did it. I should be scared out of my mind, but I'm not. I can do this. This is easy. I jumped out of bed and opened the door. Costa Rica was waiting.

"*Buenos Dias,*" Daisy enunciated, turning away from the stove toward me with a wide grin.

"*Buenos Dias,*" I ventured, feeling relieved to be rested and feeling grateful to have awakened in such a comfortable loving home.

"*Café?*" she asked as she pointed to a mug filled with the dark nectar of the morning, its aroma wafting up to greet me.

I nodded.

"Leche?" she asked, pointing to the pitcher of thick milk.

"Sí. Gracias."

We sat down at the table to a plate of the most delicious pineapple, watermelon and papaya slices I'd ever laid eyes on, their deep colors glimmering in a pool of sweet juices. I later discovered the fruit that costs a fortune at home was an everyday affair in Costa Rica. When people wanted to have a real treat for a special occasion like Christmas, they would pay top dollar for mealy Red Delicious apples.

Daisy sat down with me, chatting away, pausing and using her one-word point-to-it method when she really wanted me to understand. I nodded and gulped and slurped until I heard her say, "OK?"

OK what? I wondered.

"Doce, doce," she said.

Hmmm, I thought, *That sounds a lot of like the number two, which I thought was* dos *based on my years of* Sesame Street *viewing.*

Daisy then tried the pantomime technique. *"Doce"* she said, and then she whistled and pointed out the door, and drove a little imaginary steering wheel.

OK, I thought, *we must be going somewhere at "doce." I'll be ready at 2:00.*

With my breakfast finished and my translation reserves exhausted once more, I went back to my room to unpack, looking forward to a lazy half-day of nursing my jet-lag, resting and studying my phrasebook.

About an hour later, there was a knock at my door, which then opened to reveal a smiling Daisy wearing a bold print dress. "OK," she said.

OK what? I thought. I looked at the clock. It was five minutes after twelve.

She did her whistling gesture again with the steering wheel, and I figured that meant it was time to go.

I threw on the only dress I'd brought, a respectable floral number that fell to mid-calf and went outside to see the whole family waiting in the car. Marco explained that the excursion, which happened once a year, was a family reunion in the nearby city of Cartago where Daisy grew up. As the engine of the tiny car fired up, *la familia* blessed themselves in unison, and my anticipation and excitement accelerated.

And that's how I learned that *doce* means twelve, not two.

***

Five weeks before learning what *doce* meant, I had awakened one morning in my apartment in Los Angeles, California, and I had admitted to myself that I was unhappy. I didn't know why. Everything had seemed to be going so right. I had graduated summa cum laude from a prestigious liberal arts college. I worked at a job in Downtown L.A. where I regularly wore a linen business suit. I was studying for graduate school entrance exams. My family was healthy, I had good friends, I was casually dating. So why had it gotten harder and harder to get out of bed each morning? And why were my dreams getting worse?

Over the previous few months, I had been dreaming that I was suffocating -- that I was being strangled. And I would wake up, choking, and I couldn't breathe. Every night.

It seems painfully obvious now, almost poetically so. But at the time, I wrote it off to normal stress. That is, until it escalated. I started getting hives. The dreams got worse. More severe, more frequent, until they verged on panic attacks.

I started keeping a journal. And once I'd written it all down over the course of some months, it was much clearer to look at, like reading someone else's story in black and white.

So I decided to change my life. That is, I decided to slightly and temporarily alter my life in a very safe very limited-scope kind of way. I would learn Spanish; that would help my business school applications (notice the justification toward contribution to forward-moving path), and I would move to Latin America to do it.

To choose my specific destination, I went to the local travel bookstore, found the guidebook shelf, and observed that this place called Costa Rica had the most books written about it. *That must mean people go there. And look, there are some pretty pictures. That looks good.*

O.K. I would go to language school to help get me started. I had enough money to afford four weeks. Then I would get a job teaching English in the capital and let immersion take its course. I would stay in Costa Rica for six months, after which a close friend from college would come down and meet me. Together we would move to Buenos Aires and become Bohemians and round out one year abroad. *That* was the plan.

And I had to hurry up and do it before I actually thought about the significance of it all and convinced myself that I was crazy because it was neither logical nor well-planned-out (like every other step in my life had been), and I went to a nearby student travel agency, and I bought a ticket. Departure date: three weeks from decision day.

Telling my parents was daunting, and they told me later that even as they had driven me to the airport, they had thought, "She'll last two weeks."

Actually, I lasted about five minutes. I boarded that plane, teary-eyed but strong and determined, waving goodbye across the pre-Homeland-Security terminal to my loved ones. And the moment I sat down, panic set in. *What have I done? I was just kidding. Really. I don't actually want to go. Let me off! Let me off this plane!*

But what came out of my mouth was the well-behaved silence of a well-raised girl, and my bottom stayed pressed to that seat, and by virtue of no technical difficulties, that plane delivered me to Costa Rica whether I had wanted to go or not. And I was convinced that I should at least see it through for a week. Then a month. Then the plan went all screwy, but that was much, much later...

***

After Lionel dropped me off, I began what I will always think of as the "very long weekend." I could not speak words to anyone I actually wanted to communicate with, and yet these people were charged with my care. Amazingly, I still woke up every morning, ate with the family at mealtime, participated in family excursions, and gained my first impressions of the city. All without words. All in an environment where people smiled back at me, patiently and painstakingly pantomiming critical information, never throwing their hands up in frustration. The leap, the entrance into a new culture, is always full of newness, but the transition into life here was a soft one, having landed in the gentleness of Mama Daisy's lap. Had I chosen a different place, at a different time, things may not have been so gentle.

During the "very long weekend," I hid in my room a lot. It all seemed so overwhelming, like it took colossal effort to do so little, but strangely, if I persevered, it seemed to turn out all right -- all except for "the electrocutor."

***

I stood there amongst the mysteries of my bathroom, and I stared hardest at the shower. It still looked pretty scary to me. Loose wires, red and green and yellow and black, some with uncovered silver wiry ends, hung out of a large round device which sat atop the showerhead. Its purpose was to heat up the water as it came up through the pipe since most houses in Costa Rica didn't have water heaters. I called it "the electrocutor."

On that first day, Daisy had shown me how to use it. She had turned on the water, and stuck her hand in the stream, and I had stuck my hand in there, too, and it had been warm. But when I tried to use it the next day, it was cold. She said, "*No problema*;" she would bring the plumber or electrician or whoever she called. And in a few hours, he came out. He looked at it, I confirmed that Plumber's Crack was a cross-cultural phenomenon, he fiddled, and then pronounced that the shower was OK.

So the next day, I looked up at the wires, put on my rubber shower shoes, took my life into my own hands once again, and turned the handle. Water came out. And it was cold. The idea of a cold shower on that rainy dark day didn't appeal to me, so I got out to think about things and decided to take a pee. I flushed the toilet, then mustered up my courage to suck it up and get back in the shower, and when I stepped into the stream of water, it was warm!

Crazy. But wonderful. I hastily soaped up, and after about a minute, BAM-O, it was cold again. *Hmmmm.* My little brain started working. *I wonder...*

So I got out, and flushed the toilet again. And the shower got warm. *Success!* Soap, soap, wash, wash, then the toilet stopped running, then COLD. Jumped out, flushed again, warm. So I kept flushing and showering until I had washed my hair. Three days later, I realized the temperature of the water depended on the drop in water pressure that the flushing had *caused*, and not the actual flushing of the toilet. But after that, I had "the electrocutor" all figured out.

***

On Monday, I finally started language immersion school. I was so excited to break the code of what had been going on around me. And very unlike myself (the first of many incidents where I came to know my very-unlike-myself self), I overslept. In my own defense, I think this had something to do with yet another misunderstanding about numbers and time, and I thought that I'd better learn them soon, or I'd better get Daisy to start setting my alarm clock for me.

Anyway, Marco drove me to school which was good because I didn't arrive too late *and* because I had been terrified of getting lost taking the bus. He drove me along the route the bus traveled and showed me again where to get on and off.

When I arrived at the Costa Rican Language and Dance Academy, I was still a half-hour late. I had a brief conference with the director:

"How much Spanish have you had?"

"None. I mean, a little. I mean, since Friday."

"Follow me."

She walked me to a beginner's class and plunked me down in silence. My teacher, Manuel, who spoke *only* Spanish and no English, caught me up on the thirty minutes of class I'd missed by asking me the questions on page one of our workbook.

"*¿Como se llama?*"

"*¿Donde vive?*" (etc.)

As I answered, I looked around and smiled tentatively at my classmates who had strange looks on their faces. As it turned out, the class which was for beginners who had never spoken Spanish in their lives, had just completed the same exercise that the teacher had done verbally with me, and no one had known *any* of the answers. And I had known *all* of the answers. And I felt a little awkward. But moreover, during the long weekend, something had found its way in. And I started to wonder if there wasn't something to this concept called immersion.

PURA VIDA

On Wednesday, I walked timidly into my first salsa class, a free elective offered by the language school, and I found only one person in the room. And she was dancing. Alone. Without music. And when she turned around and saw that I had been watching her, she smiled and just kept dancing.

Eveline was a free spirit, radiating enthusiasm without inhibition, and on that day, she had channeled a Latin sway into her disciplined Swiss-German hips. Eveline made me unafraid.

She claimed that she didn't speak much English, but that didn't stop her from using the 35 words she did know to describe everything in her world illustratively and imaginatively. She spoke English the way I spoke Spanish. We communicated in the same caveman-like ways, peppered with charades and slathered with short awkward silences as the listener guessed what the speaker might be trying to say and filled in the answers like a contestant on *$25,000 Pyramid*. I loved Eveline because it was easy to be with her. She became a wonderful friend, and I was grateful for her lightness and positivity in an unfamiliar world full of daily challenges.

Eveline was studying in Costa Rica while on sabbatical from culinary school at home in Switzerland. Her specialty was breads. That girl could go on and on about braided bread and honey bread and wheat bread, sourdough bread with crispy crust and rolls as soft and puffy as clouds. And as she spoke, the poor woman's deprived mouth watered, drooling out at the corners; you could almost see the cobblestone street leading up to her home bakery, shelves bursting with golden brown delights that tickled every olfactory cell. And now, living in a land of sliced *Bimbo* Wonderbread, she was clearly suffering from withdrawal.

Eveline loved to tell stories. And she was hilarious. She had recently broken-up with her boyfriend from whom she had often been separated for months at a time because of his work. When I asked what he did, she said, "He was a semen."

She had probably meant that he was a sailor, but her way of putting it seemed far closer to a universal truth.

In our great quest for language acquisition, Eveline even managed to teach me a few Swiss-German words. My favorite was *knackarsch*. I used it every time I could. To the best of my understanding, it's a slang description of a young man's perfect bum. I loved how she explained that it incorporated onomatopoeia to recreate the sound made when biting into a hard crisp apple. And as I practiced my newly-acquired word by pointing at passerby's backsides, Eveline would feign surprise, clasp her hand to her mouth in disbelief, and then agree, complimenting me for being such a quick study.

After a few weeks she asked me if I had any plans once I completed language school, and I was thrilled to discover that she, too, wanted to travel around Costa Rica for a few weeks before Christmas. We decided to travel together and then join up with some other girls from school who were planning a trip to Panama. All I had left to do was master the Spanish language.

***

And so, the days passed. Language school went on. I learned to salsa. I learned some verbs. I learned to throw the T.P. in the waste-basket instead of the toilet, and I learned what time of day to shower in the "electrocutor" so the water pressure was uninterrupted. I learned that in Daisy's home, broccoli was served cold, or battered-in-egg deep-fried and *then* served cold. And I learned that if I didn't like something (like cold deep-fried broccoli), it just would show up the next day for leftovers anyway, so I might as well eat it the first time around.

I watched dubbed cornball TV nightly with the family, picking up vocabulary from reruns of *Mr. Ed* and *Fresh Prince of Bel Aire*. I loved how the family sat together, holding hands, sitting close, chatting above the show's dialogue.

Pascual's favorite program was *Little House on the Prairie* dubbed in Spanish. One night, we were all watching the episode where the house is on fire, and Mary (the blind sister) is trapped inside. I looked over, and Pascual was crying! Marco spotted him, pointed at his aged father and screamed with delight. Soon, Marco and Daisy were teasing Pascual mercilessly, and as he shooed them away and joined in their laughter, it left me feeling that where I came from, I could not imagine a grown man crying unapologetically in his crowded living room over a bad rerun.

***

More time passed. I got on the wrong bus. I got on the right bus and forgot where my stop was. But generally, I was making it to and from school without incident.

The city buses fascinated me. They were retired yellow school buses, each individually decorated, each with paper signs taped to the inside of the front windshield telling you where they were going and how much they cost. Each driver took pride in personalizing his bus with stickers, garlands of plastic flowers, strings of velvet pompoms and various Mary and Jesus plastic statuettes dancing atop the dashboard. Some even sported creative modifications such as replacing the floor mount for the driver's seat with a giant spring to reduce impact on the driver's *knackarsch*. And as the bus slowed (rarely to a stop), people would jump on, and I'd listen for the jingle of various-sized coins dropping into the driver's hand as he made change by feel without taking his eyes off the road.

Life on the bus gives you a meditative space. Culture is there all around you: the grandness of the National Theater with its bronze-blue operatic arches weathered by decades of rainy season, the street markets with vendors selling avocados from cardboard boxes and sticky-sweet fly-covered mangos from atop wooden stands. But inside the bus, you are protected in a safety zone, an observer until you choose to step off onto the road and become a participant once again.

I loved to stare out the window on my way to school, sometimes thinking about how I was feeling living abroad. It surprised me that for the first few weeks I didn't feel much different at all. My emotions had been mild. I had leaped, I had landed, and I felt almost like I was waiting for the other shoe to drop, waiting for something to seem hard, or exciting, or excruciating -- but it didn't. I guess I always thought the transition would be sudden, violent, during that first month in San Jose, but it felt more like a little love pat on the bum, pushing me gently forward. *That's good, all right, come on now...*

But occasionally, I'd have a rush, a flush, a *what-the-hell-am-I-doing* moment. Those times were more often sparked by overload from language learning than anything else. As I watched my progress dip and peak and drop again over the weeks, it was easy to become overwhelmed and discouraged. *Would I* ever *learn Spanish?* I eventually came to accept that this non-linear learning was part of a natural cycle, and three wise words floated in. *Everything is relative.* I spoke a lot of Spanish. I spoke a little. I understood a lot of Spanish. I understood a little. Really, it depended on who I was talking to. It depended on the day. It depended on how I felt. And eventually, I began to ease up a bit on the rigorous demands I had placed on myself to master the Spanish language in four weeks.

***

The mornings in San Jose, even in the rainy season, were dependably gorgeous -- clear and crisp and sunny, a fresh breath before the rainy humid afternoon set in. It was hard to believe that I had already spent almost a month living there. I sat down with Daisy over breakfast and told her in my own basic Spanish words that I planned to travel through Costa Rica and Panama once language school was over. I asked her if maybe I could come back to San Jose to spend Christmas with her. She answered *mucho gusto* and hugged me warmly, telling me that it would make her very happy to be my family for this *Navidad*, on the first Christmas I could not spend with my own.

As I got into the car with the family for our last Sunday drive together (their insistence to cross themselves when starting the engine still left me feeling uneasy), I sat back and watched the well-earned lines in Daisy's face, the laughing and joking and love between all family members.   People here seemed more expressive, more loving, more sad, more open-hearted, more moved. More generous, more vulnerable. More... It was so different from the armor-shielded culture that grew me up. And with this family, I felt like I was part of something -- that I was loved here, even so far away from my own home, and it had all happened in such a short time.

It's funny how you're told little wisdoms all your life, but until you're ready to hear them, they just float by. Sometimes though, there are moments when they come echoing back, when you finally have the experience to know what these widsoms really mean, not just as words of advice but as words for living more richly. Traveling seemed to provoke those lucid moments for me. And as I sat in that car watching those beautiful people, I thought about how it wasn't where I was, or what I was doing that made life feel wonderful. It was the stopping and watching and observing of small details, and the luxury of actually having the time to do that. *Why might something so basic have seemed before like such a luxury?*

An excited electric feeling pumped through me, a feeling that I was running toward something new and wonderful, even if I wasn't sure what it was. The prospect of discovery, of new observations, of learning. And that take-a-deep-breath feeling that comes from appreciating the simple and the beautiful.

And I realized then, that's what it meant -- *Pura Vida!* The Costa Rican's signature expression. Literally translated as "Pure Life," it encompasses everything that is beautiful, everything that is good, everything that does not cause worry, everything that keeps you living in the moment. It is about embracing life. Every moment of it. And I concentrated hard then, feeling it, remembering it, so that I could carry it with me, wherever I went.

CARIBBEAN TO THE PACIFIC

There are some nights you never forget, some nights so powerful that emotion rushes through you all mixed up. Some nights you'll look back on when you've earned your laugh lines, and you'll smile to yourself at the vividness of your memory and with disbelief that you actually got to live that moment. This was one of those nights.

I can still feel the hatchling in my hand, velvety-soft and covered with sand. At first a little stunned, suddenly it began scurrying scurrying as fast as it could. *I need to get to sea*, its little voice told it, imprinted by millions of years of prehistoric genetics. My sensory memory of touch changed forever as its tiny front flippers pushed softly, determinedly, against my skin. There it wriggled, cupped loosely in the palm of my hand, head to tail... A perfect mirror of its more familiar adult self, shrunken yet totally complete.

Eveline and I stood motionless on the dark beach as a canopy of stars hung sparkling in the jungle sky. No moon, and yet somehow in total darkness, Hugo, our guide, had spotted baby turtle tracks in the sand. He went right to the hole where the mother had laid her nest of 100 eggs two months before, high on the beach near the tide line, and he dug...

The fresh tracks indicated that this was the day these turtlettes had hatched from their leathery eggshells, crawled out through two vertical feet of sand, and flip-flopped their way down the beach to the sea. The hole should have been empty, but... Hugo smiled, his hand deep in the sand, and carefully pulled out the last baby turtle. All its brothers and sisters had made it out, but this one had been on the bottom of the pile and probably wouldn't have made it. Hugo placed the baby in my hand. *Won't I hurt it? Can I really touch it? Isn't it supposed to do this all on its own?*

Hugo was brilliant with wildlife, having acquired a balance of deep appreciation for animals and a realistic view of their lifecycle in a harsh natural environment. Many years ago, turtles had been a viable food-source for the few people who lived here, but as the human population grew, that resource became strained and in short supply. The turtles became rare, greed took over, and turtle eggs became a delicacy, their adult shells prizes. Hugo had lived all his life on the Caribbean side of Costa Rica, walking these beaches when poaching of eggs and slaughtering of nesting turtles was common. But all of that had changed in recent years; the Giant Green Sea Turtle nesting ground here in Tortuguero was protected by law, and poachers could be prosecuted. However, there were not enough rangers to patrol all areas of the many kilometers of beach, and so not all poachers could be caught. Guides like Hugo escorted visitors on turtle walks to raise awareness, to increase a vigilant presence on the beach, and to make a living in an environmentally-sound way.

Hugo told us that of the 100 eggs that a mama turtle lays in her nest, only one baby will reach adulthood. Predation and poachers take the rest. He assured us that it was OK to touch this baby turtle; in his opinion, we had given it a second chance by digging it out, and maybe it would grow up to be one of the lucky ones. Gently, I set it down and watched it take tiny leaps with its front flippers, making tracks in the soft sand until it reached the water's edge and finally swam away into the darkness.

***

That night, Eveline and I felt a lifetime away from San Jose, but in fact our trip to Tortuguero, far on the reaches of Costa Rica's northern Caribbean coast, was only about a seven-hour bus trip. Having both completed our language courses and now armed with an excellent set of survival-Spanish skills, we had excitedly headed out to explore the diverse beauty that is Costa Rica.

Even the journey to Tortuguero had been memorable. As we got off the bus, Hugo introduced himself as our guide and led us to a small motorboat. Moments later we were gliding through winding canals, trees towering straight up into the sky, ferns bending down to touch the muddy waters just like illustrations come alive from *Where The Wild Things Are*. We floated through a menagerie of animals big and small as Hugo expertly detected their camouflage and pointed them out to our inexperienced eyes. An orange-and-green iguana clung with needle-like claws to the top branches of a tree while a hulking black water buffalo looked up lazily from drinking at the water's edge, its head laden with heavy arcing horns. Monkeys danced from high-wire vines, Capuchins and Spider monkeys and Howlers, shaking leaves loose that floated slowly downward like tiny green parachutes in the still jungle air. And as our boat glided slowly by, a twelve-foot-long crocodile slid silently off the sunny bank into the water and disappeared into the gloom.

When we arrived at camp, Hugo helped us out of the boat as our feet sunk -- *squish* -- into the spongy ground. Our bungalow featured screened windows without glass and mosquito nets hanging above two single beds. We set down our packs and went to sit by the canal in tattered hammocks, butterflies flitting by our faces as we laid back and began to absorb all that was going on around us. After an hour or so, we walked down to the dock where a little boy, maybe seven years old, was dragging a fish head as enormous as a bowling ball away with him by the gills, its silver scales the size of silver dollars glinting in what was left of the sunlight. Hugo explained that fishermen often gave the parts they couldn't sell to the local villagers, and the little boy must have been sent to pick it up.

After dinner, Hugo asked Eveline and me if we would like to go hiking on the beach to look for nesting turtles. Although it was late in the season, if we were lucky, we might still be able to see a Giant Green Sea Turtle heaving herself up out of the surf to dig her nest and lay eggs. Hugo loaded a few supplies as Eveline and I sat quietly in the tiny rocking motorboat listening to the ominous night croaks and splashes. I strained my eyes as I looked down into the water, thinking of the monstrous-sized crocodile I'd seen earlier that day, the canal now completely dark under the shadow of the jungle canopy.

Hugo jumped into the boat, fired up the motor, and switched on the 100-Candlepower spotlight which he mounted to what was left of the raggedy canopy. He gunned the engine with unexpected vigor, and almost instantly we were whizzing through the night at top speed through the estuary and toward the ocean. At first my wide eyes were trained on the console, the speedometer needle quickly edging into the red, but soon my attention was diverted to what lay ahead. Hugo turned suddenly and without warning at sharp angles -- left, then right, then left again -- dodging fallen logs, swerving to narrowly miss muddy banks which sprung up in the middle of the canal, and tearing through lily pad patches as he snaked his way through the creature-filled waters at stunning velocity with only the immediate twenty feet of river ahead illuminated.

Eveline and I were plastered to the floor, convinced that by lowering our centers of gravity we'd be less likely to be launched through the air and into the water when Hugo finally did smack into something head-on. At first we protested politely to try to get him to slow down, but he only responded with *Tranquilla, tranquilla...* Don't worry. Our initial panic eventually grew into hysterical laughter since I felt reasonably sure this was *not* a situation to be *tranquilla* about. But it was the ride of my life... And so, we held our collective breath and prayed once again to the travel gods for our safety as we watched Hugo's spotlight reveal the occasional sets of glowing orange eyes lurking near the canal's banks.

Eventually, Hugo let off the throttle, and we glided up onto shore, securing the boat to a tree with a rope. Hugo led us down a wild deserted beach strewn with driftwood and the rotten planks of years of shipwrecks when he stopped suddenly, pointing toward the ocean's edge. A huge dark figure was moving slowly up the beach. Hugo motioned for us to sit down and be silent and still. From a hundred meters away, we watched as a Giant Green Sea Turtle labored her 400-pound body up the steep beach. When she reached the top of the high-tide line, she stopped, settled in, and then she began to dig. With her flippers, she flung sand every which way, spraying it fifteen feet in all directions, digging with bursts of tremendous energy and then

stopping to rest. Dig and dig and rest. Finally she stopped
moving. Hugo explained that once she began laying she would
be focused as if in a trance, and we could move closer without
disturbing her. Leading us with a red-filtered flashlight so our
light wouldn't upset her, we moved nearer and peeked into her
deep nest to watch the rubbery eggs drop from her warm body
into the cool wet sand. After twenty minutes, she startled us
when she swung her great flippers again, and as we slowly backed
away, she worked them in the opposite direction to move the
sand back to cover the hole.

We did not wait for her to return to the sea. She might rest
there for a very long time Hugo explained, exhausted as she was,
so we walked slowly down the beach toward the canal, silent in
our own thoughts, looking up at the stars, bright pinpricks of
light in the dark sky. And that was when Hugo spotted the
dozens of baby turtle tracks…

***

After saying goodbye to Hugo and leaving the wonders of
Tortuguero, Eveline and I headed for the laid-back town of
Puerto Viejo, a nearby destination which vibrated with rich color
and life. Green forest shimmered against blue sky, and colorful
Rastafarians in yellow and green and red striped shorts bicycled
down dusty pathways calling hello to us, the reggae beats echoing
from radios bungeed to their handlebars. Flowers as big as your
head exploded in pinks and reds and oranges and yellows, bright
giants thriving in the sunstreaks and warm rain. The Caribbean
side of Costa Rica was a place all its own; English and Creole
languages were more commonly spoken than Spanish, and its
black Afro-Caribbean culture and people were more reminiscent
of islands in the Caribbean Sea than of the Spanish and
indigenous heritage of the rest of Costa Rica.

Eveline and I spent a few days on the nearly-deserted
beaches of Puerto Viejo. Tiny windswept funnelclouds blasted
us with black sand, and powerful surf pummeled the shore in the
chaotic winter surges. Palm fronds draped out of lush jungle
backdrops making sounds like tearing paper as they shifted in the
breeze. We read, sweat, and swam on a Tuesday afternoon,
wondering aloud about where we'd be in our formerly busy lives

if we hadn't been there in that moment. Eveline leaned back, put her face in the sun and sighed.

At the end of a tranquil day, we hitched a ride back to our bungalow with a man driving a pickup that was already overloaded with coconuts and children. As he put on the brakes, the road blanketed us in dust, and we jumped into the bed. His young son opened *pipas* expertly with a machete and handed them to us. *"You are welcome here,"* he said smiling, revealing shreds of coconut between his teeth as the music of his Creole-accented English rolled off his tongue.

That night Eveline and I went out to a disco, eager to practice our salsa moves. I loved dancing in Costa Rica. Unlike the seedy nightclubs at home, when a man asked you to dance here, that's actually what he meant. He didn't mean, *Hey baby, you wanna go back to my room?* A man here asked you for one dance, and if you declined, that was OK. And if you accepted, you danced together for one song, and then he walked you back to where you had been sitting, and then later, sometimes he might come back and ask you again.

Eveline and I were sipping *Centenario* rum-and-Cokes when a gorgeous guy in a tight white T-shirt that gleamed against his smooth midnight skin in the swirling club lights, locked eyes with me. My stomach jumped as he began walking towards us. I looked at Eveline who was already giving me that *nice-knackarsch* smile, and I gulped as he approached and leaned in close to speak over the loud music to ask, "Would you like to dance?"

He extended his hand as we walked onto the crowded dance floor together and took the close-bodied salsa position. I pressed into his warm tallness, sneaking a few touches of his sleek muscled arms. The back of his shirt was wet with sweat in the warm humid night, and he smelled so like a man. It felt like forever since I'd been close to one. We danced on as the song crescendoed, a whir of feet and hips, spins and turns, trumpets blaring to the forefront of the music. And at that moment, he leaned in again and this time said, "Will you wait here one minute?"

"OK," I answered, bewildered, befuddled, feeling extremely awkward standing there alone on the dance floor.

I watched him as he walked away from me, heading towards the stereo system set-up. Then he slipped behind the booth and changed the record. As he came walking back toward me, all smiles, one song slid into the next.

"Sorry," he said with a beautiful grin. "I'm the D.J." And he took my hand again, and the salsa music played on…

***

Eveline and I stumbled home after a glorious night of debauchery, and when we reached our room, she slurringly declared, "Beer before liquor, never sicker. Liquor before beer, you disappear," as she sat down and missed the bed.

The morning after the disco, we took an easy hike along a jungle trail that meandered along the shoreline of Cahuita National Park. A kind man whom we met along the path pointed out to us our first three-toed sloth, hiding in moss-covered stillness high up in the trees. Chortling monkeys, giant spiders and iridescent butterflies abounded overhead. I was so busy looking up that I stepped right into a line of red army ants, one of whom marched into my sandal and got wedged there, mercilessly securing its sturdy jaws onto my big toe as I squirmed and yelped. I finally sunk my whole foot into a mud puddle, and I think the poor little thing must have drowned because soon the stinging subsided. When we arrived at the far end of the trail, I sat down to have a snack, and Eveline said she was going to go off in search of *pipas*. She was gone an awfully long time, and when she finally did come back, she asked if she could *please* have a tissue. I said I didn't have any, and she looked really sad. Then she confessed that she had just taken a poop in the woods and that's why she needed the Kleenex.

"Use a leaf," I jokingly advised.

She screwed her face up into little accordion pleats and said, "I did, and now it's itching."

So we jumped into the warm ocean laughing and took a swim instead.

***

Since all main highways run through the capital of the country, Eveline and I stopped briefly in San Jose to change buses, now bound for the Pacific beaches of the province of Guanacaste. Just before boarding our second bus of the day, I lost a pivotal game of rock-paper-scissors with her and ended up with the middle seat in a row of three on a very steamy journey through a very hot landscape. Quickly realizing I was simply too long from hip to knee to sit in this school-bus seat normally, I settled into the spread-eagle position until the people on either side of me could no longer endure it. My shoulders were wedged in so tightly that I couldn't get my hand in my pocket for the coins to pay my ticket, and my considerable curves overflowed into my neighbors' laps. In real time, the journey lasted six hours.

We arrived in Playa del Coco, our farthest northern Pacific destination, well after dark and located what the guidebook considered a hotel and what we considered an extra room in a nice lady's house, and settled in for the night.

In these first weeks traveling across Costa Rica, I awakened each morning at dawn, not out of a sense of obligation toward school or work or commitments I'd made to others, but out of a sense of joy, a feeling that I couldn't wait to get out and see what the world's sweet gift would be to me that day. The twitterings of tiny birds in the garden was a far departure from the mundanity of an alarm clock, and as Thanksgiving came and went almost without notice under the unfaltering sun, the concept of holidays became a moot point -- each day becoming a celebration of its own.

On our first morning in Playa del Coco we awoke to discover that most of the tourist infrastructure in town was closed for low season, so we walked around just looking for something to do. Eventually we ambled by a big wooden sign hanging above a rancho which read *Tourist Information*, and beneath it sat a young man at a picnic bench, a few papers scattered in front of him. As we approached, we could see that he had just finished writing a letter and was beginning to seal it. Now, he wasn't just sealing it -- not in the way your grandma would pucker her face at the icky glue on the back of an envelope. This boy was licking it and licking it and *mmmmm* licking it. Slowly, methodically, almost savoring it. And that envelope was soaked. Eveline whispered to me, "This is the sexiest boy of my life." She stood unmoving, enchanted, staring at him and smiling as he intently licked and licked that envelope, taking no notice of us whatsoever.

We waited until he had finished his intimate task before going closer. We introduced ourselves, and he told us his name was Alonso.

"Alonso…" Eveline repeated with hypnotic love swirls in her eyes. *"Look at his mouth when he talks,"* she whispered. *"I love this mouth."*

Since Alonso had been sitting under the *Tourist Information* sign, we began asking him our tourist information questions. He smiled and answered us patiently.

"Where was the best restaurant to order fresh fish?"

"Who could take us to see some of the beaches in the Santa Rosa National Marine Park?"

"What time does the bus leave for destinations further south?"

As it turned out, Alonso did not work for *Tourist Information*. *Tourist Information* was, in fact, closed. Alonso had been sitting on that bench writing letters because it was a perfectly good bench to sit on. But there was a friendly chemistry among us, and he decided he would try to help us find someone to take us on a snorkeling trip, eventually offering to take us himself. It seemed to trouble him that we had things we wanted to do, but no way to do them since so much was closed. And he told us not to worry about a thing.

"No me gusta las problemas," he said. *"Son malas por el corazón."* I don't like problems. They're bad for the heart.

Alonso explained that his father was a fisherman, and every day he used the family's big boat to go out for his catch, but there was also a smaller boat. He would go ask his brother if it was OK to take us out in that one. We could pitch in some money for gas. *Just wait here…*

So Eveline and I waited at the picnic bench underneath the *Tourist Information* sign (Eveline still talking about how "lucky" that envelope was), and a few minutes later almost out of nowhere, an older man came up to us and tried to solicit us for a snorkeling tour. We told him that we were already going with someone else, and we pointed down to the beach at Alonso and some of his friends who were now launching our tiny boat into the water.

He looked at what was going on at the water's edge and said in English, "I hope you have life vests!"

And he laughed as walked away.

I did not like that man.

Alonso steadied the boat for us to climb aboard, and we shoved off, putting along with the five-horsepower outboard motor and following along the coastline fringed with green hills. When we reached a rocky peninsula, Alonso grabbed the masks and snorkels and called for us to jump in. He went over the side backwards with a splash, and Eveline followed closely behind. We kicked alongside Alonso, peering into the world below as he dipped into rocky crevices pointing out lobsters and startling blowfish into inflating. The warm water lapped at our naked bellies, and the fish ran rainbow circles amidst a rocky wonderland.

We got back in the boat and putted along for another twenty minutes until we came to a tiny offshore islet where Alonso beached the boat and led us up a hilly trail. When we reached the crest, we gazed down upon the most idyllic paradisiacal beach I had ever laid eyes on. Alonso called it Playa Paraíso. Crystal clear gentle water, pure white soft sand, palm trees, and completely deserted. Eveline and I ran full bore down the hill towards the beach that danced out of our dreams, and Alonso brought over some coconuts to share that he had found lying behind some driftwood. Eveline reached over and tried to crack one open on a rock, but it simply bounced off, undamaged. Alonso took it gently from her, cracked it open on the very same rock with the finesse of experienced hands, and held it up high above her head for her to drink as it dribbled down her chin, her chest, her breasts, her legs. Eveline squirmed below gleefully, mouth open, and when she could stand it no longer, she ran into the water with a squeal. (I could have sworn I saw steam coming off her when she plunged in.) I walked down to meet her, and as we floated in the turquoise sea.

"I am so horny for Alonso. *Alonso…*" she trailed off, her head dipping below the warm calm water, bubbles of desire climbing back up to break on the glassy surface.

***

Strangely, and to Eveline's great disappointment, Alonso stood us up for our date at the Banana Bar that night, and we left the

next day never to see him again. The next morning we hiked up
to the main road to flag down the next bus headed south.

While we waited, we bought some ice creams shaped like
Mickey Mouse's head on a stick out of a Styrofoam cooler that
the ice-cream man carried around his neck. And when the bus
roared by, we jumped into the road waving our arms furiously,
climbed on, and stood in the back of the crowded bus still
wearing our backpacks because there had been no time to put
them below in the storage compartment. The bus driver drove
like a maniac down the dusty potholed road as we sloshed back
and forth from side to side in the back of the bus.

Eveline finally said, "How do you say it? He's fucking with
us?"

We joined the other passengers in laughing at our
rollercoaster ride, as we flew around like top-heavy ragdolls,
madly licking our ice creams to combat the drips of the tropical
heat.

We had told the bus driver that we wanted to get off in Playa
Grande where we hoped to see the nesting of the Leatherback
Sea Turtles, and soon he signaled that ours was the next stop. But
as the bus slowed, there was no beach in sight. Just miles more
of hot dusty road... One passenger explained that this was the
crossroads at the tiny town of Huacas, and this was as far as the
bus went. A little confused, we got off and looked around for a
way into Playa Grande. Immediately, I spotted a conspicuous
blue-eyed, blonde-ponytailed surfer-looking guy, his curls
escaping from beneath his baseball cap. *This guy has got to be from
California*, I thought. And as it turned out, my intuitions were
right. His name was James, he was from San Diego, and he was
currently living (as it so happened) in Playa Grande.

He asked if we needed a lift and said he'd take us there for
2000 colones. After all, that was where he was headed anyway.
Eveline and I thought it sounded a bit expensive so we told him
that we'd just wait for the next bus. Then he explained that there
was no bus. We looked down that hot dusty road, trying to
figure out if the guy was trying to scam us, but after some debate
we got in his 4x4 Jeep and were off. He asked us where we'd
been traveling, what we were doing and what our plans were. He
had been working for Louis, the owner of the nicest hotel in
Playa Grande, called *Hotel Las Tortugas*, for about a month.

"Louis is really the one who started eco-tourism in Playa Grande back in the 80's," he explained. "And he's the primary activist who helped save the Leatherback Sea Turtles and their nesting ground."

I told James that I'd read about Louis in my guidebook, and James suggested that Louis might have rooms available. We confessed that we were on an extremely tight budget, but James said, "Maybe he'll cut you a deal. Let's go meet him."

When we drove into town, it really wasn't much of a town at all -- just a restaurant with an attached rancho and tiny market on the corner, and then a long stretch of more dirt road which dead-ended into the beach. James turned up a path just wide enough for a vehicle, and out of the dry jungle appeared a four-story lighthouse, its sleek round white structure complete with windows encircling the tower with bird's eye views of the ocean just a few hundred meters away. James knocked forcefully at the arched wooden door, and after a few minutes passed, it was flung open forcefully. A man in his early 50s with an angular face and thin blond ponytail appeared, his faded flower-patterned shirt buttoned askew and in only two places. He wore thick glasses repaired in the middle with a glob of resin and had an uncanny resemblance to Garth from Wayne's World. He seemed nice enough (although perhaps a little manic) as he spoke with James alone for a moment, and then he walked over to the jeep where Eveline and I were waiting.

"How much do you want to spend?" he asked.

I told him, "We can't spend more than $10/person a night."

He said, "OK, I'll put you up in *Bruce's House*, but everything at the hotel is yours!"

And that was it… James drove us down to the beachfront hotel, and we got out of the car and followed him down a curving path lined with spiraled seashells set into walkways. Head-high walls of yellow and red hibiscus led us to a white pyramidal three-story Mayan temple hidden among the trees. Below lay a small glimmering swimming pool shaped like a turtle and a shady palm-thatched rancho where vacant colorful Nicaraguan hammocks swayed in the soft breeze. Hidden behind a camouflage of shrubbery for privacy, a jacuzzi bubbled with fresh water which was emptied daily and used to irrigate the garden. We followed James upstairs into the restaurant and reception area, a large dining room of simple but expertly hand-crafted woodwork glowing richly in the late afternoon's golden tones.   As James asked for our key from the receptionist, I wandered out to the restaurant's balcony and gazed down at the giant beach, wide and deep with white sand and world-class waves waiting to be surfed, crashing against the shore. *How did I ever manage to land here?*

James drove us a quarter-mile down a side-road to *Bruce's House*, which I assumed would be some little closet for $10/night, but I continued to be amazed as we pulled up in the driveway of an oceanfront mansion.   Four handmade leather rocking chairs undulated in the invisible breezes on the seaside porch.   Airy screens encircled the living room, and cool red tile led to a full kitchen, three air-conditioned bedrooms, and two hot showers. *This was too good to be true.* James explained that rather than having the house sit vacant in the low season, Louis sometimes preferred to put people in it to watch it.

"Burglary can be a problem," he said, but assured us that it was not dangerous because by occupying the house, we were acting as a burglar deterrent.   Louis was tired of replacing the small appliances and was happy to have us there.

As we heard James' Jeep pull out of the driveway, Eveline and I squealed with joy. Paradise! All to ourselves! We jumped into our bathing suits, ran into the ocean, and watched the sun set behind waves of silhouetted surfers.

✳✳✳

We made a reservation for the Leatherback turtle tour for 10:00 p.m. that night, and as we ordered a *casado* dinner of fresh mahi-mahi, Louis walked into the hotel and sat down with us. He was an amazing host. We thanked him for his profound generosity, and he asked if we'd tried the hotel's margaritas.

"They're the world's best," he claimed. "Made fresh from sweet mandarin limes grown in the backyard."

We hadn't tried them.   Much of the menu was expensive (though of exquisite quality), but in that moment, we decided that since we had gotten the deal of a lifetime with our accommodations, we supposed we could splurge…

He said, "If I treat, will you join me?"

And with that, we headed down to the jacuzzi, salted glasses in hand.

Louis was a really interesting guy. He liked to talk, liked to have young people around. He was incredibly intelligent, philosophical. I learned that he was, by training, a behavioral psychologist which meant we had quite a bit in common in our backgrounds. But something made me uneasy about him. *Why was he being so nice to us? Was he some kind of a pervert or something? What did he want?* James had told us that Louis's girlfriend, Marianela, a Tica from San José, was visiting family in the capital, and sometimes Louis got bored, especially in low season, so he was happy to have interesting people to talk to. That night (and forever forward) Louis quite often said things that were really "out there." Maybe it was because he actually believed them, or maybe he loved to simply observe others' reactions. Generally I enjoyed his company, and Eveline was a good influence on my often overly-critical mind, but I thought I'd better keep my guard up.

I couldn't wait to hear the story of a real environmental activist, and I'll admit I was a bit star-struck by the idea of hearing the account first-hand from someone who was featured in the Lonely Planet guide.

So as we bubbled away, I asked with wide impressionable eyes, "Louis, what made you decide to establish the national park?"

His reply was short. "They were fucking up my surf spot."

Then he smiled.

The long version was that Louis, a Florida native, ended up in Costa Rica thirty years ago and found his way to the tiny town of Tamarindo and eventually the empty stretches of Playa Grande. But within a few years other people found their way there, too, and they started building. As they began dredging sand from the pristine estuary to make cement, one of the world's most consistent beach-breaks began to change. With Louis's financial backing and his girlfriend Marianela's local political connections, they established the entire five-mile stretch of beach as a national marine sanctuary where no one could build closer than 300 meters to the high tide line. Trees could no longer be cut down, white lightbulbs were banned in outdoor areas where they can confuse the directional instincts of nesting

Leatherbacks, and the estuary became off-limits for anything other than small-scale fishing and wildlife viewing.

Louis and Marianela built a small hotel which opened in the mid-1980s to house turtle scientists who flocked to the area from all over the globe. And eventually they took on eco-tourists and then an ever-increasing number of surfers. They kept the place small at eleven rooms, and their only paid employees all came from the local village of Matapalo. These people who had previously made their living poaching turtle eggs now worked at the hotel as cooks, receptionists, gardeners, housekeepers and rangers. The hotel took on as many employees as it could support, much like a non-profit organization, and although as a *business* establishment it never really made any money, it employed more than thirty local residents.

I suppose my romantic version of the selfless motivations of an environmental activist had been shattered -- and it was not the last of my naïve ideas that Louis obliterated for better or for worse (usually for better) -- but in the end, the outcome was the same. Louis's waves were saved, the turtles were protected, egg poaching became illegal, a growing number of local people found skill-based work, and Playa Grande became a highly-sought-after destination for environmental tourists and nature lovers worldwide.

***

The days rolled on, and Eveline and I stayed at Louis's insistence.

"After all, you're helping me out," he'd say.

As I rocked softly in the leather chairs on the porch listening to the sea, a phenomenon had already begun to take hold of me, a feeling that I began to recognize, a feeling that slowly began to repeat. It was the ocean. It had always brought me solace, but here it also made my thoughts so vivid, so lucid. The sea soothed me like nothing else in the world, and now I was acknowledging how wonderful its constant influence made me feel.

Throughout my life, when I had been happy, or sad, or excited, or worried, I had sought it out, just to sit and be with it for a while. The sound of the waves rolling in one after another calmed me, pulled out my emotions, my passion, my love to be alive, my love to be alone, my love to be with those I love. Being near the sea always felt like coming home.

On my first Playa Grande mornings, I awakened early to gather shells, surprised at how much energy I had, how thoughtful I felt. The mornings were still and cool and quiet, and I walked alone on that big beautiful beach, not another soul in sight. Exotic shells rushed in from the deep when the sea was high; the water level varied nearly a hundred linear feet each day between low and high tide, exposing vast stretches of unfootprinted sand. There were so many shells shining there like jewels in the sun that at first I scoured back and forth picking up every one, new and exciting. Shells with thorns, shells with spikes, shells with twists and swirls and colors. Spotted cowries with teeth, and ribbed limpets with green centers. Scallops banded with pink and magenta. Cones sploched with the brown and golden patches of a jaguar. Olives that wound around and opened like tiny vases hiding purple underbellies.

As my pockets began to droop, I simply chose one path to walk, a line that felt particularly promising, and somehow there lay the most fantastic unusual shells I had ever seen! When approaching tasks throughout my life, I had often tended toward overly-thorough. I had tried to read, to research, to study, to gather, to look at *everything,* and only when I sat among my mountainous piles of information did I begin to sort and carefully discard, paring down to refinement. I was petrified that I would *miss* something -- maybe the most important something. But in Playa Grande there I was, immersed in the moment, relaxed, joyous. Missing something didn't cross my mind because any path felt so rich I couldn't go wrong. I was content to just choose one and see where it led me, trusting that it would be to a good place. And something inside me began to let go, and I knew that things were finally beginning to change.

***

On the fifth night of margaritas in the jacuzzi, Louis announced his proposal. *Would Eveline or I consider staying in Playa Grande to help him?* He had made this kind of proposal to a number of young people like James over the years -- room and board in exchange for work. James did odd jobs like fixing electrical wiring, digging ditches, and putting in septic tanks. But Louis explained that now he needed "an email specialist" to answer client questions. The hotel had recently started up their webpage, and now there were so many inquiries that it was impossible for him to keep up in addition to all his other managerial tasks. He said that the job took him six hours a day as a hunt-and-peck typist, but he thought it would take much less time for someone who could type well. When the email for the day was done, our time would be our own.

It sounded so wonderful -- again almost too good to be true -- but I had already established a plan... I had checked out English-teaching possibilities in San Jose before I had left on my travels with Eveline, and although there were some jobs available, it would be difficult to make enough money to break even financially, much less *save* money. But *this?* Well, this new offer was just *not* in the plan.

I gazed up from the bubbling hot tub at the great mango tree, its leaves rustling gently in silhouette against a small slice of white moon. And my mind began to whir... *This is a great surfing beach, and I've always wanted to learn. For two or three months until I head to South America, what could it hurt? A couple hours of work each day in exchange for room and board?* That seemed like a better deal than I could get in San Jose. Quiet and beautiful and relaxing. I could practice my Spanish with the staff, learn to surf, learn about turtles, volunteer with the scientists, swim and jacuzzi whenever I wanted, eat and sleep for free, write, draw. It sounded like paradise! Busy paradise.

And then the tortured questions emerged -- What if... *What if I stop practicing Spanish because there are so many tourists around? What if being here sucks away my impetus to travel? What if I become overwhelmed by Louis's bizarrities? Will I feel like I'm challenging myself here or just killing time? What if I get lonely? What if I turn into a--a--a surfer?*

And all this went through my head in about one-quarter of a second. Louis had paused after his question and was now looking expectantly at Eveline and me. Eveline explained that she had to get back to school for the new semester starting after Christmas. And I found myself truly surprised to be actually considering the offer. Not being prone to making decisions without heavy brooding and still a bit wary about Louis's intentions, I told him that I would think it over during the next few weeks while I was traveling in Panama. During that time I'd be able to construct a thorough list: pros on one side, cons on the other.

      ***

I didn't know it then, but I was about to begin a new life. And time didn't exist there.

I did return to Playa Grande. I went back again and again and again… And after living and working there during that first season, I was never the same. After that first season, it seemed like there was always a part of me that lived there, that belonged there.

And throughout my travels yet-to-come in South America, my life in Playa Grande echoed inside me. Maybe because of the wisdoms Louis shared which reverberated during those learning moments that come rapid-fire while traveling. Maybe because Playa Grande was the place where I eventually whittled myself down to my core. But my time there followed me wherever I went from then on, and every time I looked up at the moon as it moved through its phases, through the months and seasons, it reminded me of that magical place that was governed by the tides.

Shortly after Christmas, on the first day I had returned to begin my job there, Louis had said one thing to me, and then he had walked away… *"Take off your watch. We live on moontime here."*

My return journey, alone, back to Playa Grande was not easy. You see, I was supposed to arrive on a Thursday... When I had taken the taxi from Daisy's house to the San Jose bus terminal for all destinations Guanacaste, I was still so new at being alone. I was still so accustomed to having a set plan and depending on it, an anal-retentiveness that Latin America will cure more effectively than decades of psychotherapy. My mental resources had never been strained in the way that they were about to be on that bus journey. I had not yet reached down into my utter depths to meet my resourceful desperate self, the woman who surfaces as she faces unforeseeable challenges. The challenges are only unforeseeable, of course, because she has so few experiences on which to draw in order to anticipate what could possibly go wrong. We are at our most vulnerable as we build our experiential arsenal, stacking our adventures higher and higher until we can stand atop them and look out over the unknowns of the world to see their rhythms and patterns. That night, on my return bus trip to Playa Grande, was the first time I consoled myself with the simple thought, *Well, at least I didn't die...* And I supposed the old saying was right -- it *did* make me stronger.

The plan had been simply this: I would buy a bus ticket as far as Huacas, the town at the crossroads for Playa Grande, and then Louis would send a taxi to come pick me up at about 8:00 p.m. (the scheduled time of the bus' arrival). That taxi would then drive me the final ten kilometers over the dusty washboard road to the hotel.

But about three hours into the six-hour trip to Huacas, the bus stopped. The bridge was out, and cars and trucks and semis were piled up waiting, wondering what to do. We sat there for a very long time, and it was getting dark. Finally, the bus grinded into reverse, and when I asked the man next to me what was happening, he said that we would have to go "the other way," which meant backtracking and taking a completely different route. And although I didn't know it at the time, "the other way" meant adding an additional three hours to our trip.

So when I finally arrived in Huacas, the second-to-last stop on the bus route, the taxi that Louis had sent was not waiting there. As the only passenger whose destination was Huacas, I grabbed my bag and tentatively peeked out of the hydraulic bus doors at the total empty darkness. I began to make my descent slowly, pausing on the last step, then turned and asked the bus driver, *"Donde esta el telefono?"* explaining that I could call Louis and he could send another car.

The bus driver said that the phone was closed.

Closed? The phone is closed?

He explained that the town's single telephone was inside someone's house, and they were asleep.

(Please keep in mind that since that time, Huacas has become a bustling crossroads town between popular beaches. In 2006, a mini mall was built. Now everyone has a cell phone, there are *hospedajes* to stay in, and even an emergency medical facility. But on that night not-so-very-long-ago, when the bus driver stopped to let me off at nearly midnight, there was nothing. Just a dusty corner with a couple of young men sitting in the park, speaking in low tones in the darkness.)

I told the bus driver I wasn't getting off the bus. I was scared, and alone, and I had nowhere to go. He asked if I wanted to ride into Tamarindo, the bus' terminus, which he told me was a larger tourist town. I agreed. And so, the bus and its last two passengers bumped along for another half an hour until we drove into a town with no lights, and the driver finally stopped at another dusty bend at the end of a traffic circle.

He said, *"OK. Esta Tamarindo."*

I looked around. There was still no pay phone. It was still completely dark. I swallowed hard, and I asked him where I could go for a cheap hotel. He said they were all closed for the night. *Closed? Again?* Maybe the words "larger tourist town" were relative.

At this point, my panic grew stronger. My heart jumped into my throat as I assessed my situation. Here I was, all alone, in the dark, in the middle of the night, with nowhere to go, and no way to call Louis. So… I refused to get off the bus. And this time, I began to cry.

That poor bus driver… But I just didn't know what to do. It seemed like I was out of options, and in a last desperate plea, I asked the driver, *Please, please, can't I stay at your house?* I don't think this thought would have ever occurred to me before I had moved to Costa Rica. But the Ticos had been so warm, so welcoming, so hospitable. People hardly ever said no, and when they did, if you asked again, they usually said OK. The bus driver looked at me, his brow furrowed, his eyes full of pity. I'm sure he wondered how in the world I'd gotten myself into this situation. He said I couldn't stay at his house, but he did have a niece that lived just outside Huacas, and he would drive me back there in the bus, and he would ask her if I could stay. It was 1:00 in the morning.

So back we went, bumping along the dusty road. This time, I sat up in the front seat next to the driver, hoping with all hope, praying to my little travel god that this mysterious stranger would find it in her kind heart to take me in.

When we arrived back in Huacas, the driver told me to stay on the bus. He walked slowly up a narrow pathway flanked by a small garden toward a house hidden in the shadows and knocked on the door. For a moment, it was just cicadas and silence. Then, a light came on, and the door opened to reveal a young woman with long tangled black hair and a pink satin nightgown. I strained my eyes in the darkness, my ears in the murmurs, and thought I could make out the nodding of heads. And after a few minutes, the bus driver walked slowly back toward the bus and said, "OK."

I burst into tears all over again, overwhelmed, relieved, and threw my pack up onto my shoulder, whispering *Gracias, gracias señor*, as I padded up the walk behind him.

The bus driver's niece was my first angel. She led me inside, put a mattress down on the floor in the front room, gave me a sheet to keep the multitudes of mosquitoes at bay, cooed soft comforting words into my ear, and turned off the light as she walked into her bedroom, one thin wall away. I didn't really sleep. But it didn't matter. I was so grateful to be in a home, not to be standing alone on a dark corner in a town I didn't know, waiting for whatever inevitability was lurking in the night. Women are taught to be afraid of the darkness, of the unknown out there waiting to "get" us, the innocent, the beautiful, the feminine, and leave us in ruin. Women live with a phantom rapist, a specter murderer over our shoulders, and however fantastical those tales-that-go-bump-in-the-night are which are created to keep us dependent, to keep us from going out and being *sola*, they are hard to shake out of our collective imagination.

In the morning, the bus driver's niece awakened me early when the light was soft and the air was cool. She said that her cousin usually drove his truck this way to work, and maybe if we stood on the corner, we could flag him down and he'd pick me up and take me into Playa Grande with him.

And before I knew it, a truck with a dozen men ready to work construction laying down cinderblock homes for wealthy ex-pats, pulled up, and the bus driver's niece shouted some words to the truck-driver over the rumble of the diesel engine, and I jumped in. And within twenty minutes, I was walking up the stairs toward the reception desk at Hotel Las Tortugas to find a bedraggled Louis sitting at a small table drinking coffee. I gave a weak smile as he said, "*Where* have *you* been?"

WELCOME TO PANAMA

After several weeks exploring Costa Rica (including our first foray together into Playa Grande), Eveline and I had met up with eight language-school classmates to begin our trip to Panama, a trip which had given me much time to consider Louis's offer of employment. During our overnight bus journey from San Jose to Panama, I had shared a bench seat with Mie. An elegant flower, Mie hybridized refined Japanese mannerisms with flawless porcelain skin and wide wondering almond eyes. She slept peacefully with her head, no more than a feather, on my shoulder through the neck-whipping curves, erratic stops, and tire changes that are part of any public transport journey. This bus, however, offered more than the usual set of surprises. After a few hours we started munching on the snacks we had brought which we had stowed in the overhead racks. And that was when we had found the *cucarachas*. Lots of them. The tiny kind, and in the thousands. They were in our food, in our seats, in our hair. And when our bus inexplicably stopped for three hours in the desolate reaches of the far south in the wee hours of the night, Eveline jumped out of the vehicle's stagnant swampy confines, climbed up on its back bumper, and wrote with her finger in the dust on the window, *Shit Cucaracha Bus*. Then sat down in the dirt and curled up under the stars.

When we arrived at the border the next afternoon, twelve hours after our departure, the handwritten sign in the window of the customs office said that the official passport-stampers had gone home for lunch and a siesta. We unloaded our gear and waited under a shade tree as I watched the bus turn around and just drive away. And it didn't come back. The what-ifs soon followed the feelings of abandonment. *What if the customs office doesn't even open today? And if it does open, what if I don't make it across? And if I do make it across, then what?* No one really knew. I'd gone through customs before -- at the airport in San Jose and on the trains of Europe -- but there was something different about standing here at this land crossing, just waiting. This was not a slick air-conditioned airport that saw thousands of international travelers a day. This was a concrete one-room square, sitting heavily in the red dirt, bars across the windows, without so much as a bathroom nearby. I imagined standing, my passport -- my livelihood -- in hand, offering it out to an official-looking stranger with absolute power, hoping that my smile and respectful answers to simple (and hopefully comprehended) questions would allow me to pass, and the gates to the next land would open.

Eventually, two mustached customs agents returned. After a moment of breathless silence, each of us approached the men in the khaki uniforms. They looked at our customs forms, they looked at us. They looked at our passports, they looked at us. And they paused. And then, *stamp stamp*, we were ushered through the building to the other side. All except for Mie...

From the blinding sun outside the cinderblock structure we looked back into the dank shadows to see Mie standing alone, on the opposite side of the border from the rest of us, patiently listening to the officials explain that her entry stamp had been carelessly generated at the airport, and now only half of it could be read. Unfortunately, the half which was omitted was the half that contained the date of entry, and now she could not prove that she had not overstayed her visa. We sent our best Spanish-speakers back to the window, and after an hour of light-hearted debating, pleading, showing of airline tickets, and more pleading, the matter was settled suddenly and without explanation. Mie officially left Costa Rica, and the customs agent pointed *that way*... Out.

But our border-crossing experience was just beginning. As we looked along the custom agent's finger, there stretched a rickety bridge of wooden planks, about a hundred meters long, five feet wide, standing about fifty feet above a river which ran through a political and geographic no-man's-land. And beyond that bridge, stood Panama -- and another immigration office. You see, what we had not realized was that we had to do this twice: once to leave Costa Rica, and then again to enter Panama. And in that moment, we were somehow standing in neither.

We heaved our mighty packs onto our backs again, and tottering under their great weight, wobbled across, stepping carefully among the missing slats. Rotten boards flipped up without warning, nails having rusted away long ago, and as our legs burned and sweat dripped from the tips of our noses in the midday heat, we balanced step by careful step, crossing this narrow bridge without a guardrail, across a river without a name, in a place that was neither Costa Rica nor Panama. And ten heart-thumping minutes later, we reached the other side. *Stamp, stamp!* Welcome to Panama.

As we stepped out of the immigration office cheering, two men were waiting, leaning against an old battered pick-up truck. They explained we could hire them to take us by taxi to the launching dock of Bocas del Toro, a group of well-touristed islands off the Caribbean coast. After negotiating and agreeing on a price, the driver opened the door to the truck against which he had been leaning, and his friend got in. Somehow, I had supposed they would lead us around the corner to a fleet of taxis, but there was no corner, and there was no fleet of taxis. Instead, we had apparently negotiated a price to squeeze the ten of us, plus the two of them, into this *one* pick-up!

The three smallest girls pressed into the fold-down backseat, and we pushed the boldest woman into the front between the driver and his friend. The other six of us, buried beneath our ten enormous backpacks, loaded ourselves into the bed while one girl ran to buy cold sodas for everyone for the long hot ride. And as we sped though the tropics of Panama, down the once-upon-a-time-long-ago paved road, the islands of asphalt were more a hazard than help. We wedged ourselves further beneath our luggage to keep from launching through the air as the driver floored it, the rickety truck bouncing and scraping through the dips and bumps. It was like a giant game of Twister: no one knew whose fallen-asleep legs belonged to whom, and as we drank and laughed and sang songs, we quickly discovered the drawback to combining bumpy roads and soda drinking. It's a lot like shaking up a pop bottle. Tummies bounce and swell to thrice their normal size, and it sounds a lot like this... *Belch, belch, laugh, laugh, bounce, bounce, belch, belch* -- times ten girls -- flying through the countryside, hair whipping in the wind, palm leaves flapping at our faces.

***

An hour later when we arrived at the boat landing, the water-taxi drivers for Bocas del Toro met us with astounding boldness, haggling aggressively for our business, both with us and amongst each other. The money our group was about to lay down (at $4 a piece) could feed a family for a month, even with the exorbitant price of petrol. My stomach tied in knots as I realized we were the source of this domino effect of crazed competition amongst colleagues which was quickly escalating into a screaming match. In an effort to get out of there, we split our group between two boats, and as we trailed away, I breathed out slowly as the dock grew smaller and smaller and all I could feel was the fresh sea-spray blowing against my face.

When we landed, we learned about the good news and the bad news. The good news was that we had unknowingly arrived during festival time. The bad news was that all the hotels were full. By this time, we had been awake for the majority of thirty hours and were all exhausted, hungry, irritable and just wanted a place to lay down. Some of us settled into a little restaurant and had a Panamanian beer (which was cheaper than water or soda), while others went off to see what they could find for accommodations. The boldest (that is, pushiest) girl returned to report that she found a man who was willing to move his family out of their house for us for $10 per person per night. I was horrified. Could *anything* be bought for a price? Another girl suggested that we use the pay phone at the restaurant where we were sitting to call and check for vacancies at a few hostels listed in the guidebook. The only place with a vacancy said that they had a room for seven of us, but got frustrated and hung up before we reached consensus. We decided to go look at it anyway, so we asked the waitress, "Donde esta *Las Deliciosas?*"

She paused, tilted her head a little sideways, and said, "Esta aquí."

It was right there! We had been sitting there the whole time and had somehow managed to call this woman inside the restaurant from outside the restaurant. Apparently they had a *pensión* upstairs.

The woman agreed to put foam mattresses on the floor to accommodate our whole group, and we climbed the splintery stairs to the attic to get settled in. The place was an absolute dump but better than sleeping on the beach. Three of the bottom bunk-beds sagged to the floor, and the double bed collapsed when Eveline sat on it, nearly crushing one of the girls who was checking underneath it for spiders. By the time all ten of us had showered and dressed to go out to the festivals, eight of us had fallen asleep.

Over the next three gorgeous days we snorkeled amongst neighboring islands, lay on the warm sand, skinny-dipped in bathtubby waters. The beaches did not compare to the beauty that we had seen in Costa Rica, but we were pleased to be there and spent days adventuring, packing into long narrow motorized canoes that nearly sank under the weight of our ten big bottoms, and touring the islands for secret hideaways. And every night, we found a new dockside restaurant, and sat under thatched canopies, and ate fresh fish, and watched perfect sunset after perfect sunset.

***

When we arrived in Chiriquí Grande a few days later, we were yanked from a well-sheltered tourist world back into the desperation and poverty which was the reality for the rest of the country. When we got off the bus, children were stationed like sentinels, ready to grab our bags and carry them for tips. Their aggressiveness was shocking. Seven- and eight-year olds with dirt-smudged faces and tattered clothes trying to grab my sixty-pound pack out from under the bus' cargo hold and then right out of my hands. When that didn't work, they clamored together all around, grabbing at our pants, pulling at our shirts, begging for money. Stricken by their desperation, conflicting emotions tugged at me; I felt so cold-hearted wading through the knee-deep crowds of these tiny people feeling like I had to do something but feeling too overwhelmed by their sheer numbers to do *anything*. Yet as the persistent children encroached ever closer, my travel-smarts, green as I was, also triggered a self-preservation response, and I clung to my pack for fear it would spring legs and run away.

While all that was going on below four feet, fully-grown taxi drivers accosted us at eye-level, all talking at once, trying to convince us to go with them to the town of David, our next destination. Slogging through the heavy crowds, down the wet street, around the corner, we finally found the minibus stop, albeit without any help from our intrusive entourage. And there, still idling at the curb, sat the minibus we had been searching for. And it was full -- or so we thought. So I went to the bathroom in a neighboring restaurant knowing we would have to wait at least an hour for the next bus, but when I returned, I could see the other girls inside the bus yelling at me to hurry as the man who sold tickets jumped down from tying our things to the roof, ropes still dangling. I ran toward the bus, and when my face broke the plane at the doorway, the temperature and humidity rose ten-fold as compared to outside on that stormy day. Extra seats had been folded into the aisles, and children had been moved to sit on parents' laps to accommodate the *gringas*. I climbed over my friends to the last remaining seat and settled into a makeshift chair whose backrest ended just below my kidneys. The ticket guy jumped on, and so little space was left inside the vehicle that he hung out the sliding door, calling out our destination to passersby until the highway began to whir under our wheels, the land turning to green hills trickling with rainy-season waterfalls behind windowpanes of breathy fog.

It rained during most of our time in David, but there was one attraction from which rain could not deter us -- the Caldera Hot Springs, located about an hour outside of town. Seven of us decided to venture out to find the natural thermal baths bubbling up from underground. They are said to have healing properties, but to me it just sounded like a warm thing to do in a cold damp place and a chance to get out into nature. We started on foot early in the light morning rain with determination in our hearts but without any real knowledge of what bus to get on, or even where the local bus station was.

As the sky darkened, we flagged down a passing taxi to ask how much it might cost to drive us the fifteen kilometers out to Caldera.

"$60," the driver answered with a sneer, watching our fallen expressions with a sort of perverse glee, and then rolling up the window of his warm dry car and speeding off.

Determined to avoid further tourist rip-offs, we continued our march toward the bus terminal but bickered among ourselves as we became more and more lost. A shiny red truck, with the word *t-a-x-i* painted in yellow letters across its door, slowly drove by and stopped at the curb as we approached.

"Taxi?" he asked.

We asked him for a price to Caldera, and he told us $20. Our agreement was instantaneous and unanimous, and we soggily piled in, lap-sitting three girls in the front seat with the driver, while four climbed into the fold-down backseat. Although merely one week ago it would have seemed laughable to travel a muddy road full of rocks and potholes with eight people squished into one truck like clowns in a circus car, it is amazing how quickly one adapts. We were grateful to have found Giovanni, our thirty-something soft-spoken driver, and he seemed quite pleased to have seven girls in his car. I peeked around Mie who was sitting on my lap and gazed out the front window through the giant Jesus windshield sticker that was so big it almost obscured oncoming traffic. Giovanni chatted with us as the storm clouds opened, and we asked if he thought his truck could make it down the road to the springs or if he'd have to drop us off at the crossroads, a wet three-kilometer walk from the springs themselves. We had read in our guidebook that a 4x4 was required to navigate the difficult mud track, and we could see that Giovanni's truck was clearly a two-wheel drive. But Giovanni was a bit of a macho, and I could tell he didn't want to disappoint us. He assured us that he would get us there…

As it turned out, Giovanni was a madman. You'd better believe we took that dirt road -- stones, puddles, ruts, boulders -- and you'd better believe we took it all the way. As the truck's underbelly scraped against rocks threatening to rip it apart, as the tires spun in the mud and jumped the bank, as the vehicle hung up and teetered on boulders lying in its path, I was sure we'd have to get out and push -- or that Giovanni would tear his truck up from the inside out. But he was insistent. He even drove across a suspension bridge that I was convinced was intended for pedestrians, just so he could let out his precious cargo within eyesight of the springs. And we were impressed. And so, when he asked if he should come back and pick us up since it was unlikely that any other taxi would happen upon us out there in the middle of nowhere, we said it would be much more fun if he just came with us.

Lying inconspicuously amongst a group of leafy green trees, the hot springs were a bit smaller, muddier, and less glamorous than most of us had hoped for, but they were warm and certainly welcome. We began excitedly stripping away our raincoats under which we were all wearing our bathing suits -- all, of course, except for Giovanni. He disappeared behind the trees as we settled into the *oohs* and *ahhs* of the warm springs. We dipped our heads into the soft water, inhaling the light sulfury fumes and opening our mouths to the raindrops falling on our faces. Actually, we were so wrapped up in the moment that we'd nearly forgotten about Giovanni -- until he emerged, that is, wearing only his tighty whities.

Dios mió! Do you think this man knew he would be doing this when he woke up that morning? He walked confidently towards us, led by his hairy beer belly, his chest draped in gold chains and crucifixes. And slowly, he slid between us into the hot springs, closed his eyes, and fell instantly into a state of bliss that had absorbed us all. We sat quietly, listening to the rain fall on the leaves as the healing properties of the sulfur springs bubbled away our worries. And when we got out and started to dry off, Giovanni climbed out onto the rocks and sat quietly peeling an orange, absorbing the energy from the green meadow full of wildflowers like it was nothing to sit there in his wet white underpants with a bunch of strangers. As the day came to a close, we piled back into the truck and drove safely back to town, each of us with many new stories to tell.

***

After about two weeks together, the ten of us arrived in Panama City where we found one huge cheap hotel room in a relatively safe area and bunked down together like a giant slumber party in order to save money. By this time, we were all a bit edgy, the idiosyncrasies of one another's personalities beginning to wear a bit. I put in my earplugs and pretended I was alone.

We visited the Casco Viejo, the old section of town with colonial hotels and churches, and we climbed to the top of the bell tower to look out over the city. We walked together toward what we thought was the shopping district, but it turned out to be a pretty rough area of town. It was difficult for us to stick together among the open market stalls in the unrelentingly rain, and soon I had lost track of Eveline and Mie. That was also about the time I remembered how much I fervently disliked shopping, so I caught a cab and went back to the hotel for some peace and quiet. When Eveline returned, she was all a-flutter with excitement, and she had a new story.

She and Mie had been shopping when some guy tried to snatch her purse, but she had been carrying it looped diagonally across her body, and so instead of grabbing it quickly without her noticing, he ended up trying to run away with it while she was still attached! She grabbed at her bag, and soon the purse-snatcher and she were pulling it back and forth, tugging and yelling, when she lost her grip in the rain. Just then, Mie, the elegant flower, came out of nowhere and smacked the guy over the head with her umbrella! He pushed her, and she went flying into a vendor's cart, knocking it over. Then he ran off empty-handed. *"Just like a movie!"* Eveline exclaimed, dazzles dancing in her eyes.

***

At four a.m. the next morning I waited alone on the dark quiet sidewalk in front of our hotel for a taxi. By the time I arrived at the tiny airport which services exclusively San Blas province and its islands, I had already walked into another world.

Nearly every passenger at the airport was four-and-a-half-feet tall. The men were dressed in western-style shorts and shirts, but most of the Kuna women wore their straight black hair cropped short with long bangs hanging out from under red-and-yellow scarves which rested untied atop their heads. Some women wore colorful print blouses to which were sewn *molas*, squares of traditionally-embroidered cloth that are hand-stitched with intricate designs representing stories of the islands.

365 islands, to be exact -- one for every day of the year. The exquisite beauty of the San Blas Islands falls right out of the imagination. Tiny idyllic cays of pure white sand, broken by nothing but palm trees bending gently in the warm wind. Some islands are uninhabited. Some have villages. Some house a single family, a solitary thatched hut and three perfect palms perched atop pearls of quartz, swimming in turquoise crystalline seas.

But perhaps the most unique feature of San Blas is that it is autonomously governed by the Kuna people, a distinctive cultural-ethnic group who differentiate themselves from mainland Panama not only by their rich traditions but also in the self-governance of their province which is geographically located within Panama. To visit San Blas is to visit a place like nowhere else, a small uniquely-evolved complete and independent system, distinctive in dress, customs, language, mannerisms and economic systems. If there is ever a reason to travel, it is to experience feeling different, to experience a place that is like no other. And I would not have missed San Blas for the world.

Sitting there in the airport looking around from my plastic seat in the waiting area, I felt like an albino giant, so alien from everyone else in the place. But no one seemed to pay much attention to me. An older woman with thin beaded bracelets wrapped up her arms to her elbows, sat down next to me, gave me a glance, and then looked quietly straight ahead. I felt a little nervous now that I was all alone, having left the other girls to go out on this adventure for a few days. I was shocked that no one else had chosen to go to San Blas. The trip was on the far reaches of any backpacker's budget, but I decided I'd rather eat saltines and mangos for a week to make up for it than miss out on this. I was learning that no matter who I traveled with, I had to make my own decisions. And sometimes that meant splitting off from people I'd met along the way. I learned I was unwilling to compromise my agenda for companionship, and I was forced to step out and travel *sola* which seemed hard at first since I'd become accustomed to being with other people.

For a total of $100, I bought a plane ticket (the only way to visit the archipelago) and a made reservation at the only budget-friendly lodge whose price included room and board as well as transportation around the islands. And I never looked back. Those exquisite days were some that I will never forget…

***

A man with shoulder epaulettes and a clipboard walked into the waiting area and began calling passengers' names. I followed him out to the runway to a small ten-person plane into which he ushered the Kuna families. I waited outside as the plane filled, and the man told me to get in the front seat.

"You can be the co-pilot," he said in Spanish, and I chuckled at his joke.

But he just kept looking at me, straight-faced, so I got in, sat down, and there, right in front of me were all the controls! I kept my hands folded tightly in my lap as the man climbed up into the pilot's seat, wiped the inside of the fogged windshield with a handkerchief, and started up the engine. As the propellers whirled to life, I looked behind me at the eight other passengers who didn't seem to be worried. I held my breath, and we took off!

The view was incredible! I felt like *I* was the one flying -- on a magic carpet, without a plane at all. I had never been in such a small plane, and certainly never in the front with a full windshield's view. It was like being part of the clouds. We took off over the Pacific, circled around, and flew over the lush jungle and mountains of mainland Panama until the breathtakingly blue waters of the Caribbean came into sight. The sun had started to rise over the ocean, and there I was looking down on it in its pinks and golds as it lit up the hundreds of islands below.

About thirty minutes later we began our decent toward a tiny island that wasn't much more than one very short runway and a hut. When we touched down, the grandson of the owner of the hotel was there to meet me. He introduced himself as Danny and said he would be the one taking me around the islands for the day. As we got into his small wooden boat with an outboard motor and headed towards the hotel on a neighboring island, he said, "Yesterday we had thirty Americans. Today, it is just you."

***

When I arrived at the hotel on Nalunega Island, home to about 400 Kuna residents, Danny introduced me to Griselda, the cook, and showed me to my airy room where the walls were draped with palm-leaf woven mats. I wandered around the grounds looking into the general store and the bakery, watching a few Kuna women in their traditional dress walk by and finally settled into a laid-back wooden chair on the beach at the edge of the water. There was not a voice, not a sound but the waves lapping against the shore, and a feeling of tranquility washed over me as I stared hypnotically into the most crystal-clear turquoise water I'd ever seen.

Danny found me at the water's edge, and we were soon whizzing across its surface, bound for a tour of the nearby islands. The sun beat warmly on my shoulders, and its light danced and twinkled on the water's calm surface. I peered over the side of the boat as the sea's color changed from one subtle shade to another as we passed over sandbars and seaweed.

We arrived at Isla de Perro where we jumped out onto sand so fine it was almost dust, velvet under my toes. As we waded into the water for a swim, Danny said there was a sunken ship nearby where I could snorkel. I asked if he was coming with me, and he said that in all the years he'd lived there, despite taking tourists to the wreck a few times a week, he'd never snorkeled there.

We swam out together, and I felt currents of warm and cool rushing around me. The small ship which sunk thirty years ago was now rusted and broken up, making it a perfect habitat for sea creatures. Magnificent schools of tiny black fish glittered with brilliant blue stripes that shone and sparkled as the sunlight penetrated the water. Giant red sea-stars stuck to the ship's underbelly, and as I swam around and around the ruins, I noticed the currents were quite strong on the far side. I felt like an explorer, discovering archeological treasure amongst delicate anemones and soft yellow corals. But the ocean seemed so big and open and full of life that I noticed myself becoming a bit paranoid, and the idea of sharks snuck into my mind. I finally asked Danny if there were any.

He said, "You want to see sharks?"

"NO!" I exclaimed, maybe a bit too loudly.

"OK then. There are no sharks here," he said.

Hmmmm… Not two minutes later, my bikinied bottom bobbing, I felt something nip me hard, and when I jerked around, I saw a huge white fish swimming away. Wow, did I get out of there fast! I tried to play it off and pretend like I had just swum away to get a different view of the ship, but when I looked up, Danny was already laughing.

***

After lunch we motored over to Isla de Hierba where I laid my towel down on an untouched white sand bar that stretched far far into the ocean and sighed deeply as I lay soaking in the sunlight. When I had left home to travel three months ago, I hadn't had many expectations. In fact I'd tried not to think about it too much. But as I lay on a heavenly tropical island in the Caribbean, I was sure that *that moment* was what my travels were supposed to be about. I was where I was supposed to be.

I told Danny I'd like to go for a walk and asked how long he thought it would take to walk all the way around the island.

"Ten minutes," he responded dead-pan.

And as I began my circumnavigation (it was hard to get lost even for one who is directionally-challenged), I gathered hollow puffy shells once the bodies of sea urchins and noticed the shoreline changing. Some parts of the island had waves while others were totally calm, their waters softly lapping at the shore. A few steps later there were areas covered in rocks, then coral, and then pure white sand -- all on one island which I could walk around in ten minutes.

I watched as the sun fell lower toward the horizon, and my heart sank when Danny said it was time to go back to the hotel. I wished I could have stayed on that speck of sand forever. The afternoon winds had picked up as we crossed the now-choppy seas, and white clouds dropped onto the mountains of Panama, the sunset sky turning pink and red. In that moment it was truly the most beautiful place on earth, preserved as it had been for centuries. Life was simple and beautiful and pure, and I felt privileged to have been able to experience just one day in it. Dark storm clouds moved closer as the waves grew bigger under our little wooden boat, and all I could do was stare out at the beauty.

As we neared the hotel, Danny asked, "Do you like *langostinos?*"

Lobsters. I nodded enthusiastically. We veered off-course and headed for a nearby island to talk with the man who sold the lobsters. As we pulled up to the dock on which his home sat, the man invited us in, pulled up a trapdoor in the floor, and we looked straight down into the water! The man pulled on a rope that led down to the sea below, and when the other end came up, it was tied to burlap sack from which he emptied out a dozen lobsters!

"Which one do you want?" he asked.

I picked one, feeling guilt pangs as I sealed the little guy's fate (yet my mouth wouldn't stop watering), and the man threw it in a bag and put in on a scale. One kilo! Then Danny tossed it into the bottom of the boat, and we got back in. I pulled up my bare toes onto the seat, tentatively looking over at the twitching crustacean until Danny explained that *langostinos* have no claws. It flopped around as we drove it back to the hotel (I think it knew), and we brought it into Griselda.

While I waited for dinner, I swayed back and forth in a hammock, listening to the ocean and watching the color drain out of the sky. Then Griselda called me into the kitchen hut where I sat alone over a plate of tender lobster, pulling its meat from the shell and licking my fingers coated with coconut milk and rice.

With full belly I walked out onto the beach under a midnight-blue canopy of a billion twinkles. From sea to sky everything was crystal clear on San Blas. Danny came to find me and ask if I'd like to walk with him to see his village. He led me through the locked gate meant to keep tourists from bothering locals, and into the village in complete darkness. The only electrical generator on the island was at the hotel, and even there electricity shut off at 10:00 p.m. In the blackness I could make out the palm-frond-roofed huts with bamboo walls which Danny assured me expertly held out the rains. Hammock beds hung from ceilings above dirt floors. And in this bare minimum of material things, children played amongst the trees, and the elders chanted for the sick, and women talked quietly, and people seemed to be happy to live life the way it had always been lived. Tradition was something about which I knew so little.

Danny showed me "the party house" where the village gathered to celebrate and drink for four days when the girls came

of age.   He showed me the basketball court, and the primary
school staffed by two Kuna and two Panamanian teachers.   And
then we walked out onto the dock where the children were
running and laughing and playing.   Since I was a real giant in
Kuna society, the children spotted me right away, even in the
darkness.

One little boy told Danny, "Shine the light," and Danny
pointed the flashlight into my face, completely blinding me.

The children took a step backward in surprise but were soon
touching me, squealing, running away, laughing, and touching me
again.

As we walked back toward the hotel, Danny stopped in to
show me his mother's house that he grew up in.   His mother and
grandmother were sitting on a bench, dressed in their traditional
best, and soon drenched me in turquoise beaded bracelets the
color of the sea, winding them from wrist to elbow just like the
woman who I'd seen in the airport.   I sat with Danny's bright
inquisitive ten-year-old sister who asked me questions all about
America as Danny's mother laid out exquisite *molas* to sell me.   I
was pleased to be able to buy them from the women who made
them, and I chose an intricate design with birds as a gift for my
mother to symbolize her beautiful singing voice, and one for me
with colorful fish swimming together so I could remember my
time snorkeling in San Blas.   Danny's mother gave me a small
mola with a picture of an iguana so I would always remember my
time here.   Truly, I could never forget…

In one day's time I've seen the sun rise and set and rise over the ocean.
I've swum in the purest most beautiful water of turquoise I've ever seen.   I've
learned about handicrafts kept alive by tradition.   I've listened to the complete
tranquility of an island sleeping in the darkness.   I've observed another way
of life, an ancient one.   I've lived in the moment for no one but me.   I've been
to a different world -- not just one beautiful view, or one beautiful beach, but
an entire land of paradise.   And as the sun rises, it begins again.   And that,
I suppose is the essence of what this year is all about.

***

At 5:00 a.m. I awakened in complete silence, laying there in the
half-darkness, absorbing the peace resounding in a hush all
around me.   Sitting on the cold sand, I watched the sun rise over
the ocean, again.   Waves lapping up on the shore, stars and moon

in the west, gray clouds and a red ball of fire in the east. The ocean, the island and me.

I hadn't heard Griselda come up behind me. She offered me coffee, and much too soon Danny had arrived to motor me back to the airstrip. We exchanged addresses and watched the plane come in and land on the tiny strip. The pilot motioned for me to sit up front again, and sooner than I was ready, Panama City came into sight.

***

The girls from language school were already packing up the hotel room, and we caught the TicaBus from Panama City directly back to San Jose. I found myself so immediately in the familiar surroundings of Daisy's home that I almost wondered as if I'd dreamed the trip to San Blas. Eveline left for Switzerland a few days later, and we spent our last night together dancing at the salsa club. I was sad to see her go.

But Christmas was in the air -- the season for sharing and loving and family. And amongst the festivities, or maybe because of them, my attention turned to the unshakeable fact that I was in a foreign country all alone. I was endlessly grateful to share the holidays with Daisy and her family, and it certainly made my first Christmas away from home much less emotional, but it didn't stop me from crying like a baby at midnight mass on Christmas Eve as the church choir belted out the second verse in Spanish of *The Little Drummer Boy*. I cried so hard that a withered little nun came over and gently held my hand during the service, assuring me that everything would be OK, as my lower lip quivered with every gasping breath.

On Christmas Day, we ate *tamales*, and Marco invited me to Zapote, a giant fair of rides, bumper cars and cotton candy. Festivities filled San Jose that week from bullfights to the Tope, a parade of hundreds of horses and masterful riders along with traditional Costa Rican ox-carts painted in signature bright oranges and blues. I even saw one rider atop a proud white steed, shining in the silver gleamings of his cowboy attire, talking on his cell-phone as he pranced down the parade route. Next came Carnivál, a tradition brought over from the Caribbean side complete with wild rhythms, deep drum beats, uninhibited dancing, and skimpy costumes of strategically-placed sequins and feathers.

When it was all over, I hugged Daisy tightly, told her I would be back in a few months, and with some anxiety and much excitement, began the fateful bus journey towards Playa Grande to begin my new life...

After I stepped off that diesel truck and finally made it back to Playa Grande, I figured things could only get better. And they did...

After one week I had quickly become competent in my new job of organizing and answering client email inquiries for the hotel. I had begun surf lessons with Louis which I had negotiated as part my contract in addition to room and board. And, I had met "the girls."

The staff of Hotel Las Tortugas had been created out of Louis and Marianela's vision to provide jobs for the families of former turtle-egg poachers who lived in the nearby town of Matapalo. And from the hotel's small beginnings, a core group of women came together to work as receptionists, cooks, waitresses and maids. That had been twelve years before I had arrived, and now that assemblage of matriarchs who virtually ran the hotel from the inside out, were impenetrably close-knit. "We are family," one of the girls explained, and it was true in the literal sense for many -- having all come from the same small town -- as well as being undeniably true in the symbolic sense.

This core group of fifteen women who were informally referred to as "the girls" or *"las guilas"* in Spanish, were savage in their loyalties, ferocious in their defense of their own, passionate and unyielding in their ideas of how things were supposed to be.

I felt sure that this different breed of feminist would have been the first to be burned at the stake at the Salem witch trials. I had to admire these women. They were incredibly tough. Some of it was due to their birthright of being Guanacastecan, raised in the wild cowboy northwest of the country where people's existence for generations had depended on being suspicious of outsiders. Some of it was that these women lived tough lives. Nearly all of them had a story of their lover or husband or father running off with a younger woman, leaving his wife to raise the family alone, and perhaps that was one reason why these women had come together in protection and support of each other like sisters against the world.

But despite how their toughness had evolved, they were unrelentingly resistant to outsiders -- including all clients -- which made it kind of a challenge to run a hotel. And then there was me, the newest and most suspicious outsider of all, who appeared to be staying.

And so during my first week, Louis had sat me down and explained things. He said, "You *are* an outsider. And you are a woman. And you are my friend. And the girls are going to think automatically that I have brought you here as a lover." I cringed, perhaps visibly.

"Well, I'm sorry," he continued a bit hurt, "But that is just what they are going to think. Where they come from, a young beautiful woman and an older man are not just friends. And because of this, you are going to have to live with the *chisme*."

Chisme was the word for gossip. And Louis warned that over the next few weeks, or maybe even months, it would run rampant. The staff had no real explanation for my presence there since Louis had never had any other foreign women working there, and few of the staff understood the scope of my new job with computers and webpages. And because I would be unable to explain myself satisfactorily due my lack of language fluency, *las guilas* would make up whatever stories about me suited them.

"You are just going to have to live with it for a while. They are protecting my girlfriend, Marianela. They love her, and they will protect her relationship with me until the end. That may make things difficult for you. But be nice to them, and slowly, slowly, you may be able to win them over. You'll figure it out."

But I wondered if I would. I had always wanted to be liked by *everyone*, and the first few weeks with the girls were torture. I'd walk into the kitchen with a smile, and have it returned with sharp unintelligible comments that flew from one woman to another, followed by shrill laughter. Luckily, I had other things to keep me busy.

It was a unique situation. And although the girls wouldn't let me in, I loved watching their microcosm with all its stringent rules which to me were foreign and unpredictable. Louis said that the only way to manage the girls was to not manage them. After sporadic mutinies he had figured out that you cannot manage a machine whose cogs willfully refuse to turn. And so, although the girls treated Louis with great respect and a deep familial love, everyone knew full well who was *really* in charge, and if Louis wanted to make any changes about how things ran at the hotel, first he had to get the girls to buy in, or it was like a lone locomotive engine chugging uphill hoping the rest of the freight cars would decide to follow.

As time wore on I came to know the *guilas* as individuals apart from their collective identity, gathering tidbits from Louis or from Spanish conversations in the kitchen that they didn't think I could understand.

The two senior Señoras, the toughest of the tough, were Carmen and Juanita. Carmen had been the very first employee at the hotel. Her father, Don Chico, had been the only Costa Rican who owned property in Playa Grande when Louis established the preserve and bought the land for the hotel. In an effort to support the people who supported the park, Louis and Marianela asked Don Chico's bright daughter, Carmen, to be the receptionist at Hotel Las Tortugas, and Marianela taught her everything from working the reservation book to doing the accounts. Since that time Carmen had become the reigning queen of the pack.

Carmen was short with the customers and shorter with me. Sometimes clients would ask me, "Why doesn't that lady like me?"

"I don't know," I'd reply. "She doesn't like me either."

You see, Carmen's favorite word was "No."

"Excuse me ma'am, may I have a towel?"

"No."

"Hello Miss, could I change this large bill?"

"No."

Ring, Ring. "Hello, do you have any rooms available tonight?"

Carmen would look at the empty reservation book, sigh a tired sigh, and "No."

In those first few days I had the distinct impression that Carmen particularly loved to torture me. We worked closely since we had to coordinate the reservation book -- she with the telephone reservations, me with the email. And so, I would break out my dictionary and carefully translate my question for her ahead of time, and she would bark something back at me which inevitably ended with the word "No." Sometimes, she even blocked me from eating. I'd go in and ask, *If one of the cooks wasn't too busy, would they mind making something for me for dinner?* And if Carmen was sitting in there chatting, sipping coffee, she would simply shout back, "No," and then they would all laugh. I ate a lot of ice cream those first few weeks.

Carmen sat at the front desk for over twelve hours each day. She saw everything. She knew everything. When a pesky client asked her a question, she would shake her head adamantly and say, "No Iiing-lish!" But I knew it was a cover. She understood a *lot* more than most people thought. I'd even seen her speaking broken English when she didn't know I was watching. But because she'd convinced most of the *gringo* world that she didn't understand English, people spoke in front of her like she wasn't even there. And *that* was why Carmen knew *everything. She* was the *chisme* source.

Now, ten years later, I consider Carmen one of the most loving loyal friends I have ever had.

Then there was Juanita, Queen of the Kitchen. Juanita was the senior cook, and no one -- no one -- messed with Juanita. Not Louis, not Marianela, not Carmen, not no one. You see, Juanita loved her knives. She sharpened them ritually at least twice a day, and when finished, would stand with intense focus in her immaculate white cook's uniform, clutching a carving knife and assailing slabs of red meat as the blade thrust back into the air with each deliberate pleasureful stroke.

A commanding woman with an imposing frame, as wide as she was tall, Juanita had *indio* features that spoke of her indigenous ancestry, an unusual look among Costa Ricans. In her mid-forties at a squat 200 pounds, Juanita was the most desirable woman in Matapalo. When I met her, she had five children from five different men and had never bothered to get married. I don't think she had kids because she loved kids; I think she just liked to have someone's ass to kick. And for all the years I knew her, it seemed like she was always pregnant, dashing from the kitchen toward the bathroom whenever someone ordered fish.

I was enamored with Juanita. She was brave and unapologetic, and it took many months before I realized that she had the dirtiest mouth I had ever heard (always something about sausages or empanadas or other food-sex innuendos). As the weeks rolled by, I'd ask permission to come into the kitchen and wash dishes to help out during busy dinner-rush times. Eventually, she let me pull up a stool when the girls were having coffee during a lull, and when an order came in, I loved to watch her broad strong arms chop heads of cabbage to bits, or throw fresh mahi-mahi fillets onto the sizzling grill from meters away with confidence, accuracy and flair.

But when Juanita was angry, you stayed away. I've already mentioned the knives, but sometimes I could hear her yelling -- bellowing -- all the way out by the pool. If you'd done something to piss her off, she let you know about it, usually right away, and often with the threat of raised fists. Juanita never, never lost a fight.

So compared to Juanita and Carmen, the other girls seemed much less intimidating. There were two other cooks. Mayella was stunningly beautiful, always smiling and joking, gold jewelry dripping from caramel arms. Johanna, the third cook, was warm and smart and curious. She was one of the few of the girls that ventured out into newness; she sought out Chinese and Italian recipes, took classes at the community center and was anxious to have me describe places I'd traveled to. Of all the *guilas*, Johanna was the easiest to get to know right away because she was so full of love, a love which spilled out into her cooking, just like *Tita* in Like Water for Chocolate.

There were two waitresses. Shirley was good-tempered and approachable. She was bold in speaking English with the customers and had a quick wit which meant she was usually

Louis's accomplice in playing pranks. And Shirley loved to dance. *Salsa, merengue, cumbia.* Whatever came onto the stereo, her hips swayed almost subconsciously, and her seemingly never-tired waitress-feet lightly danced trays of food across the dining room.

And then there was Sandra. Sandra was not really part of the inside crew. She and I got along quickly, maybe because she was a bit of an outsider herself, or maybe because she loved to slather motherly attention on me, just short of what Daisy had provided. But one would never guess by her generally-gentle demeanor that Sandra had a temper. Short but sturdy, she played on the local soccer team, and Louis said she'd been known to kick in other players' shins. She was full of fire, full of life, full of stories, full of worries and full of drama. She and Juanita were constantly going at it, and I could often hear her in the kitchen standing up for herself against the bullying from the other girls. Her biggest allies were the clients, who absolutely adored her, bringing her gifts from abroad, far and wide.

Nearly thirty people worked at the 11-room hotel, the four apartment rentals, and the two beach houses that Louis and Marianela owned or managed. And most of them were women. I got real pleasure watching the *guilas* push the men around who numbered in the minority among the employees. *Get the drinks, bring in another case of beer, the meat truck is outside ready to be unloaded...* They were amazing. And in the beginning, I had to stand at a distance in awe and admiration of them because I was not allowed closer. And at first, the *chisme* flew. And sometimes it hurt, although I couldn't really understand much of what they said anyway. But eventually, I guess they accepted that I wasn't after Marianela's Louis, and that I wasn't all that bad. And slowly, I made my way in. But *las guilas* had made their way into my heart from the moment I had met them.

PART II:
CHILE & ARGENTINA

SANTIAGO

Flying through a sky of diamonds, I arrived at Santiago international airport at a pitch-black 6:00 a.m. to be shocked into wakefulness by a phenomenon nearly forgotten. Cold. Deplaning from the familiar warm humid body smells carried all the way from Costa Rica, I was born out into a world of harsh refrigeration. It was winter in Chile. I breathed out slowly. *Fascinating...* I could see my breath as I crossed the terminal to customs where I was greeted with an official "Stamp, stamp!" It was perfect. All the ink evenly distributed over the page. A red-and-blue work of art.

Upon exiting the airport a door-to-door shuttle driver gave me some Chilean coins to call a hostel, and then he sped me into the city. I checked into a room whose bed had a decadent four blankets, whose toilet flushed, and whose hot-water shower reliably produced hot water. It was my first introduction into the relative efficiency of Chilean society. I was refreshingly delighted.

Over the next few days, I discovered that in Santiago there were at least five payphones on every corner, and all of them worked. The buses were painted one uniform color, they were all numbered, and an electronic sign flashed their destinations. There were street signs. You got a receipt for everything, but luckily you also got a bag for everything, so at least you had some place to put your receipt. And at stop signs, people -- brace yourself now -- actually stopped. I found it surprisingly comforting to be in a cosmopolitan city. Gobs of stores, gobs of restaurants, gobs of people in high-heeled shoes. Tall buildings, commuters, a metro system. It was sort of like New York with a few cathedrals sprinkled in.

After a few days exploring museums and coffee shops, I called Paulina on a whim, a girl whom I had met in Playa Grande when she had vacationed there with her family. Paulina was born in Santiago and was Chilean, but she had lived in Washington D.C. for many years where she had learned impeccable English during her father's high profile diplomatic career. Months before, she had suggested I visit if I ever came to town, and I had hoped to see her for a few hours, maybe even have dinner. Instead, she picked me up in her car, whisked me off to her house, and adopted me as part of the family for weeks. I was left wondering if I would ever have a "normal" backpacking experience.

Together we rode buses up and down the *cerros* of Valparaíso, gazing at the hundreds of brightly-painted tightly-packed houses that clung like rainbows to the ocean bluffs. We explored Pablo Neruda's house, La Sebastiana, its four stories filled with eclectic art and treasures from all over the world. I thought someday I'd like to have a house filled with treasures. We strolled through Museo Cielo Abierto, a museum of graffiti art and poems by Chile's best-known modern artists who've displayed their work in spray-paint along a chosen neighborhood's narrow alleyways.

While Paulina was at school, I spent hours in the parks in Viña del Mar, crunching leaves underfoot on crisp sunny days, lines of uniformed school children passing, two by two with bows in their hair and navy knee socks. Elderly people walked hand-in-hand, leaning on canes as they shuffled along Avenida Libertad. I found myself inspired by usually mundane things -- the smell of Chilean women's perfume, the brilliant blue sky without a cloud, buses barreling by. And as I walked from place to place down long avenues of trees and sunlight and color, my life became a poem I recited in my head. Thirsty for life, I drank and I drank.

***

One day, Paulina and I went to get our legs waxed. The only defensible explanation I have for subjecting myself to such a horrifying masochistic practice was that it was a cultural phenomenon. Truly. Chilean women wax. They don't shave. They rip the hair out of their legs, armpits, eyebrows, bikini line voluntarily and on a regular basis. And although I acknowledged it as a form of torture, it came at such a reasonable price! I could just *try* it. When in Rome, right?

And then I realized why it was so cheap. As the woman in the white lab coat spread the melted hot wax from the vat brewing in the corner of the room onto my shins (which tensed in disbelief), I noticed that the wax had a number of foreign objects floating in it, like tiny insects trapped in amber. And as the "aesthetic technician" ripped the follicles from my legs, first I screamed... And then, I watched as she put the used strips of wax *back* into the simmering vat, melting them down once again for the next victim. Now, that's the best deal in town!

Paulina treated us both to fat slices of triple chocolate cake to celebrate our hairless transformation; it reminded me of when my mom used to buy me ice-cream after I went to the dentist. (The legs hurt more, by the way.) When we got home, we tittered wildly about the next phase of my journey. I had decided to head south, traveling toward the far reaches of the tip of the continent and "El Fin del Mundo" in Patagonia, romantic visions of untamed wilderness dancing though my head. I got so excited about the whole thing that, fueled by the sugar buzz, I crawled into my sleeping bag, zipped it all the way up, flipped the hood over my head, and started hopping around. Paulina, between hysterical fits of laughter, decided that this is what I would look like in Patagonia: bundled from head to toe, hopping with my backpack and wiggling like a worm on the ice.

"Cold, wet and alone," she said, "floating on an iceberg with a penguin!"

She had never been to the south of her country, but she could only imagine this is how it would be! *Cold, wet and alone.* Four small words that echoed in my mind over the next few months. *Cold, wet and alone.* We shall have to see about that...

***

When it was time to say goodbye to Paulina and her gracious family, her father said to me, *"Mi casa es chiquita, pero mi corazon es grande."* *My house is small, but my heart is large.*

Somehow during my travels, I often managed to be made to feel like family, be made welcome in a town as more than just a visitor stumbling around with a map in front of my face. When people here invited you to come stay with them, they *meant* it. And it was not a burden. It was a joy. How many times had I ever offered for a distant acquaintance to come stay with me if they ever happened to come to town, knowing full well (and with a certain relief) that the offer was nothing more than a polite gesture. That was not how it worked here. I learned quickly that this was a place of many things genuine.

And so began the first of many Chilean bus experiences. "Easy" does begin to describe it. I walked up to the counter where I stood in an orderly line and bought a $9 ticket for a nine-hour direct trip (that means no stops!) to destinations further south in a huge new nearly-empty bus with cushy seats that reclined. The porter (yes, there were *two* people who worked on the bus, a driver and a porter) came by to ask if he could assist me in putting my backpack up on the shelf above. There was a sign that stated, "No driver drives more than five hours continuously." My legs didn't even touch the seat in front of me, even when I reclined! Air-conditioning and a skylight. And cup holders. And a bathroom. No one on this bus was crying. In fact, it was totally silent, and when I dropped a battery I was trying to put into my walkman and it fell to the ground with a clunk and a roll, the porter came to see if everything was OK. Yes, this was a very, very good start.

VOLCÁN VILLARICA

I am an ordinary woman. But once I did an extraordinary thing. I climbed a snow-covered active volcano -- by accident. I say by accident because I hadn't ever intended on going all the way to the top. I really just wanted to wear the crampons because I thought they were cool, and snap a couple award-winning photos of me in my red-and-blue issue snow gear, ice axe proudly by my side. You know, to impress my friends, hang in my office. Just for a day, I wanted to play mountain climber (in a safe, picturesque and photogenic environment). But what ended up happening opened me up to look at the womyn inside me, and I saw that I had a lot of growing to do.

***

I had begun to work my way down the 2800-mile stretch of Highway 1 that runs the length of Chile, taking in sweeping ocean vistas, winding country roads, and handicraft markets spilling over with silver and lapis lazuli jewelry made by the Mapuche, the indigenous people of the region. And soon, I found myself in the Lake District. Widely-regarded as the country's most picturesque province, the Lake District is a canvas of quaint Alpine-style villages dotted along green hills and crystal lakes, all nestled before a backdrop of breathtaking snowy Andean peaks. A fellow traveler had recommended Doña

Sonia's hostel in the town of Pucón, and when I arrived late at night in the pouring winter's rain and walked into her warm living room with the fireplace blazing, I knew this was the kind of place where something wonderful might happen.

It rained every day that week, and the supposedly imposing Volcán Villarica which I'd come so far to see, was nowhere to be found. *How could something that big hide?* My guidebook clearly stated that there was a magnificently dramatic snowcapped active volcano sitting just on the outskirts of town, and as if that wasn't enough of a thrill, it was apparently possible for travelers with little or no alpine experience to actually climb it since it did not require technical skill. While I impatiently waited, I filled my time by taking long wet walks, making vegetable soup in Doña Sonia's kitchen, and accompanying her to a local exposition of handicrafts, sculpture, painting, and photographs where a folklore troupe pulled me up on stage to dance the *Cueca* with the mayor. If blushing was any indication of the impression it made on both of us, I imagine we're both still talking about it.

Since Pucón is known among backpackers as the *Mecca* for outdoor adventure travelers, there was plenty of natural scenery to enjoy while I waited for the volcano to appear from behind the storm clouds. Ojos Azules, famed natural pools noted for their clear blue waters, were little more than overflowing muddy puddles, but the hot springs of Termas de Huife were as welcome as they had been back in Panama. As I bubbled away in the waters heated by the area's volcanic activity, I felt a bit of nostalgia creep in for Eveline, wondering what she was doing now. I hoped she was making bread. And I was quite sure I'd never be able to sit in hot springs again without vivid images of our driver, Giovanni, flashing into my head. They made me smile...

I river-rafted down the Bio Bio and Futaleufu rivers, Class IV rapids swollen with winter rains and bordering on an upgrade. Exciting and terrifying, I held on with all my might, bouncing around on the raft among swirling whirlpools, crests and troughs, and when we had safely made it through to calmer waters, I wished I could to do it all over again.

And then one day, the sun came out. It started with a little blue spot in the sky, and then it got bigger and bigger, clearer and clearer, and I began to see the green hills all around town, and then the rocky mountains behind them. I ran toward the lake as the layers of fog began to dissipate, lifting higher, and soon I could clearly see the other side for the first time. After an hour of walking around in a town bathed in the glorious soft glowing sunlight of the late afternoon, I briefly ducked into a shop, and when I came out, THERE WAS A VOLCANO standing right there in front of me! It had appeared in a matter of moments. It was enormous, and its base seemed to start at my very feet. *How could* that *have been hiding?* But there it was, covered in snow, staring at me, waiting for me, imposing as the Matterhorn.

This was why I had come. I ran to the mountain expedition office and was giddy at the news that yes, there would be a climb tomorrow. And as I skipped back toward Doña Sonia's, I stared and stared at what seemed like an illusion with its instant appearance out of thin air. And then the crisp air grew cold, and the sun began to set, throwing pastels against the sky, against the snow, and then in a dramatic finale for its last magnificent magic trick of the day, the entire volcano turned pink.

***

I arrived at Turismo Trancura Expeditions in the wee hours of the next morning where I met Alvaro, one of the hiking guides, who loaded me up with gear. He was a gentle guy in his early thirties, a few days of stubble framing a kind face and unforgettable smile. I slid on waterproof pants and a jacket, gaiters, a hat and gloves. He gave me a backpack filled with mysterious items whose purposes would reveal themselves over the course of a day. These included crampons (metal spikes you could strap to your shoes to prevent slipping on the ice), a gas mask, and an ice axe. I got into the van filled with two guides and numerous other anxious "adventurers," and in the dark we drove to the base Volcán Villarica. Little did I know that I had a life-changing nine hours and 1800 vertical meters ahead of me.

***

My body burned, and my legs had turned to Jello within the first hour. Alvaro held my hand as I climbed through volcanic dirt and ash to the first resting spot. I was surprised he didn't leave me for the buzzards right then. The terrain was loose and deep, like trying to climb up a sand dune; every step up meant a coinciding slide down. I was ready to turn back. I almost did. The trek was estimated at six hours up, three hours down. *If I feel like I can't take another step now after only one hour,* I thought, *then how on the earth can I expect to make it though the next eight?* It took everything I had not to fall down and spin in oncoming dizziness. Blackness loomed from my peripheral vision creating the feeling I was looking down a long tunnel. All the blood in my body surged through my temples. I looked up at the top of that snow-covered mountain. There was no way in hell.

But I felt a little better after a rest, and I was just fine for the next fifteen minutes. Then the intense fatigue started in again. The burning in my legs. Shaking. Gelatin. I was sure they'd simply give out.

I looked up. I looked down. *There's no fucking way.*

OK, I need a distraction. "Alvaro, de que piensas cuando subes el volcán?" I asked. *What do you think about when you are climbing the volcano?*

"I think about the climbers," he answered in Spanish.

That's not what I had been looking for. "No, I mean, to take your mind off things."

He smiled and replied, "I think about Cancun."

Hmmmm. I wondered if Alvaro had ever been to Cancun. But at that moment, an inner monologue began to chatter away in my head, and for the first time, I heard it. Acknowledged it. Listened. A little voice was talking to me, tellin' it like it is, tricking me into moving beyond the tough spots, and every once and a while, reminding me that I can do anything, whether I know it or not. Once awakened, that little voice never went away, and I consider its discovery one of the greatest gifts of my travels. I keep it with me always, and since that day I try my very hardest to give it the respect it deserves.

OK, Cancun. Beautiful beaches. STEP, STEP, STEP. *Sunsets, romance. Oh Costa Rica. What the fuck am I doing climbing a volcano? I could be surfing. OK. Surfing. Do you remember how hard that was the first time you did it? At first, Louis was very helpful, and then he kicked your ass. Then you hated him. Then he won back your favor. Is this working?*

I looked up. *This thing is huge!* I looked down. I could still see the van. *Damn I'm tired. When can I stop?* After the first hour, I never intended on really making it all the way to the top. *Look how far that is. Look at all the snow, and you're still on the ash and dirt at the base. OK, just walk until you find a respectable quitting point so you don't look so defective in front of the group. I could really care less about this kinda stuff. I won't feel like a quitter. I'll just know I wasn't cut out to climb mountains.*

Hey, what's this? Snow? Wow, cool. This is kinda fun. Look. I don't even have to blaze a trail. I just put my foot into the footprint that the half dozen people in front of me have already made. Hey, that's not so bad. STEP. STEP. STEP. *When the guy in front of me takes his foot out, I step in. Hey great. Didn't my legs hurt? Couldn't I barely pick them up? Well, this is much better.*

Look up. Look down. *God! Stop doing that. It's making you tired. If you look up, it's hopeless. If you look down, first you get dizzy, then you see how far you've come and realize how tired you must be, and finally, it makes you realize that when your body finally collapses, you're going to plunge down that very long hill.*

But check that out. STEP. STEP. STEP. *That's not so bad. Terrifying, yes. Look how steep it is. Someone else's footprints are the only thing holding you on the mountain. But hey, you're not as tired as you were before.*

My friends would be so proud of me if they found out I climbed a mountain. Random thought... Who cares? I mean, I know I don't have to prove anything to anyone, and I'm sure as hell never doing this again, but yeah, I think they'd be proud of me.

Yeah, STEP. STEP. I started to think about when my college roommate and I used to run the stadium steps at the baseball field. *And I thought that was hard. 50 steps? Maybe 100. Do you have any idea how many steps I've taken this morning? Oh my God, I'm tired.*

And in that moment, my foot slipped off the side of the cliff, and I was instantly sliding down the mountain. Fingers clawing, gloves digging fiercely into the snowy bank, I slowed quickly, but was significantly shaken. It took two guys to pick me up, and six to give me advice. STEP, STEP, STEP.

Look up. *Ahhhh, STOP IT! But hey, are they stopped up there? I'm saved. Are they eating? Oh, thank you. Lunch.*

OK, lunch. Good. Stop. Eat. Feel better. Have to pee but can't take off all my snow clothes. We must be almost there. I can see the top. It doesn't look very far. All snow, yes, but it doesn't look very far.

"OK people," the bellowing voice of the head guide echoed, jolting me from my inner narrative. Alvaro's boss continued, "It's going to be cold up there. Put on all the clothes you brought. This is how to put on your crampons. This is how you use your ice axe to stop yourself if you fall. 2 ½ hours to the top."

W-H-A-T   T-H-E   @%e~*$!!!!!   TWO-AND-A-HALF HOURS??!!!!

"If you can't make it," he continued, "We'll send one guide down with you. We'll decide if you should go down. If you're very slow, we may send you down."

AH-HA! This is my chance. He's looking right at me. I'm the last one in the group. Earlier that day, I had learned that every other person in this group had climbed before. Some were even self-proclaimed experts. Me? Trekking? Never. Climbing? In gym class on a rope once, and I hated it. Failed miserably. Too hard. *What the hell am I doing? Oh well. It's pretty cool I climbed half way up a snowy volcano. And now I'll even get to say I've used crampons and an ice axe.*

Yes, I'll get to say that. During my phone calls home. To my friends. Pictures. Take lots of pictures to prove it. And I'll make up some exaggerated excuse why I had to come down. My bum knee? Yes, that should do it. Actually, contrary to my hopes, my old knee injury was faring amazingly well. No pain. My boots were warm and toasty, and the equipment was functioning perfectly.

That's it. That's why I came. To be able to tell *people I climbed a volcano. Not because I wanted to climb it. Not because I thought it would be particularly rewarding. Not because I had always dreamed of climbing a mountain. But to say, hey, look at my photos! Look at my equipment! Look at my Chilean adventures! I climbed a mountain. And now I'll say, I climbed half a mountain. Whatever. I don't care. Let's get out of here. God, I thought I was beyond being concerned about what everyone else thinks. About appearances. I guess not. Some ugly things show through in times of crisis.*

Alvaro started off, leading the experts of the group in the front. The head guide stayed with the second-string climbers, and we started up a few minutes later. *Well, here we go.* My legs tired only ten minutes after lunch. Now it was very steep. *Just take it slow. You'll never make it 2 ½ hours more. You shouldn't have even made it this far. Good job. God, my legs are burning. I can't keep up with my group. I'm almost last. There's only one couple behind me. I could slide down this mountain any second. I could slide down and hit those rocks and die. That is a long long way. My legs are NOT going to hold me. That's it. I'm done. Where is the fucking guide? What?! Why is he in the front?! He's supposed to be back here to catch me if I fall. Stupid shit. I'll just wait until he stops and then tell him that's it for me. I have no pride. Dignity, yes, and it would be better if the people behind me would give up first. Wow, I spend a lot of time thinking about how I'm going to give up. Why is he so far ahead? Hey! Back here! I'm done!!!* But I didn't call out.

Soon, I had lost the group entirely. *That head guide is one hell of an SOB.* He and the others had disappeared, and I was precariously balancing on a mountainside of ice with only two other climbers whose abilities were arguably as weak as mine. We had made it to the switchbacks. I was stopping every few meters, trying to look pitiful enough for the guide to come back for me.

Then the two climbers behind me, passed me. They were a couple, and the girlfriend was hurting badly, beyond pure exhaustion. I could sympathize. All I wanted to do was stop. In front of her, her boyfriend had hold of her hand.

"Come on, baby. You can do it. Just a few more steps. You can rest on the turns. Don't cheat yourself. Come on. COME ON! DO IT!"

Encouraging, angry, annoyed, he dragged his girlfriend up the mountain.

I worked off his words. I stopped when she stopped and pushed when she pushed, only a few meters behind them. I couldn't catch my guide. *There was no one to take me back down. Why not keep going? What else do I have to do today? This sucks. God I hurt.*

Hey, I don't want to be that lame girlfriend. I AM that lame girlfriend. I don't want to be her. I hate pain. I hate this. I hate things that are hard. I almost started to cry -- twice. *That's not going to do me any good.* I could hear the boyfriend calming her.

"Shhh, shhhh, come on. Just to the next turn."

No trail. Just footprints in the ice... Small rockslides. Slipping. And a save with my ice axe. *No one to catch me.*

"Don't cheat yourself. You're almost there," he said.

I looked up. *We're NOT almost there. I went into a zone. So much pain. One step.* STEP. STEP. STEP. Just one step. Then one step. *Hard. Strong. Crunch the crampons into the ice. Don't slip. Sure steps.*

I don't remember much more until he said it again.

"Come on baby, you're almost there."

I looked up. And we were. Almost there. I could see Alvaro and all the others.

Alvaro shouted, "Ten minutes, and you're at the top!"

I knew at this rate, it was going to me more like thirty. BUT I WAS GOING TO MAKE IT! I couldn't believe it. Emotion overcame me. My heart pumped. I began to cry. I screamed inside. I'M GOING TO MAKE IT! I can't believe it! I didn't mean to. I don't deserve it. I gave up a long time ago. I gave up in hour one. And now it's hour six. AND I AM GOING TO MAKE IT!

It didn't hurt anymore. I just did it. Although my mind had given up, my body was a machine. It kept on stepping. It didn't have a choice. I had intended to just kill time until the guide could take me down. But I MADE IT. ALL THE WAY. By accident.

***

We stayed only a short time at the summit. A storm was coming quickly, and I could see the clouds swooping in. I put on my gas mask, crawled to the edge of the active volcano's crater, got down flat on my belly, and peered in. A delicate layer of black film covered a boiling pot of lava, a few tell-tale orange bubbles percolating up to make their point. The fumes from the volcano burned my lungs as I gasped for breath from altitude and sheer exhaustion. And all I could think was I CAN'T BELIEVE I REALLY MADE IT.

Over the next three hours, the group descended the mountain by sliding down on our butts like toboggans on the snow. We used our ice axes to slow us down, and I laughed deliriously the whole way. When I reached the ash at the base of the mountain, my legs were so weak and wobbly that I fell every few steps. I didn't care. Total exhaustion. Total elation. Alvaro held my hand.

I know what it's like to climb a mountain. I have more insight into those metaphors now. I have more insight into myself. It was the beginning of recognizing something new -- a strong body, but more importantly, a strong mind that can take it anywhere. From that time on, I was a trekker, and when the going got tough, I told myself, *You are not that lame girlfriend. YOU are strong.* And the going did get tough. But I never felt weak again. *Do not be afraid. Your body will not break. Your mind will not let it.* I had discovered the zone, I had discovered my inner voice, and together, we could do anything.

***

Alvaro and I had a drink that night in front of the roaring fireplace at the neighborhood bar, and by the time he walked me home, it was raining again. I lingered on the hostel steps, hoping he might lean in, press his wine-kissed stubble into my face. But he just shuffled his feet a little and dropped his head, his soft brown eyes turned towards his shoes. And then he said goodnight and ran out into the rain.

"I took one of my hands from his and placed my glass of wine at the edge of the table.

'It's going to fall,' he said.

'Exactly... Try to understand that I've broken things within myself that were much more important than a glass, and I'm happy I did... Our parents taught us to be careful with glasses and with our bodies. They taught us that the passions of childhood are impossible,.... that people cannot perform miracles, that no one leaves on a journey without knowing where they're going. Break the glass -- and free us from all these damned rules, from needing to find an explanation for everything, from only doing what others approve of.'"

<u>By the River Piedra, I Sat Down and Wept,</u> *by Paulo Coelho*

***

The fireplace blazed downstairs in Sonia's living room, warming me from the chill of the freezing rain. The ceiling blurred under my heavy eyelids, and I wondered what the moon looked like high above the low thin clouds.

When I fell into bed, I felt like I'd been run over by a truck. As my muscles ached and my body vibrated with energy, I thought back to a different time and place that had first dared me to break the glass. A new world of people to test me, question me, challenge me. A place where mountains were made of water -- surging up, crashing down, my body inconsequential amidst the sea's profound energy and rhythm. And as I often did throughout my travels in South America, I soon drifted to sleep, dreaming of moontime and Playa Grande.

WAXING GIBBOUS…

For the first few weeks after my return to Playa Grande, I enjoyed the decadent courting rituals to which I had become accustomed -- long seaside chats, delicious drawn-out meals and nightly margarita parties in the jacuzzi. Marianela and Louis knew better than to move me into the Rancho right away. Instead, they shuttled me from vacant hotel room to vacant hotel room. But as high season wore on, there was nowhere else for me to go except…

THERE ARE FROGS IN THE TOILET

There are frogs in the toilet
And crabs in the shower
And spiders in the sink
And iguanas on the fence post
    There are cats in my room
    And raccoons in the kitchen
    And ants in the sugar
    And monkeys in the yard
And this morning I woke up for my 6am surf
And went down to the bathroom
And put down my toothbrush

Almost on top of a spider.
      But this spider wasn't anything
      I used to shriek over in California;
      This was a Costa Rican spider
      So it had big fat legs
      And a little hair.

I live in a land
Where the wind is so warm
It feels like kisses,
And I live in a rancho
With a palm frond roof
With garbage bags over the top so the rain doesn't get in.
I live in the corner,
Above the laundry room,
Amongst the rafters of broken surfboards
In the building where old French-fryers go to die.
Where one wall is made of plywood
And the others of palm fronds
And they're all covered with sheets
To help keep out the visitors,
But I still get some...

      Yesterday a big gray beetle flew in
      With the sound of a helicopter
      BUZZZ
      It was uniformed in armor
      With a hard gray shell
      And antennas that were four inches long.
And I DOVE for my bed
And I squeaked under the mosquito net that hangs from the ceiling
And I tucked the edges under my mattress
And I knew I was safe.

It's just us, the Four Little Pigs, who live in the Rancho.
And all day and all night
The Big Bad Wolf tries to
      Huff, and Puff, and Blow our house down.
The Papagayo offshore winds are great for the surf
But not so good for a house made of palm fronds and garbage bags.

At 2:13am I wake up.
I am sure the place is coming down
And this is the end of me.
And there goes the roof,
Part of it.
The wind whips through and clears my shelves
And blows my mosquito net into a little ball,
And I can hear the waves crashing up on the beach below me.
> *And I live here in a rancho*
> *With all the creatures*
> *And the windy nights*
> *Here in* verano *in Playa Grande.*

The Rancho was a far departure from Bruce's House. My morning rituals changed significantly. Now I got up, rinsed gecko poop from my toothbrush, surveyed my room to determine which wild animal had thrown up where, and shook my clothes violently before dressing until the potential-for-scorpions fell out. I was probably the only person on earth to live in a storage building, and still have a cook and a maid.

The Rancho was a two-level accumulation area for extra things and extra people, the bottom floor of which housed the hotel's laundry facility, a small bathroom, and a series of head-high piles of discarded items from broken halves of yellowing surfboards to old cookware, from rotting lumber to rusty tools. In the first days of the hotel, every ounce of material had to come from San Jose, and thus Louis had developed (and hung on to) a hoarding mentality which unfortunately meant nothing could be thrown away. And over the years, the piles had grown taller…

At the top of the rickety wooden un-railed staircase were four bedrooms. Mine was located in the southwestern corner and was the biggest of the closet-sized rooms. It would have had a million-dollar view of the ocean if it had had a window. As I pushed open the creaky plywood board that served as a door and ducked my head below the frame, its sparse furnishings revealed themselves in all their functional glory. The narrow bed stood beside a small unlatched cupboard, and on a single shelf stood a rusty dusty rotating fan, tiny swirling funnelclouds dancing on the splintery floor.

But the Rancho was magical in its own way. Living there, one could not deny that you were unequivocally in the heart of the tropics. The outside was forced in, and I quickly became environmentally synched, waking naturally at first light, telling time by the sun, menstruating with the moon. Of the entire stretch of Playa Grande's three mile beach, the Rancho was the nearest structure to the sea, sitting amidst the ground vines of succulent plants which marked the high tide line. And on the nights when full and new moons brought the highest high tides, the pounding surf would shake and rumble my bed as I lay awake feeling its immense power. Moonbeams poured through the gaps in the roof and stroked my face. Violent winds regularly jolted the footings of the building as gusts came flying through the gaps in the walls. The sun's midday heat baked into the rooms, while creatures, great and small, crawled and squeaked and chirped alongside me in my little cubbyhole. There was no doubt, either in times of wakefulness or in times of sleep, that nature lived there right beside you, inside you.

There were four of us *Rancheras* who had found our way to Playa Grande and whom Louis had taken in either because we were useful or in a moment of quickly-regretted charity. The first was Alex. Alex, the gay laundry boy. No one remembered what part of Costa Rica Alex had come from, or even how he had found his way to the hotel, but he had lived there for nearly two years. He spent his days meticulously folding white towels, singing pop songs and dancing to the music on his boombox as he watched the loads go round and round in the dryer. Marianela had tried to teach him to clean rooms, but due to his nasty habit of smoking, guests complained that their rooms smelled worse after he was finished. So he stayed and danced and smoked in the laundry room.

His thick long black eyelashes fluttered for emphasis with every flit of his intonated speech. I had never seen anything like those eyelashes. The envy of Tammy Fay Baker, of any woman -- and why shouldn't they be? Alex was a self-described *mariposa*, a butterfly, which reminded me a lot of his eyelashes and his mannerisms, but which was also a slang word for *gay* in Spanish. Alex was truly a beautiful creature. Soft features set dark in a baby face, a clean white ribbed tank-top clinging to his slim teenage figure.

Alex and I shared a wall in the Rancho -- a wall made of wood scraps nailed together, full of knots and spaces and imperfections. And I suppose I should have taken Louis's warning about peepholes a little more seriously. It was perfectly reasonable to think that Alex could peek through any number of spaces right into my room had he wanted to. But that didn't really bother me so much. Alex wanted more than anything to be a woman. He told me he *was* a woman. I could not imagine what it was like to be him in the cowboy-up province of Guanacaste. And so, with just us ladies in the Rancho, I didn't worry about the peepholes.

One night, I arrived home, and there was Alex, dancing on the ground floor of the Rancho which had recently been waxed and buffed by the maids. And he was wearing *my* dress. My tight little black dress. The one I had bought in San Jose to go to salsa clubs with Eveline. And I can only assume that Alex obtained said dress by sneaking into my room while I was out and taking it. He was mid-flourish when I walked in, and when he came around from his ballet turn and spotted me, he landed off-balance, and his feet slipped out from under him, and he fell right on his butt -- the dress flying up above his thighs, exposing his striped boxer shorts.

"Oh no," he exclaimed in English, looking more embarrassed than injured. "You saw my vagina?"

***

Marianela's niece, Sabrina, occupied the third upstairs room. Louis referred to her as "trouble on a stick." A beautiful nineteen-year-old from San Jose with wide eyes and a tiny kitten-like face, Marianela brought Sabrina into the rural lands of Guanacaste to keep her out of big-city trouble. She was a bit of a wild one, that Sabrina, and her mother had been worried about her. Marianela had tried to make her work as a maid, but Sabrina was much more interested in partying than working. As she proceeded to clean rooms in her signature red string bikini, she was followed without fail by a long unshakeable trail of I'm-on-vacation-so-let's-party-with-the-local-girl guests, who followed her bouncing butt from room to room.

I liked Sabrina. She was smart and fun and positive. Vivacious and curious and full of the spark of life. Maybe she had some growing up to do, but at least she knew how to live in the moment. She took me to local fiestas and bullfights, taught me the lyrics to merengue songs, and convinced me that my Spanish was flawless after three *Imperial* beers.

But Sabrina didn't last long… After she'd slept with a dozen guests ranging from film producers, to actors, to semi-pro surfers, Marianela sent her home, sighting that she was just too much to handle. Louis, on the other hand, thought she was great for business.

***

And finally, there was Jenny. Jenny showed up at Louis's doorstep shortly after I had come to stay in Playa Grande. Originally from Argentina, she now spent her summers windsurfing and her winters working abroad as a masseuse and yoga instructor. Louis offered her full access to the hotel's clientele as well as a free room in the Rancho in exchange for free massages for Marianela and him. Marianela took full advantage of the offer whereas Louis, after his first massage, complained that Jenny tried to pull his leg over his head and look at his butthole. And that was the end of massages for Louis.

At a ripe ole' age of thirty-two, Jenny was already hardened by life, an unusual trait for her line of work I thought. She was extremely opinionated, her favorite phrase in English being, "You are completely wrong."

Jenny and I were like sun and moon, earth and sky, hard and soft, hot and cold. Opposites, it seemed, in every glass-half-empty, glass-half-full kind of way. She loved to taunt me, stating that all I did was sit around and read and surf and hang out with old people like Louis, and that I was blowing it, and that I was young and I should go out and have fun.

I questioned myself for a while, and then I went back to reading. She could give me a bad time all she wanted, but it didn't appear that how she was living her life was making her happy. She went out every night to the nearby bar (appropriately named Rancho Diablo), got drunk, screwed guys left and right -- favoring the ones who were leaving town the next day -- and then spent the next week pining over them. And although she claimed to be desperate to start a family, she seemed hell-bent on seeking out the most dysfunctional relationships possible. And when those relationships inevitably failed, it made her even more angry. Her tough front seemed a thin disguise of fragility. I can't say I loved living with Jenny, but she helped me care less what other people thought of me. She made it easy -- other people weren't always right. And I will always be grateful to her for that.

AGE OF DIURNAL INEQUALITY…

"Every person, all the events of your life, are there because you have drawn them there. What you choose to do with them is up to you." Illusions: Adventures of a Reluctant Messiah, by Richard Bach

As the weeks slipped by almost unnoticed, my friendships with Louis and Marianela deepened in the *pura vida* of Playa Grande. We sat and talked, talked and sat, and watched the moon sink big and yellow into the nighttime sea with an almost-audible hiss.

As for Louis's personal story, the details slightly varied based on his mood, the audience, and the number of margaritas consumed, but basically, it went something like this: Louis in his early-twenties found himself in his home state of Florida, married and with a new baby. As a white male behavioral psychologist in an equal-opportunity market place (which didn't seem so equal to him), he was out of work but grateful to have successfully avoided the Vietnam draft by convincing the mental health evaluator that he was crazy. (Studying the DSM in graduate school did come in handy.) But life took a turn for the worse the day he came home from his temporary construction job to find his wife in bed with another man, an affair that was later revealed to have been going on for some time.

He left the house to his ex-, bought a small plot of land out in the swampy boondocks nearby and lived under his overturned sailboat for a year until the municipality offered to buy the lot because they wanted build a highway through his land. Now freed, financially and emotionally, he grabbed his surfboard, his brother and his best friend, and they got in the car and drove south. Very south... And a few years later, they crossed into Costa Rica and stumbled upon one barren light-bulb hanging from a single shack at the end of a beach called Tamarindo. The palm and plywood hut was owned by a man named Nogui who today owns a restaurant in the same location now amidst the shopping boutiques and four-star hotels. Nogui let the guys camp on his land, and they discovered an entire bay of perfect unridden waves. Louis and his brother started a fishing business to attract the first flickerings of a tourist industry, and soon Louis had started a new life -- that is until the burgeoning construction in the area threatened the waves. (You'll recall the "They were fucking up my surf spot" motivation for establishing the national park). That was about the time when Louis met Marianela. They fell in love, joined forces, and established the reserve and the hotel. Marianela provided the political connections, her father being a well-known radio personality in San Jose. Louis put up the money. And the rest is history...

As for Marianela, she was the queen of her realm and the queen of the party. In the public sphere, she filled the room, her laughter perfectly-timed, her extroverted personality charming her fans. At home, she spent her days lounging in her giant round bed, watching satellite television, eating popcorn and drinking Chianti Reservo out of oversized goblets while maids cleaned gingerly around her propped-up feet. I was shocked when Louis told me of her more humble beginnings.

At the start of their relationship twelve years earlier, they had had nothing. They camped contentedly in a tent on the property where the hotel was being built for a year, living on beans and rice, making bonfires and scooping up field mice as pets with their bare hands. It seemed unbelievable. The Marianela I knew loved her stuff, her leisure, her power -- and it had aged her. It was hard to imagine her poor and young and happy.

I wondered how the enormous rift I now observed between Louis and Marianela had become so great. Day after day, they fought and yelled and fought some more. And it was all very public. When Louis recounted their early days, he seemed almost joyful. But now, he put Marianela down, made fun of her, picked fights with her, and talked about how he wished he could get rid of her. Then just as quickly, he'd turn around and say how he wanted her and no one else. And despite Marianela's seeming confidence and gregariousness, she felt her life in Playa Grande with Louis slipping away. I was left utterly dumbfounded, but unfortunately I was also left utterly surrounded by it all.

Over the next season, the gap between their lives, expectations, and daily activities continued to widen at an alarming rate. Marianela slept in and got bi-weekly massages while Louis ran around frantically tending to client crises. Whether his mania was warranted or not, I could not be sure, but Louis was constantly in motion... When he was at home, he was balancing the books, making small change for the reception desk, setting aside travelers checks to take to the bank. At the hotel, he was greeting guests, plunging toilets, renting out snorkel gear, giving surf reports. I could see how he could feel resentful towards such a seemingly lazy partner -- that is, until I heard from Marianela about "the arrangement."

When they had started the hotel, they had decided together they would work hard building the business for ten years, and then they would go into semi-retirement. It was the twelfth year. And Marianela had lived by her word. But Louis, he just couldn't stop... And it was making them both crazy. And I had a front seat. And Louis only had one outlet -- surfing.

***

1) SURFING IS ESCAPE:
I'd look up from my computer duties mid-keystroke, and there he'd be, tucked behind a cement column -- *psst* -- board under his arm, motioning for me to follow him. Careful to avoid eye contact with anyone who could impede our escape, we'd jog down the beach for a half a mile, despite the fact that some of the best surf in the area was right in front of the hotel. Down the sandy stretch and out of sight, we'd paddle though the punishing rows of pounding waves without looking back.

Once out past the breaking waves, the sea was totally calm. And if you sit just on the edge of the ever-shifting line where the motion begins, you find yourself suspended in a secret place, floating and bobbing, apart from everything that was your existence just moments before, a mere observer looking back at the shore of wild green trees and dusty golden hills, or gazing out to sea at the Farmer's Row clouds that dotted the brilliant blue sky. Nothing can touch you anymore; the ocean stands between you and all your worries, stresses, people, problems that are there on land. They all melt away into emeralds dancing in the water, the golden sun's heat falling on your back. And you breathe out slowly, melting, returning to Mother Ocean's warm and constant womb.

When Louis was surfing, he was alone -- even if I was sitting there next to him. Sometimes he would talk, usually to give me an instruction about a wave that was coming or which way to paddle, but usually we were silent, watching the brown pelicans glide in and ride the updrafts created by the waves, gracefully maneuvering inches from the spinning faces and then shooting down the line and up into the air as the wave exploded into foam behind them.

Louis had been surfing all his life. Even today, at sixty years old, he is still my favorite surfer in the whole world to watch, endlessly patient, wave racing, gliding weightlessly with grace and precision. But if a guest from the hotel happened to float down and find us in our secret spot, Louis would pretend like he didn't recognize him, which was easy enough because he was nearly blind without his glasses. If the client called out to Louis, he would paddle off against the shoreline current so that the person would just drift away. Sometimes I wished that life worked like that.

2) SURFING IS DANGEROUS:

"Surfing is dangerous," Louis said, as he lectured about the risk involved in taking a hard unforgiving fiberglass surfboard into an unpredictable power source such as the ocean. He illustrated with numerous graphic examples.

Not two weeks before I returned to Playa Grande, there was an accident involving an experienced surfer named Joyce, who was the girlfriend of James, the guy who originally picked Eveline and me up at Huacas crossroads. Joyce had a head-cold and had been taking mind-dulling decongestants for a week. And on that first day back in the water, she had stopped paying attention for just a moment. And when she fell off her board, the wave took it and held it, and when it let go, the leash snapped back like a rubber band, and when she popped her head up from underwater, the board headed straight for her like a missile. In a fraction of a second, the spear-like nose of her board tore her left cheek off. Nothing left but a flap of skin, hanging there limply from the side of her face. The force of that board being held back by the wave and then let go, was enough to break her nose and as the board continued in its trajectory, tear the side of her face resulting in 63 stitches. Louis had driven her to the Tamarindo airport, put her on a plane to San Jose, and she was in the office of the best plastic surgeon in New York in six hours.

"She didn't even cry," Louis detachedly reminisced as he gazed blankly out to sea. "That woman was made of steel."

I knew I would have been scared out of my mind, and that I never would have surfed again. But Joyce is still an avid surfer, and Louis told me that she sent photos a few months after the accident, and amazingly you can barely even make out the scars.

Not everyone is so lucky. Although most surfers have scarred shins and ankles and feet, sometimes even a sliced Achilles' tendon from accidents with a surfboard's knife-like fins, Louis's second wife in Tamarindo lost her eye to her surfboard. Like Joyce's accident, the board came back at her unexpectedly snapping against its leash, and in the early 1970s, that poor girl spent two days in a local Costa Rican clinic alone, waiting for surgery to put in a glass eye. Those stories scared me. And my enthusiasm quickly turned to thoughts of, *Do I really want to do this?* Louis assigned me a very spongy, very un-cool boogie board for my own safety for the first few months of my training.

"First," he said, "You will have to learn the basics without the worries of riding sharp objects. Learn how to read waves and where to ride on them."

And on Day 1, he molded little mounds of wet sand with his feet and talked for hours about the physics of waves.

3) SURFING IS HARD:

Learning to surf was the hardest thing I had ever done -- it still is. Ten years later, I am still learning. With surfing you're *always* learning, because you're never in control. Maybe you've honed your skills and strengthened your muscles, but unlike a ski slope or a skate ramp, in surfing the medium is a force of nature, ever-changing, ever-shifting, even as you approach, even as you ride, even as it throws you from its previously-gentle shoulder and pounds you into the sand below. There is a constantly-in-motion interplay between you and the wave. You can do your best to learn the waves' patterns, and where the sand bars are, and what the tides do, but when you're riding that wave, you are at its mercy, and it is going to move in a way that you can never anticipate for certain. You have to let go, trust the exchange, and let things flow. And maybe that's what's so beautiful. You *have* to let go…

Allan Weisbecker in my unequivocally favorite surf novel, In Search of Captain Zero, explains, "At any given time the sea is not only what it is (calm and tranquil, say; a soothing influence), but it is also its capacity to be something else (a medium for wave riding); and then, a moment later, something else altogether (a destroyer and a killer). Imagine gazing at the *Mona Lisa* with the knowledge that her little-girl smile could at any moment transmute to a viscous snarl or a lascivious smirk or a goofball grin."

Surfing is not a forgiving activity. Even on a boogie board, I struggled and sputtered and picked sand out of my teeth on a daily basis. I was pitched from the top of waves on late take-offs, drilled by the lip on bad judgment calls, and sent through the washing machine more times than I'd care to remember. Wash, rinse, repeat. But after a few months, I had learned how to read waves and which way to take off, where and when. Even with that knowledge, when I graduated to a real surfboard, the physical and mental bumps and bruises were daily, and an afternoon ritual evolved, sitting in a hammock and reading a book with an ice-pack pressed tenderly to my flavor-of-the-day injured body part.

Because of Louis's strong convictions about surfing, he felt it necessary to set up a contract if he was going to agree to help me. It was being ever added to, ever amended, but the core of the contract read something like this:

LOUIS'S CONTRACT FOR BOOGIE BOARDING LESSONS:

- The only teacher you're allowed to listen to is me.
- I'm not responsible for where my hands go.
- I'm not responsible for anyone else's bathing suit.

THE RULES:

1. Keep your butt down. (It was attracting too many other surfers and no one likes a crowd.)
2. Keep your mouth closed. (I'm not sure how many gallons of saltwater I swallowed in those first few weeks.)
3. Don't run over your teacher.
4. Get the whole thing...

The last rule was where the relationship between surfing and life started to become more clear. You have to catch the wave from its peak; it's the scariest place to take off because the drop is the steepest, but it's the fastest place to launch you into flying. You can take off from an easy shoulder and get a decent ride, or you can take off from the deepest darkest pit where the risk is high and the payoff unequalled. And this concept was starting to make sense to me in a much broader way...

4) SURFING IS ENERGY:

If all of this was so hard, why then, you might ask, did I continue? Could anything really be so great that I was willing to endure such abuse? I was the least masochistic person I knew, often avoiding activities entirely (maybe more than I should have) simply because my aversion to pain kept me from taking risks. But there was something about surfing that made it all worth it. It was a feeling...

Louis once said to me, "Surfing is the closest thing you'll ever know to flying."

Surfing is the transference of energy. It took me a while to understand that -- to believe it. But when I paddled into a wave and slid into a spot that was both so still in its glassiness and yet at the same time so fast moving, so powerful, so terrifying, the energy -- which had traveled from storm to sea, from wind to water, from continent to continent -- is sent up through my body. The waves of the ocean connect with the waves of my being -- you know, in a quantum-physics vibrations kind-of-way. There is no other reasonable explanation for how surfing could make you feel so amazing.

I would close my eyes long after I'd hit land, vivid images of empty green tunnels spinning around me, and I could still feel the waves moving. The energy which comes from surfing is so emotionally-altering that it takes only one amazing ride flying across the horizon to feel lifted up higher than you have ever felt. But when you have a bad surf day, you can walk out of the ocean feeling like a failure, not only in surfing but in life, and a depression can settle in and last for days until it is washed away once again by another beautiful wave.

Maybe it was the transference of energy that fosters mysticism which started me thinking about the big unanswered questions when I became a surfer. Maybe surfing forces you into a state of meditation as you sit out in the middle of the ocean floating in space with nature all around you -- up and down and all-around sideways -- focused, immersed, concentrated. Maybe more people would hear about this awakening except for the unfortunate tagging of surfers as illiterate stoners not to be taken seriously. You must have heard the profound words that surfers use to describe their world; you probably just didn't recognize them as brilliant since they are book-ended with "dude" and "man." But when surfers describe the way it feels to be in the perfect spot on the perfect wave, they go into a place -- you can see it in their eyes. A high. And their voices quiet to almost a whisper. And they talk about being in exactly the right place, and paddling only a few strokes, and slotting in and riding -- no, flying. A feeling of ecstasy. A feeling like no other as their faces contort as they describe it. Waves, flying and orgasms...

It may be impossible to articulate or even understand the magic, but I suppose that's what keeps it all locked up in secret. Allan Weisbecker explains: "I could remember nothing of the final couple hundred yards of the ride, except an odd sensation, which I can only describe as one of suspension. I was flying and I was walking on water, and yet it was also as if I were standing still -- as if I were *stillness itself* -- and *everything else* was moving past *me*... It is not the water, not the sea itself, that is ridden when one surfs. The water is only the medium that carries the energy that *is* the wave, much as one's body is the medium, the carrier, of one's consciousness. I had perceived, in a deeply intuitive way, the seamless integration of matter and energy -- without the artificial duality, the either/or-ness the human mind is prone to... Then it hit me... *I did not know how surfing worked."*

5) SURFING WILL RUIN YOUR LIFE:

If there is one thing about my first surf lessons from Louis that I will always remember, it was the warning he issued.

"Surfing here will ruin your life," he said looking intensely into my eyes.

I thought it was a strange thing to say. Silly for someone as disciplined and forward-moving as myself. *What? Like I was going to become a surf bum or something?* But there is nothing quite like ducking through the warm Costa Rican water, waves backlit against the setting sun sending golden outside-set lips gliding over your back. The sea glows steely blue in the north and deep purple in the south, and the sky explodes in pink flames. You are unencumbered by wetsuit, feeling nearly as free as the day you were born, bobbing in the temperate water, looking down into an aquarium. Surfing anywhere, I learned, will also ruin your life. But surfing in the tropics is like nothing else. And once you have lived it, you will spend the rest of your life trying to get back there, having tried second-bests and having found yourself utterly unsatisfied. There is no such thing as a surfing fanatic. It is simply redundant.

At the time of this writing, I am thirty-three years old, I am happily unmarried (to an amazing man), happily without children, happily regularly unemployed, happily unmortgaged, and have not lived more than a few miles from the beach for more than a month at a time for the last ten years. I can't say he didn't warn me...

TORRES DEL PAINE

After leaving the volcano climbs, quelled romance, and numerous excursions of the Lake District, I journeyed further south, welcoming the solitude of La Grande Isla de Chiloe. A land of hilly farms overlooking the sea, of shingled houses puffing smoke from chimneys, of toothless grandmothers weaving llama-wool sweaters to sell at the weekly market, this large Chilean island left the city far behind.

From the bus station, I trudged through the rainy gray, following hand-painted *hospedaje* signs to find myself staring at the home of one Señora Elvira. I dashed under the awning overhanging the front door and shook the water from my hood.

Knock, knock.

After a few moments, an elderly woman with a head full of curlers cracked the door and peered out at me.

"Good afternoon, Señora. Do you have a room for tonight for one person?"

Pause. She looked down the walkway. *"Sola?"* she inquired, eyebrows raised.

"Si, Señora."

Pause. She peeked around the corner to my right. *"Sola?"* she came again, this time with a rising tone.

"Si."

Pause. She pressed her lips together. *"En invierno?"*

"*Si, Señora.*" I was freezing and wondering if she was going to let me in.

Then slowly, her expression cracked into a smile. "*Que valiente,*" she said softly as she opened the door wide to show me in.

Señora Elvira led me upstairs down a long hallway flanked with a dozen doors. Then up another set of stairs to a short wooden door which she unlocked with an oversized key and opened to reveal a spacious room with a low slatted ceiling, a single bed and dresser, and a tiny round window. Her huge house appeared to be empty of all but her, but I did not ask why I'd be staying up in the attic. At the price of $7/night including breakfast and her company, I was happy wherever she thought I should be.

And there it began on the cold gray island of Chiloe that I started to find comfort in my loneliness -- in my aloneness. The only tourist in town, and apparently the only woman traveling alone in winter to ever cross Señora Elvira's path, I began to feel alive by it all, the quietude, the romance of being alone with myself in a faraway place, the splashes of color that sparkled amidst the dreary landscape.

In the mornings I walked down to the docks and watched the fishermen bring in crate after crate of giant red crabs. Blue and orange boats bobbed on the water as the short stout men in yellow rain-slickers and pants held up by red suspenders tossed their catch up from the bottom of their boats into empty crates waiting on the pier. When the plastic crates were piled high with crabs, the fishermen jumped out of their boats, swung the crates up into their arms with a grunt, and hefted them up onto the handheld spring-scale which their fellow seaman tried to support by bending backwards to counter the weight. "Twenty kilos! Thirty kilos," the fishermen called out as the crabs snapped and clattered. And every morning they were out in the early gray damp, doing it again.

I walked along the sea, following its curves along flooded streets, watching wiry men shovel mud from the road, watching women bail water from their houses because of recent storms. Although many people lived in these *palafitos* typical of Chiloe, basic wooden-slat homes built on stilts which stood in the ocean, sometimes the architectural advantage was not enough; the floods, rain and climate assured that these people remained among the poorest in Chile.

The artisan market in the town of Dalcahue was filled with exquisite handicrafts, the softest *llana-llama* woolens in all of Chile -- thrice spun, then woven by women on Chiloe's tiny neighboring islands who came into town by rowboat to sell each Sunday. A handmade pair of gloves cost less than a stamp and a postcard, and a sale would feed a family for days. I decided on three purchases from three separate merchants that my shoestring budget could afford: a thick gray-and-white wool sweater embroidered with snowflakes, a long soft scarf that wrapped three times around my neck and covered my chest, and a pair of purple mittens with yellow lightening-bolts that flashed across the backs of my hands. I would think of these women's faces as I ventured south, toasty and warm and grateful.

The island of Chiloe is a place of contrasts, gray and color, cold and warmth, poor and comfortable, Catholic and animist. With ancient traditions and rich cultural beliefs, Chiloe is considered the folklore capitol of Chile; stone statues and plaques line parks and walkways and tell the stories of *Trauco*, the mischievous troll of the forest, or *Pincoya*, goddess mermaid who keeps fishermen safe at sea. But the island also has a strong religious history, and a dozen 19th century Jesuit churches dot the island in brightly-painted wooden rainbows standing out against the gloom. La Iglesia de San Francisco in the town of Castro is purple and brilliant salmon, and in the town of Chonchi the church is royal blue and yellow. When I knocked on the heavy imposing door of Iglesia Nuestra Señora del Rosario, the priest welcomed me inside (even though the church was closed for lunch) and took a break from pulling nails to tell me about his single-handed restoration.

But despite my small forays into the island's towns, I didn't speak aloud very often for those few weeks except to have tea with Señora Elvira and practice my Spanish, and to order my one big meal at lunch. For three dollars a day, I feasted on huge platefuls of fresh salmon, topped with onions and vegetables. The days were dark and near-freezing until about 10:00 a.m., and the almost-constant rain permitted only a few hours each day to walk around town without getting soaked.

And so I spent long hours in my journal, in my books, in my Spanish study material, snuggled up in that attic, coming to revelations about what "cold" really meant.

YOU KNOW IT'S COLD WHEN...

- You wake up and you can see your breath -- inside.
- The sweet old lady of the house brings you a hot water bag to heat your sheets.
- You cling to that hot water bag all night like it was the man of your dreams.
- Your best friend is a Polar Guard sleeping bag.
- You go to sleep in wool socks, long underwear, a fleece jacket, gloves and a scarf.
- You wake up still wearing all of those items and wishing you had a face mask.
- You've been so cold for so long that your nipples have actually worn through your bra.

In addition to becoming intimate with the subtle nuances of being cold, I also began to get in touch with what it meant to travel alone. To be alone. Sometimes it meant being sad, feeling lonely, eating lots of chocolate... Sometimes it meant marching out into the world, electrified to think of what I might discover that day. But whatever I was feeling, I knew I was feeling it because of me -- not because I was being influenced by a moody traveling companion, or an overprotective boyfriend, or feeling stressed by a deadline at work. Every emotion I felt was pure, and after this period of hibernation, of nurturing my introverted self, I felt ready to burst out and fall in love with whatever, and whoever, crossed my path. It was then that I boarded the Navimag.

***

"Each friend represents a world in us, a world possibly not born until they arrive, and it is only by this meaning that a new world is born." Anais Nin

It was a four-day voyage aboard the Navimag cargo boat through magnificent fiords, sounds, and straits from Puerto Montt to Puerto Natales, the jumping-off point for trekking in Torres del

Paine National Park and the Patagonia territory. In the high season, the ship can hold 200 tourists. On my trip, there were fourteen -- and each one fascinating. Veteran travelers and fresh blood. A journey into South America. A journey of self discovery.

As I stood in the one-room building that served as a waiting area to board the ship, I looked everyone over. There was a group of girls, chattering away in excited crescendos. There were two extremely tall young men with tiny backpacks. There were young people and older people, friends and couples, all talking in groups. And then there was one guy who sat alone, olive-green ski cap pulled nearly over olive-green eyes. He seemed intent on a spot on the floor, listening to headphones, deeply absorbed in something inside his head. The whistle blew, and the doors opened.

As we boarded the ship in an orderly fashion, we all followed the First Mate up a wooden plank to our "economy" quarters. Bunks were stacked three high against each of three walls in a small wooden 8'x 8' room just off the bow. In the kind of group-bonding that comes only from strangers being stuck together in a ridiculous and challenging situation, the nine of us took turns entering the room and working together to make room for everyone's bags (nearly as big or bigger than the body accompanying it). The only configuration during which we all could fit in the room at once was if we all slid into our bunks like pizzas in a commercial oven. Watching Willem and Michiel, the two Dutch brothers who both were nearly two meters tall, attempting to perform the necessary contortions, sent all present into fits of hysterical laughter.

We filed out onto the deck to watch the ship take off, and I realized how big the boat was. *I wonder what is on the rest of this boat.* I saw semi-trucks drive up onto the ramps, I heard sheep baa-ing from unidentified areas, but the biggest secret had yet to be revealed.

I went below deck to wander around when I ran into the green-cap-guy coming out of a door. Simon spoke a language that he claimed was English (from the Northern part), but I missed about 40% of what *the good ole chap* said. He told me that this was the door to his room. I peeked in. Three sets of double bunk beds, and he had it all to himself! I said I didn't know there were other rooms down here.

He said, "Yes, actually the whole ship is empty."

EMPTY!! Then why are we sandwiched up top like a bunch of cross-cultural sardines? He said he'd paid the economy rate too, but had asked just before boarding if there were any other rooms available. *He just asked… Amazing. I'm gonna try it.*

It took me an hour to work up the nerve (and compose the Spanish required) to approach the First Mate. I crossed the deck when I saw him.

"Excuse me, but are there other rooms available? Our room is very full."

He smiled, gave a conspiratorial glance and looked over his shoulder. *"Vamos,"* he said. Let's go.

He jingled his set of keys as I trailed him through a below-deck maze; then he opened a door. There before me stood a warm room with no wind whistling through the boards, two sets of bunk beds with enough room to sit upright in each, a private bathroom with mini hot-water shower, a heater, and a tiny porthole with a view of the ocean. My jaw dropped.

"I'm not really supposed to let someone stay here because this is low season, and we have no one to clean it. But if you clean it yourself before you leave, you can stay."

I wanted to hug the man but restrained myself to an emotional *Gracias*, and ran upstairs to grab my gear. I learned something important that day, and I've lived it every day since… *It doesn't hurt to ask. What's the worst that can happen?* They can say no. And then you're no worse off than you were before. The world's possibilities kept getting bigger every day.

***

Once settled in, I returned to sit out on the upper deck of the ship to write in my journal and watch the scenery drift by. I sat up there alone for hours, my fingers so cold I could barely control the pen. Cold bit my windpipe as I inhaled every breath, and I listened to nothing but the wind whistling and the whirring motor of the boat. I was in Patagonia! I was actually doing this! A 360 degree view of the world in pure amazement.

That night I took a hot shower and danced naked to the sounds of Shakira on my walkman, gazing out the porthole at the midnight ocean. The moon shone on a choppy silver sea, and I lay down to sleep (without a sleeping bag or a face mask) in my heated room for the coziest dreams in months.

I awoke to sunrise over the Andes, the cloud-covered sky streaked pink and gold. *How many people ever get to write those words?* Onshore, I could see the snow-capped mountains across the sea. Peak after peak, as different as each snowflake that covered them.

Feeling guilty by breakfast, I watched the crumpled "economy" travelers make their way to their porridge and Nescafe. I asked the Dutch brothers if they'd like to move in with me since they seemed the most in need. Simon invited retired Robert and his 70-year-old dad, Ralph, to share his place, leaving the girls and Andrés, the accident-prone Austrian, with the economy room to themselves. And we all slept a lot better.

***

As for the fourteen characters aboard, each was fascinating. To be the few, the hearty, the valiant backpackers who travel Patagonia in winter took a special something (and maybe some cranial mis-wiring), and I felt honored to be among them.

Willem and Michiel were the very tall Dutch brothers. Willem was a nurse who had traveled all over the world with Doctors Without Borders. Michiel was the dummy in the family; he spoke only five languages. From them, I learned how to pack ultra-light (not that I was able to put that knowledge into action until many years later). They showed me their shower shoes, only 1/8" thick. They showed me their soap which they had cut in half, and their toothbrushes which had the handles lopped off. They showed me, more often than I would have liked, their only two pairs of brightly-colored bikini underwear which hung like prayer flags from the edges of their bunks, drying in our room in a constant cycle of washing.

"Why would you need more than two?" they asked at my incredulity. "You only wear one at a time."

There were the three girls from California on their junior year abroad: Nuri, Lindsay and Laura -- giggles galore. Robert, a retired Air-Force pilot who first pointed out the Southern Cross to me, and his dad, Ralph, were traveling together for the first time in 20 years.

There was David, a surfer kid who knew someone I had gone to high school with. There was Janine, a nun-to-be, theology student at Berkeley. There was Joelle and Martin, a honeymooning couple from Quebec traveling on the world's tightest budget. Joelle said, "Martin and I, we have traveled together for nine months, and I have been on top (she gestures to the bunk beds) the whole time."

There was Simon. Even though I really never got a handle on either his accent or his vocabulary, I liked Simon from the start because he talked to himself. On the first afternoon, I found him up on the deck in an animated discussion alone with his headphones on. *Was he singing?*

"What are you doing?"

"Talking to myself," he replied matter-of-factly.

Maybe it had something to do with traveling alone for the last six months (south from Quito, Ecuador). Maybe it was that traveling alone brings that inner voice to the forefront like it did for me in Volcán Villarica and forever forward. Or maybe it was that until then, he had had no one to talk to. But Simon became my closest friend on the boat. He was quiet, undemanding, and enjoyed looking out at the world.

And then there was Andrés, the accident-prone Austrian. If ever there was a more unlucky human to walk the planet, I have yet to meet him. Unassuming and almost invisible, he was quiet for an entire day until Simon brought him out of his shell.

Each day, Andrés unraveled his turbulent travel tales in broken English as he drew increasingly bigger crowds, and always had everyone in stitches, endearing him to us all.

"I was in Pucón," he began a bit quietly, "And I wan to go with zah kayak. I never go before, but zhey say is OK. I go in zah morning with zah group, and zah river is very big because of zah rain, and very fast. And I get very scary, so I go to zah side. And zah river, it go two way. I go one way here. My guide go zah different way. And my guide he pass me and zah group pass me too. And zah river make my kayak go up... Boom!" he gestured.

"Upside-down, Andrés? Did your kayak flip over?"

"Yes, and I fall out, and I grab to zah plants, and I hold. And I am scary, and I swim to zah land. I am very cold now and very wet, but I wait for zah guide to come for me. I wait but it is dark now, and so I walk home. I walk for many hours, and I fall many times. I have no shoes. I have only zhese pants and one shirt and one, ummm, zhis orange for zah water?"

"A life vest?"

"Yes, and I walk and I fall in zah bushes and some blood come out here. And I see one light zhere in one small house, so I go to zah door, and zah Señora she open zah door and she scream. And she close zah door. So I am sad and I wait. And zhen zah police come and zhey take me home."

By this time, we can't even breathe we are laughing so hard. The poor guy...

"And zah next day, I sleep in my bed in zah afternoon because I so tired now, and I turn on zah radio and I am on zah radio! They tell zah story from yesterday, and I am zah star!"

I can hear it now... *"Yesterday, a foreigner was found in the woods after being separated from his tour group..."* And that is how Andrés became a star.

***

The day was bright, green and full of sun. The passengers gathered together on the upper deck, taking pictures, talking about travels and life, sharing stories, and enjoying our amazing surroundings.

The captain called out in Spanish, *"Six dolphins starboard side!"* And there they were -- gray backs and white bellies, jumping out of the water like popcorn. They raced alongside us in pairs, in groups, changing formation, playing tag with the boat, as beautiful and graceful as the landscape.

We had been traveling through relatively calm water channels between the coast and a scattered group of islands, but all that changed on the second night. We entered the open sea about 8:00 p.m. and played a challenging game of charades, flying up and down the deck while trying to manage the compounding effects of Pisco (a local hard alcohol) and Dramamine. At 2:00 a.m. we crossed the Golfo de Paine, infamous for its rough seas, and when I lay down to sleep, I realized that the bunk-beds are positioned so that you don't actually fall out no matter how big the swell gets. You just rock up and down all night dreaming that you're standing up, then standing on your head, standing up, standing on your head.

The next day the rough seas passed, and the landscape transformed into the mist-covered mountains of a lost world. It felt like we'd fallen into a prehistoric time, and I fully expected to see a dinosaur sneak by behind the trees on the harsh and wild distant shoreline. By the afternoon, we were driven inside by the rain. I washed my clothes in the sink, hung them to dry on the heater (which I learned from the Dutch boys), and then we docked outside Puerto Eden to let on local passengers. Puerto Eden, one of the only towns between Puerto Montt and Puerto Natales has a population of 280. I even saw an island with only one house on it, a Patagonian version of San Blas.

In a few hours we entered Campo Hielo Sur, the second largest freshwater reserve in the world (only after Antarctica) where the wind blows east to west so that the ice falls into the channel, making conditions dangerous for navigation but ideal for spotting icebergs. We fourteen watched vigilantly, but without a sighting. Perhaps the crew and passengers of the Navimag knew what was in store for climate change before it even had a name.

The next day we motored through the Kirke Pass, the narrowest channel on the trip. Although its breadth stretched one hundred meters wide, only 60 meters are passable because of underwater rocks. To my nautically-untrained mind, that sounded daunting based on how enormous the Navimag seemed, so after the uneventful crossing, I climbed up to the wheelhouse to talk with the captain and gaze over the charts and lines covering his table that meant nothing to my novice eye. I asked about what other animals I might see on the trip.

"Are there a lot of seals?" I asked in Spanish.

"Not many seals... *Focas pocas.*"

Focas pocas? They were the funniest two words I'd heard put together in a long time. I imagined a magician wearing a black top-hat waving his magic wand over the seals. "Focas pocas," the magician would proclaim as the seals appeared and disappeared, popping up to the surface and then dipping down out of sight beneath the ice.

***

When the sun came out again, we all stood up on the deck, and suddenly Willem looked down and asked Andrés, "Andrés, what happened to your boots?"

"I was walking in Lima, and one man ask me for shoe shine." (It is so common for people to earn a living polishing shoes in South America that I once had a man ask to polish my sandals.)

"So I say no, but zhis man say he need money, so I say OK. Zhen I watch, and I zhink zhis man cannot see, you know?"

"He's blind, Andrés?"

"Yes. And zhen he put zhis color black on my shoess, but my shoess zhey are brown. And now my shoess, zhey are black."

The captain called out, *"Four whales off the bow."* I ran to the front of the boat! I had never seen whales before and was the first to the railing. As I peered down into the water at their beautiful giant sleek bodies swimming in pairs, I heard a soft poof as mist sprayed from their blowholes, their hot breath condensing in the cold air. They didn't linger long near the boat, and I watched through Ralph's binoculars as they swam into the distance. One set of flukes pointed high to the sky before disappearing for good.

That afternoon the landscape changed from dense green lost-world islands to sparsely-forested rocky cliffs. Sharp, barren, dramatic. Thousands of waterfalls, like liquid quartz rushing down the cliff faces, disappeared then reappeared into the next majestic waterfall.

That night Simon came inside from the upper deck to get us. "The stars are amazing," he said, and we all hurried outside.

The sky was crystal clear and covered in diamonds. I'd never seen such a bright Milky Way. Robert showed me the Southern Cross and remembered aloud when he'd first seen it from the deck of his military ship 30 years ago. The wind was completely still for the first time in the entire trip as I stood on the deck of that boat in the Pacific Ocean in the middle of Patagonia watching that magnificent sky.

And on our last day, I saw penguins! A whole little island full of them, thirty or forty strong. They were supposed to have moved on for the winter, and the captain had said the likelihood of seeing them had been very slim. But I was dancing on lucky stars. An hour before we docked, my magical seals materialized.

Focas pocas became *focas muchas*, jumping in and out of the water, playing and swimming alongside the boat.

As we approached the dock at our final destination of Puerto Natales, I felt a sadness come over me to think that this was the end. As it turned out, it was far from it... The Dutch brothers, Simon, David, the three girls and I agreed there and then to hike Torres del Paine together. Andres had decided not to join us, and although I felt a sad parting, I honestly think we all felt a little relieved. When I had boarded the Navimag I had assumed that I would hire a guide to go into the park, but the Dutch brothers were confident that we could do it ourselves.

After an amazing four days, our group disembarked the Navimag together to be greeted by exuberant señoras with *hospedajes* and polished sales pitches. We split into two groups for the night and arranged to meet the next day.

The evening was a flurry of activity. We shopped for our food for the trip since we'd have to pack it all in with us. In the park, there was one ranger's station cabin (*refugio*) that was still open for the season to stay in, and it had a kitchen, but no staff or meals supplied for us in the low season. We repacked our bags, left the un-essentials in the *hospedaje*, and before midnight were poised to catch the 8:00 a.m. bus to the trailhead of Torres del Paine National Park.

***

It was a cold dark morning. Our group awoke before 7:00 a.m. for Nescafe and toast slathered with caramel *manjar* and were out the door before the winter's far-latitude sunrise. Our group filled the bus ride to Torres del Paine with laughter, and I was comforted to know I'd embarked on this journey with newfound friends. I gazed dreamily at the dry golden grass, the shrubs and thorn bushes as we bounced down the dirt road. I must have dozed off because I jolted awake and nearly jumped out of my skin when the bus skidded to a stop, just in time to avoid colliding with not just one, but an entire herd of cows that the driver hadn't seen because of the rising sun's glare on the dirty windshield. My heart and I both felt awake wide awake after that.

By the time we arrived at the Ranger Station at the entrance to the park, it was past noon. We had an estimated five-hour walk ahead of us to the only open *refugio*, and couldn't count on our daylight lasting past 6:00 p.m. The Dutch brothers were off like a shot. They hoped their giant strides would carry them beyond the refuge to a more isolated site to pitch their tent by dark. The three giggly California girls took off at a sprint, full packs a-bouncing, to try to get ahead of David who was trying to tell them (and everyone else) what to do. I walked with David and Simon. With David, the self-proclaimed hiking guide at the helm, we soon passed the girls who'd taken a wrong turn. For the first hour, I kept up at full speed. But soon I began to wonder how my pack had gotten so heavy, filled with only clean undies, socks, soap, toothbrush -- and a week's worth of food.

The walk was stunning. The jagged snowy mountains that I'd seen in the distant mist when we had docked at Puerto Natales, suddenly stood directly in front of me. Like broken shards of glass dropped from the sky, the frosted spires climbed magnificently upward until they disappeared into a blanket of gray clouds. *The Torres*. The Towers, as they were called. As the wind came up, I leaned forward to meet it. Traversing open meadows of tall golden grass, I followed rushing rivers of icy blue, climbing a path into a forest of black and white dead trees, all at the foot of the towers. As the wind's strength increased, the drizzle turned to razors; I was warm beneath my Gore-Tex layers and just my eyes and nose met the near-freezing needles of rain. I had fallen to the back of the pack, slightly ahead of the girls, having stopped to eat an apple. I walked a few steps in front of Lindsay, who had hurt her foot, to help block her wind. At one point, a wind gust knocked Nuri face-first to the ground. From there, temporarily pinned beneath the weight of her own pack, she looked up, dumbstruck. A crack spider-webbed from the right lens of her horn-rimmed glasses, a smudge of dirt hung on the end of her nose.

By then, we were starting to worry. We were only three hours into the hike, the sun was completely obscured by the storm clouds, and we had not yet reached the lake which was a halfway marker between the trailhead and the *refugio*. A sudden gust of wind nearly lifted me off the ground, full pack and all, and at that moment, fear struck -- this was more than simply following others down a well-worn path. I was in the middle of the Patagonian Andes. The Patagonian desert. The inner voice spoke up. *We have no map. We are inexperienced hikers who are beginning to doubt if we are on the right trail. We are fighting the setting sun and the harsh elements which are ripping through the mountains and valley. Don't worry. We have plenty of food. Warm sleeping bags. We could always find a natural shelter if it gets dark. My equipment is good. I'm warm. I'm tired, but I don't hurt. Just don't stop; you learned that at the volcano. Hey, didn't I swear I'd never do this again?!* Amy Alyson, this *is why you write things down in your journal -- so you learn from experience. Well, here I am again. A five-hour trek. Maybe I'm getting stronger. Maybe I have a terrible memory. Just keep walking. Step. Step. Step.*

I caught up to Simon who had set up his tripod to take some photos. He didn't appear worried. He stood relaxed, casual even, holding his jacket open to shelter the camera from the rain. We moved on together, walking side-by-side along the path. His calm calmed me. He was wearing his walkman singing along, then without a word handed me one side of the headset. *Wow, that's more like it.* Tracy Chapman. Then, Brandy. (What adult man listens to Brandy?) I stopped and looked around me. *It's all part of it. The music, the mountains, the water, the rain. How amazingly beautiful. Music changes everything. Perspective changes everything.* I forgot about the weight of my pack. The *what-if*'s melted away, and suddenly it was a different journey.

After nearly an hour, the trail narrowed, and we could no longer walk two abreast. I disappointedly relinquished my half of the walkman to Simon who took it back with a smile and fell behind to stop and take more photos in the fading light. And on I went... Up and over the ridge. Scan the horizon. Nope, no lake. Up and over another. Nah-uhh. The next ridge was a killer. *This ain't no Stairmaster! This is the real thing. Almost there! Ooof -- and over.* And there lay the most beautiful lake I'd ever seen in my life. Ice blue. Green. Colors I had never seen before. The colors of cold. Of glaciers and snowmelt. Paine Grande, the largest of the Torres, stood directly in front of me like a snowy mammoth. Monstrous and unmistakable. I was on the right path. And I had made it only halfway to the shelter.

Two hours later: Up and down. *Amy, are you still talking to yourself? Hug the cliffs. Gusts of wind burst suddenly. OK, Amy, let's not fall off the path and plunge into the icy lake 100 meters below.* I'd totally lost sight of the others. I was pretty sure Simon and Lara were about five minutes in front of me. Nuri and Lindsay were probably fifteen minutes or more behind me. All I wanted to do was get there. I just hoped I hadn't accidentally wandered off the trail and was now lost and all alone! It hit me again. *People get lost here. People freeze to death here. Up and over. Up and down. Up and ahhhhh! There it is!* The warming hut. A little house! With lights! And a roof! *Faster. Walk faster. Be careful. The path is muddy, slippery.* I can barely see the rocks on the dark trail that I'm trying not to trip over. A few more steps, and I opened the door, warm and safe. Cheers emerged from four friends who sat warming themselves by the fireplace. *Thank you, my guardian angel.*

***

The next day, the exhausted hiking crew overslept and left the *refugio* at 9:30 a.m. instead of 8:00. It was still dark as we wobbled down the stairs to the front door, aching, groaning, freezing. The hiking groups had rearranged themselves. David and Lara walked ahead. Nuri, Simon and I poked along at our own pace. Lindsay stayed at the refuge to rest her hurt foot. We planned to hike to the Grey Glacier. I'd seen amazing pictures and couldn't wait to see it with my own eyes. Planned time: Two hours to view the glacier, three more hours to stand next to it. The Dutch brothers passed us on our way there; they were off to another part of the park. *Wow, they were fast!* Maybe they knew something I didn't; I then considered lopping off the handle off my toothbrush, but it seemed a little late now.

We started an uphill climb, and I was surprised to be huffing and puffing after only the first few minutes. I wondered if we should have waited to attempt this difficult hike, having hardly recovered from the previous day, but heck, I came to DO, not sit around.

The weather was amazing. The sun peeked out timidly at first, then shone brightly in the crisp cold air. Some bushes still retained glowing orange leaves the color of tangerines, of fire, of the sun. One or two green leaves clung to each hibernating tree. The sky glowed blue, bright and magnificent. The enormous mountains were right there. We caught a glimpse of Lake Grey, and there were those amazing indescribable colors again. My steps crackled against the first ice on the frozen path. I squealed with glee. I was doing it!

We reached the viewing point for the glacier by 10:30 a.m. in an impressive 1 ½ hours. It had been a steep uphill trek, and I was grateful to have left my big pack at the *refugio* for this day-hike. Once we cleared the ridge, there it was: my first glacier. Gray Glacier stretched as far as I could see. Frozen to the horizon. Whipped cream frosting puffs on the top, jagged and white, sneaking up to overtake the lake. Now, I was ready to go touch it!

The hike down to the glacier was difficult and slow. *Down, down, down, down.* Descending from the mountain through deep valleys, through forests and rushing streams (so much for keeping my feet dry). There were fallen logs to cross, hand-over-foot scaling of banks, near misses and falls as we helped each other through the elements. Beautiful. It seemed like it went on forever. And although I tried to absorb every ounce of beauty around me, I couldn't help but wonder, *Will I be able to get back up?* Absolutely exhausted, legs shaking, the group separated. It was a race against the daylight, and David and Lara knew it. Simon, Nuri and I were the laggers, but what was the hurry? You can't hurry through life, through this once-in-a-lifetime place... What was the point of that?

We followed the tiny sign at the fork in the road: "Ice Hike." Luckily, we were closer than we had thought and got another glimpse of the glacier. *We can make it.* We climbed out onto the rocks, pulling each other by the arms, pushing each other up by the butt. Higher, farther, to the edge. And there was the glacier... Blue. Glitter. Enormous. We looked down inside of it, just a few hundred meters of lake separating us from the ice. Then we heard the shouts. We looked across to the other bank and saw the others.

"Hurry. It's late!" they said.

"Yes, but we just got here," we shouted.

It was 2:30 p.m. I looked up at where we'd come from. *Uuh-ooh.* I watched the black clouds move in. And then... BAM! Rain. Gusts of wind. The rocks instantly transformed to slippery and dangerous. The weather had double-crossed us. We scrambled across the rocks towering above the lake, a 5 ½ hour return hike still ahead.

Once we were in the shelter of the valley, the weather calmed. Up, up, up, we went. Back up the bank. Back up the mountain. Back over the trees. Step, step, step. Nuri and I talked about home, and Simon sang audibly to his John Lennon tape a few paces back. I guess that we had assumed in the back of our minds it would get dark. Simon had a flashlight, but we had eaten all our food. We filled our water bottles with glacier melt from the river, delicious ice-cream headaches, and just kept step-stepping. I felt the urgency, but I also felt the beauty, the wanting to stay there, in the moment, forever.

By 5:30 p.m. it was very difficult to see, the sun having set at such an early hour behind the mountains. *Damn the winter. Damn the tilt of the earth.*

Our walk had turned silent, and I tripped over stones and roots. *Careful. Concentrate. Faster, we've got at least another hour of walking. We waited for Simon who was in the mellow world of his walkman to catch up. Stick together. Man, my knee hurts. Darker, darker. Trip, stone. Trip, twig. Trip, twist. Down, down, down. Ouch, ouch, ouch. Why does* down *hurt so much?* We later realized that everyone's joints were being badly battered with every step from the shockwave of clomping atop newly-frozen ground, pounding knees, ankles and toes, mile after mile.

And then it was completely dark. The wind howled like a lonely wolf through the snowy mountains and sent shivers across my skin. *Amy, not so smart -- again.* Simon walked in front, holding the flashlight behind him to light Nuri's and my paths. He said not to worry; he ate a lot of carrots so his eyesight was very good. We had to retrace our path a few times because we couldn't see the trail markers. The possibility of taking the wrong path was not something I had anticipated. *There was only one path, right?* We soon began to doubt that. This certainly didn't seem like the path we took this morning. And with it being winter, there was no park staff, no search-and-rescue to come find us if we got lost.

The moon rose over the mountaintops after about an hour of pure darkness, and the first stars appeared. Simon and Nuri both agreed that we must be on the wrong trail. Lake Pehoe, the lake aside the *refugio,* had come into view, but there were no cabin lights to be seen. We decided to climb across the ridge to see if the cabin was on the other side. Maybe we were one valley over. Simon kept the stress down with the timely offering of breath mints. Nuri was quiet. In my head, I was a basket-case. But I was quiet too, an eye-blink from tears. I felt them welling up inside me.

Then Nuri said, "I think I see a light."

I'd never been so happy to see it (not even as happy as I had been the day before)! The *refugio* twinkled in the distance, and we yipped with joy, hugged each other, and quickened our pace. When we arrived at the hut, we pulled out our cameras to commemorate the moment for posterity. The others, who had arrived hours earlier, stared out at us from inside the warm cabin as we danced and jumped in the clear night air. They could not understand that the universe had now bonded the three of us together. Travel is often like that, connecting people who might have otherwise never connected, through shared experience, shared fear, shared elation. Still laughing and hugging and patting each others' shoulders, we brought our joyous delirium inside, warmed some tea, and slept like babies in our bunks.

***

I hiked 64 kilometers in those first three days, and the adventures continued (albeit at a quieter pace) for a week. We got better at planning, getting up earlier, not setting out more than we could do in a day-hike since Lake Pehoe was the only *refugio* open. The ten- and twelve-hour hiking trails had been designed for summer months when there were 16 hours of daylight. In the winter, there were seven.

After a week, a few of us decided we were ready to hike back out of the park. The girls stayed behind to relax for a while. David went back to the glacier. And Simon and I decided to hike out, go back to Puerto Natales and continue our journeys south. The only bus which left from the park entrance back towards town departed at 2:00 p.m. daily. The hike would take us at least the full 5 ½ hours it took to get in, maybe more. We decided to leave the next day at 7:00 a.m.

But we didn't. We left at 9:30. And, as always, we were in a rush. And, as always, we couldn't rush because there was breath-taking scenery to enjoy. We headed across, up and then down the first hill, once again burdened by the rucksacks we'd had the luxury of leaving in the refuge all week. All of our joints ached because of the week's trekking upon unforgiving icy trails. Up and down the second hill. Simon tied a sock around my knee as a support brace. Up and down again.

At 10:30 a.m., we stopped to confer. "Can we make it in time for the bus?" I wondered aloud. If not, we'd be stuck in the middle of nowhere with no shelter.

"Do we have a choice?" Simon asked. *Let's go!* The wind blew hard at our backs. We felt sure it was the gods of Patagonia screaming, "Hurry up! You're going to miss the bus! Walk faster!"

And the wind blew like crazy. It almost blew us over. I whimpered and swore on the downhill as my knee creaked and popped. I began singing to myself to disguise my grunting. Torres del Paine. Towers of Paine. And now I know why...

Simon wasn't doing any better. He'd badly bruised the arches of both his feet, and his pack was too heavy. We took turns being the inspiration. Back up, and over, and down the valleys and mountains. Back through the forests of hibernating trees, white and black. Back through the flat golden grassy meadows. As the gods of Patagonia did their calculations, the gusts came suddenly. "Hurry up! You're going to miss it!" We plodded on, sure we couldn't take another step. Sure there was no other option.

Hours passed, but fatigue never overcame me. I focused on the magnificent Torres, on the patterns the grass made when the wind blew. Simon and I cheered each other on. Finally, he had to sit and rest. His feet wouldn't take much more. Time ticked away almost audibly. We had merged with the main road, and I knew the ranger station couldn't be far. I decided to walk ahead and hold the bus. At least one of us had to make it before 2:00 p.m.

I focused on the pain. Somehow it sent me into a high, and I began to sing a little song. It was nonsense and didn't rhyme, but I stepped to the beat until I saw the Ranger Station -- screamed, cheered -- and it goes like this (chanting):

I'm hiking through the Torres
I'm a strong strong woman
And I know I'm gonna get there
If I just keep on going
So I gotta keep on walkin'

And I gotta keep on steppin'
Cause I'm a strong strong woman
And I'm hikin' through the Torres... (etc.)

It went on with different stories emerging as they appeared around me. It got louder and louder and stronger as I marched. I made it just in time, and with a little pleading with the driver to wait just a moment more, Simon and I boarded the bus in time for departure.

The driver let Simon and I sit shotgun, and delirious with relief and excitement we ate jam sandwiches as the magnificent Torres del Paine moved by. Along the road, we spotted two very tall men with tiny backpacks striding along the pavement as they turned to flag the driver down. The Dutch brothers climbed aboard, as surprised to see us as we were them. By the time we got back to Puerto Natales, I was so exhausted that I couldn't move, so I took the world's longest bath while the Dutch boys went to buy me the first hamburger I'd eaten in years.

LUNAR ECLIPSE...

Each morning I sat in the same wooden chair and ate overripe papaya and sweet bananas and drank coffee and listened to the sea. Tiny ants crawled around in the cracks of the table and got into the bindings of my books as I read and wrote beneath the almond tree, its leaves flashing orange and pink in the sunlight, framed against a bright blue sky with swishes of clouds. Palm fronds whispered and stirred forty feet in the air, releasing streamers of leaves and confetti pollen that skittered across the surface of the water. Along the tin roof iguanas scritch-scratched with long claws, sliding down -- *thump!* -- into the canopy below. I walked for hours along the Jekyll-and-Hyde beach watching the tides eclipse the soccer-field-sized golden space into a narrow steep slope, waves building and breaking and crashing on the sandbar. And although I still struggled with what I was supposed to be doing -- what I *was* doing -- here in Playa Grande, it was hard to maintain that kind of futile energy in the presence of the tropics.

The *Papagayo* winds ravaged the beach, pelting and stinging my feet with a metaphorical hourglass' very real grains of sand. *Time does not exist here*, I heard Louis echo, and indeed I no longer knew what day it was -- and it did not matter. Every dawn had the same potential for magic, the deep mystical calls of howler monkeys rising from the dry forest as the dreary gray sky blossomed with the first pinks of the day.

As my self-imposed need to appear productive gradually gave way, I began to *notice* things... The iridescent turquoise glimmering under a dragonfly's wings. A big bright blue moon rising over the treeline, its glowing spotlight mixing with the early evening pastels still left in the sky. They had been there all along, and yet now nothing had ever seemed so exciting.

I had been in Playa Grande forever. I had just arrived. And swimming in this pleasant simplicity of discovery, I gave myself permission to pause every quarter century and take inventory. I deserved time to reflect on my life, far from the stage on which it had been taking place. And after 25 years of living a society's dream, it was time to figure out what mine was. It was time to go *some*where. To do *some*thing. To explore. To see what it felt like to be someone new for a while. And it would all stay secret here with the mango trees.

I was melting -- into my books, into the ocean, into a world of possibilities that exploded exponentially like the Milky Way in the clear night sky, galaxies of light being born into a hungry vacuum that had been just waiting for the nourishment and the courage.

***

Las guilas started to warm up to me, their stone wall crumbling one pebble at a time until a small pile of rubble had accumulated at its foot.

I told Louis, "But they're still laughing at me."

He said, "That's good. If they didn't like you, they'd just ignore you."

And so I got a little braver, and things got better with *las guilas*. I practiced my Spanish with them (which provided them substantial entertainment.) They refused to correct my errors outright and instead would squint their eyes as I spoke as if concentrating enormously to decode my meaning.

One afternoon I was standing behind the reception desk with Carmen and Johanna when a man dressed in a powder-blue uniform came in and greeted us politely. He was a vendor for Bimbo bread, a popular product in Costa Rica which, similar to

American Wonder-Bread, was white, sticky, dependably squishy, and had a shelf-life of about 400 years.

When he went back to his truck to get samples (as if he were peddling fine wines), I hurriedly made my case in Spanish, "You can't serve that bread. It is full of *preservativos*."

Carmen and Johanna looked at me, eyes wide, then looked at each other, unblinking, and then looked at me again. And then broke out into the loudest belly-laugh I had ever heard emitted from them.

"*Preservativos? Preservativos!*" they echoed.

But I had no idea what I had said until Johanna was finally able to breathe.

"*Preservantes, Amy. Preservativos son condones.*"

Carmen had taken off her glasses and was wiping at her streaming tears. Apparently, I had advised against buying Bimbo bread since it was full of condoms...

***

The dusty dusks of the dry season summer blew away as Sabrina, Jenny, Alex and I met up with *las guilas* at the fiestas in Matapalo to drink *Imperial* beers and sit atop the bullring made of horizontally-laid tree trunks. We watched as ropers and bull-riders showed off their expertise, and once the rider had been bucked off, the bull ran freely around the ring chasing drunken spectators who had jumped inside, Guanacastecan cowboys and flip-flop-wielding gringos alike, in search of a macho adventure story. Base beats of cumbia and merengue pumped from the dance pavilion, and the night's *baile* called men and women in their evening-best to swing their *cinturas* 'til dawn.

The fiestas went on for months -- every weekend hosted by a different local town -- and their end marked the half-way point of the dry season. One afternoon soon thereafter Louis's friend tossed me her rental-car keys with a smile, handing me my freedom with a jingle and a clank. She knew that as beautiful as Playa Grande was, it was easy to feel a little stir-crazy after months of living in a one-mile square patch of paradise.

Always under the watchful eye of *las guilas*, Shirley quickly came over to mention that she owned a car which she had bought from her cousin months ago, but she didn't know how to drive.

"Come on, then," I said, and soon half the hotel staff was streaming down to the parking lot to watch.

Shirley got into the driver's seat of the hatchback, adjusted the seat, and made small circles in the lot before confidently signaling and turning left onto the wide dirt road.

When we returned fifteen minutes later, everyone was still outside waiting for their lesson. Johanna was next. The gentle-natured cook, brimming with enthusiasm and curiosity, posed a problem however. She was barely four-and-a-half feet tall. It took three romance novels from the hotel's lending library, a Bible and decorative pillow for her to see over the steering wheel; still her feet could barely work the peddles. But eventually we jerked down the dirt road to the cheers of the crowd.

At the end of shift, I offered to drive the staff home. We wound our way through the country roads toward the *pueblo* of Matapalo where they lived, passing perimeters fenced with cactus and great swaths of shady fruit trees, the smell of fallen mangos rotting with a sickening sweetness in the sun. Brahma cows ambled along the hilly stretches of dry golden grass, their rib-bones squeaking through loose skin, their extra chins flapping side-to-side as they ambled along. Dignified old-timers wearing stiff white cowboy hats watched while dust from the road choked their homes as the now-daily onslaught of 4x4 Hyundais with surfboards strapped to the roofs roared by on their way to hurry up and enjoy their ten-day vacations. Brightly-painted houses dripped with magenta bougainvillea, and empty turquoise benches sat sentry in the plaza awaiting school children or tired shoppers or lovers. Colors as vivid as the country.

I dropped the girls off one by one as they waved goodbye from the top of their walkways, and I drove home alone, silently watching green parrots squawk across the sunbursting sky to land in the broad canopies of the flowering Guanacaste trees. As the sweet warm wind drifted in through my window, I was reminded of why I loved Playa Grande. It was a secret. A secret at the end of a dirt road that invited to her exactly who needed to be there.

***

"Do not believe that he who speaks to comfort you lives untroubled among the simple and quiet words that sometimes do you good. His life has much difficulty and sadness and remains far behind yours. Were it otherwise he

would never have been able to find those words." Letters to a Young Poet, by Rainer Maria Rilke

As time went on, I became much closer with Louis than Marianela. Maybe it was because I had met him first and he had looked out for me. Maybe it was because I was intrigued with our surprisingly similar backgrounds despite our seemingly contrary personalities. I looked forward to the daily hours we spent sitting atop my boogie board in the sand talking about life and relationships, physics and metaphysics, love and life paths, almost as much as I looked forward to the surfing that followed. I gradually grew out of my standoffishness as my doubts about him went unrealized, and I soon found myself energized by his eccentric views and deeply-powered insight.

We seemed to fill a void in one another. I was on the beginning of a journey. He had followed an unblazen path for decades and felt compelled to share knowledge. I would ask him a question and then wait for the rhythm to flow as he fell into extended monologue. He was the first person I'd ever known who was so far removed from political correctness that he cut through any bullshit with one clean stroke. His unsoftened personal truth was often hard for me to hear and held no one sacred, but despite the sweeping generalizations and frequently shocking conclusions, I felt strangely like I'd gained some wisdom simply from listening to him. And although I knew I needed to find it all out for myself, I began to feel stronger, smarter, every day. Over time, I thought of his collection of perceptive rants and astute conclusions as "Louisisms." And as I traveled throughout South America and beyond, those little wisdoms came floating back to me, in his voice, in a time of need, like a perverse little guardian gnome squatting atop my shoulder.

SELECTED LOUISISMS:
"The truth always makes a better story than a lie."

Louis loved to tell stories. Radical stories. He had been some radical places and done some radical things. Jostling with locals at aggressive Puerto Rican breaks, vigilante justice in Costa Rica, confrontations loaded with unapologetic opinions, love affairs with famous women... I'm not saying that sometimes the details didn't vary slightly, but for the most part Louis had lived such an extraordinary life that he had no reason to make things up to shock people (and he loved to shock people). Unsurprisingly, it wasn't uncommon for guests to respond to these stories with disbelief.

"No way" or "You're lying," they'd gasp, and without a word Louis would get up from the table and retreat to the safety and solitude of the Lighthouse. He just couldn't stand liars.

<u>"We all should have as much love as we can get."</u>

"Far be it for me -- or anyone else -- to be selfish enough, possessive enough, controlling enough to want someone all to myself," Louis would say.

Basically this translated to an open relationship with Marianela which included not just former lovers, but also varying degrees of intimacy with friends. In Louis's view, it was all the same.

"We all need to get, and give, and share, as much love as we can," and getting that kind of attention, whether it was sexual or platonic, from people around you meant that you gained energy and that you became a happier person because of the exchange. And when you're a happier person, you're better for your partner and you're better for yourself.

To me, Marianela and Louis were not the picture of a happy relationship so I wasn't convinced that the philosophy worked. But maybe it once had; maybe it would if both people got equal attention from others. But what I took away from it was that people need individual lives, individual interests, in order to stay strong and interesting and compelling.

<u>"The happier and healthier I am, the better off you are."</u>

This was Louis's basic advice on couples. You have to be happy with yourself if you expect to be happy in a relationship. You have to continue to stretch and grow and experiment and find joy on a personal level, and you cannot rely on your partner to do it for you.

Louis believed that Marianela had gotten lazy. Whether his perception had any bearing in reality didn't matter; his perception *was* his reality. He believed she no longer did anything to push herself while he was out every day surfing, meeting people, twisting his brain around new ideas. And that, to him, made her very uninteresting and very unattractive. There was no spark because there was no energy to exchange.

<u>"Do everything you can while you're young and you have your strength."</u>

Obviously Louis never believed in doing things the ordinary way. He had tried to live a conventional life when he was younger, but fate kept booting him out of it. So he had to adjust. What he ended up with was a rich active life throughout his youth and his middle age.

Think about all you've wasted if you wait until you retire to start living. Your body is finished. Security is a myth anyway so you might as well enjoy every moment, and the younger you are, the more fully you can physically live.

Don't waste your time, your body, your spirit on anything that doesn't love you back. Find out what you love and do it now; anything else is disrespecting the cosmos.

<u>"Take care of your body. It's the only one thing you really have."</u>

I don't think I ever appreciated my body until I met Louis. I looked at it. I pushed at the bulges on my thighs and sucked in the Buddha-belly and wished I could iron out the cottage cheese. I knew that if I dressed in a way to hide my "flaws," I could look pretty cute, but I never felt *proud* of my body. But after months of a daily surfing regimen, walking in the sand and eating fresh fish and vegetables, my body had started to change.

By the time I noticed it, muscles stretched along the length of my calves from the hours of kicking around my boogie board. Outlines of my triceps peeked through my upper arms from paddling my surfboard. There was muscle-definition all over my body. My dirty-dishwater-colored hair had grown long and blond like a mermaid, dripping wet and salty down over my breasts. I liked my golden tan. I liked that my stomach was getting flatter. I liked surfing. I liked being in the water. I liked being one of the only women in a town of surfers, and the male attention was more than I'd ever known. I didn't want to hide anymore. I didn't need to compensate. And my confidence grew -- which made me more beautiful.

Louis told me that if he was a woman, he'd want to be me. "You have good basic machinery," he said.

Suddenly all those "flaws" that I'd always been embarrassed about, that I'd always accepted as my cross to bear, that I'd always dealt with by just hiding, had changed. I had changed them. And I realized that I was in control of my body. Beautiful bodies weren't just for gym rats. If I wanted one, I deserved one. I had made one, without even knowing it. And finally I had learned to treat my body with respect. After all, it was the only thing I'd ever really have.

There were more Louisisms. Endless Louisisms, really. I wrote them down in my journal if they seemed to stick. They'd come up at the oddest times, and although some provoked hours and hours of thought, some needed no explanation at all:

- *"Someday, if you keep working, what you think will align with what you feel."*
- *"Guilt is a useless emotion left over from our previous Catholic selves."*
- *"Men are romantics. They're the ones who can't stand to be alone. It's just that sometimes it comes out as sex."*
- *"Jealousy is when you think the other person is having more fun than you."*

***

One day I told Louis that I would get into phases where I loved to sleep because my dreams were beautiful, sometimes better than real life he said, "Maybe you have an artist deep inside."

"I don't know how to get it out."

"Maybe you never will," he said.

I wanted to.

Looking back, I realize that Louis was very intuitive. He could see the *me* I was learning to let out, not the *me* I was trying to hide behind. He could see who I would be in five years, in ten years, and he inspired me to grow in that direction. And I couldn't remember the last time anyone else did that in such a non-judgmental, non-child-rearing, non-this-is-best-for-you kind of way. And he was not the last. Sometimes I wonder who I would have settled for being if I had not crossed his path.

***

Louis had been telling me for months that he knew all the answers to all the Big Questions. One night at a margarita party in the jacuzzi he said I could ask him one Question, anything I wanted to know, and he'd tell me the answer.

OK. "What is the meaning of life?"

"The reason we're here is to live our lifespan. We're just a stepping stone in evolution. Some people are only here to contribute to the gene pool. Others are here to push us ahead and hit the window of opportunity to propel us into the future."

And then he made some sort of wisecrack and abruptly changed the subject. And that was it. Question time was over.

Of course sometimes it seemed that Louis's gift for philosophy was stronger than his gift for logic. One afternoon I knocked at the door of the Lighthouse, and when he called me inside, there he sat on his big round bed, the laptop computer's circuit board in tiny pieces all around him. In his hand he held a soldering gun and strewn around his crossed legs lay various screwdrivers, two pairs of pliers and a fork. The tropics were very hard on electronics.

"What are you doing?" I managed to stutter.

"I'm fixing the computer."

"Louis, I don't think you can just open it and fix it like that."

"That's how I fixed the blender."

Well, he did fix the computer. I don't know how, but Aesop said it all. *This was the jungle, man.* You had to do what you had to do. And sometimes it worked out.

And I guess what I learned from Louis overall was that he was unafraid. He pulled shit apart just to see what was inside. Electronics, people... He risked and he tried, and he thought up crazy schemes (like driving down to Central America to find a good surf spot), and he went for it. And sometimes he failed, but most of the time he didn't. And I think it was because he was so utterly committed. Persistent. Sure. *I could use a little of that*, I thought. Confidence. Certainty, that once I made a decision it would be the right one because I *made* it the right one. And Louis did that for me.

***

As the months in Playa Grande rolled on with Louis and *las guilas* and the Rancho, I did wonder more and more about the next phase of my travel. The longer I stayed, the closer it seemed that moving on was eminent. The Louisism that reverberated through it all was perhaps his favorite: *Do what's happening.* Live in the present. That was still hard for me.

And then, one day, my safety blanket was snatched back.

My former college housemate, J.B. Sloan, was a good friend, a free spirit and totally non-committal. He was the one with whom I had concocted this whole plan of moving down to South America. The reason I even considered doing the first six months alone in Costa Rica was because the *plan* was for J.B. to come down and meet me, and we'd do the next six months in South America together.

First he had wanted to live a Bohemian lifestyle in Buenos Aires; then he'd wanted to live with the Incas in Cusco. Now he wanted to travel to Nicaragua to live the real human suffering brought on by Hurricane Mitch. Whatever it was, one thing was certain -- he would change his mind tomorrow.

I guess I should just know that after seven years of friendship. But somehow he got me every time. For months I had been trying to pin him down to at least a city and a month I might meet him. No can do. He had no plans and said he liked it that way. Now he said he wanted to drive across the U.S. and then maybe just into Central America. Not sure how much money he'd have, if any. And after months of Louis's stories, I had learned a bit about what you can expect from people: *Past behavior predicts future behavior, and the only one you can depend on is yourself.*

I had to do what I wanted and not depend on anyone else -- not count on something that might never come -- or I could be waiting a long, long time. *Amy, it's all you. You chose this, now do it -- all by yourself.*

I didn't come here to learn to surf. I came here to learn Spanish, and my Spanish is shit. I came here to travel, and I'd done so little. I felt resolute. Determined. And when I sat down in the hammock to read my Lonely Planet South America book, I felt excited. *Ecuador, Peru, Chile, Argentina. Who knows??!!*

And then I got the email from J.B.

J.B. Sloan, true to his nature, true to the Louisisms that had preceded him, was not coming. And with his message, the last remaining thread of my solid well-lit plans abroad darkened. I could no longer see anything ahead of me because there was nothing left to see. The slate was completely terrifyingly blank.

Strangely, it wasn't more than a moment before the darkness from the eclipse passed, and what had begun as a small twitter inside me crescendoed steadily to elation. For the first time, deep within my heart, I was completely *sola*, and I was completely free…

EL FIN DEL MUNDO

Upon returning to town from Torres del Paine, joy surged through my exhausted body after the intensity of the previous week. My heart felt so big, and the world so open and full of possibilities. I had narrowly escaped -- multiple times -- some sort of calamity. I was living amidst one of the world's most exquisite natural galleries, its beauty and wonder absorbed through my skin and channeled to my very center. I felt full.

Living below a latitude of 50 degrees in Puerto Natales was full of surprises. For example, the hostel observed the standard practice of turning on its water heater for only a few hours each morning in order to conserve electricity in a country with a severe power shortage. And on the first day I went out with a wet head in the extreme weather (this womyn ain't gonna carry around no hairdryer in her backpack), I discovered that wet hair freezes solid after about an hour outside and snaps off in chunks like icicles letting go from a rooftop. I walked to the nearest salon and told the hairdresser to take those golden locks that hung in waves to my mid-back (a significant part of my feminine identity through my entire life and the hair that had made me feel so beautiful in Playa Grande just a few months before) and chop them to my chin. It really looked quite horrible. But it felt great. Light. Free. And in two snips I had been stripped of it all;

another extraneous layer had fallen away. I went outside whenever I wanted, and I stopped looking in the mirror.

I shared a room in the hostel with the Dutch brothers and Simon, a room which always looked as if it had just thrown up, packing and repacking and sorting for the next adventure. Simon and I spent our days recovering, eating pancakes, trying to connect to the world's slowest internet, and playing on the town's playground (although the see-saw was a challenge since I still couldn't bend one knee).

We walked around town laughing most of the time, grunting when our worn-out joints had to step down a curb. One day we were carrying our filthy clothes around in plastic shopping bags looking for a laundromat when we stopped into the grocery store to buy a snack. After checking our bags at the front desk (common throughout South America) and buying ice-cream for me and cigarettes for him, we went back to retrieve our bags from the attendant. Unfortunately, the guy handed them to us upside-down, and all the mud-encrusted items spilled all over the floor. By this time, we were all embarrassed, me because of my tacky insufficient luggage, the attendant because of his faux-pas, but it got worse when I looked up to see him holding out, at arm's length, my dirty *knickers*.

I guess I should fill you in on how I managed to spend so much time with an Englishman whom I couldn't understand. The accent was something I just had to get used to. But as for the vocabulary, I started making a list. When I got an explanation, I scratched down the translation. I'm not sure which foreign language was harder to learn -- Simon's English or Chilean Spanish.

SIMON'S DICTIONARY OF "ENGLISH"

a boggie	a booger
the bin	the garbage can
trainers	tennis shoes
a jumper	a sweater
knickers	girl's undies
trouser	pants
rucksack	backpack
naf	tacky
jay cloth	dish cloth

biscuits	cookies
crisps	chips
chips	French fries
nackered	*so* tired
a sod	a jerk
Sod's Law	Murphy's Law
sodding	bloody, darn
bugger off!	go away!
braces	suspenders
suspenders	garter belt
lad, lass	guy, girl
bloke	guy
mucking it up	messing it up
dodgy	sketchy
polarneck jumper	turtleneck sweater
creased ourselves	laughed ourselves silly
pissed ourselves	see above
trolley	shopping cart
a lorry	a semi-truck
the loo	the toilet
bog paper	toilet paper

***

After a few days recovering in the relative comforts of Puerto Natales, the four of us decided to head farther south toward the border-crossing with Argentina and into Tierra del Fuego, *Land of Fire*. From the bus, the sun set in orange clouds and purple deserts. As white country homes with red roofs moved past the window, hundreds of sheep blocked the road. And as the bus wiggled through, four dogs barking at its heels, one solitary rosy-faced shepherd turned toward us and smiled as we rolled by.

The end of the earth... *El Fin del Mundo!* Ushuaia is the farthest southern city in the entire world! *The end of the world, Amy, and you are here.* We got into Ushuaia after dark, and Simon, the Dutch brothers and I bargained a price for a shared hostel room.

The next morning, I visited the eclectic Maritime Museum which housed the original map Magellan used to navigate what became his namesake Strait; there were relics from the first European sailing voyage to sail around Cape Horn, photos of the first people to land on Antarctica, and artifacts from the Yamana indigenous people of Tierra del Fuego who were wiped to extinction by disease thanks to helpful missionaries from Europe. And I visited the old prison -- where the baddest of the bad were sent. *OK Mister, I'm sending you to prison at the end of the earth. That should keep you out of trouble.*

When the museum closed, the thermometer read –5 degrees Celsius, and Simon and I stopped into a café to drink hot chocolate and eat dinner since we couldn't bear the thought of walking back to the hostel in the cold. We arrived in the late afternoon, and when the waitress came back later to tell us she was closing up, I was shocked to see my watch read 11 p.m. *Where had the time gone?*

Things with Simon were that way. We could talk for hours without even realizing it. Travel friends are different than regular friends. For starters, you're usually together 24-hours a day, so you spend more time with each other in one week than most friends spend in three months. You share intense experiences -- all of which are new -- and help each other out of dire situations on an almost daily basis. You are intimately connected by virtue of time, space, and unique experience; you share everything, and no one but that person, in that moment, can completely understand. And it's all coming rapid-fire. And before you know it, in even a matter of days or weeks, you feel as if you've known that person your whole life.

Later that week Simon and I took the bus to where the Pan-American Highway ends at Tierra del Fuego National Park and hiked to the water. The distant mountains shivered against the cold sunny day in stunning shades of lavender, but for the rest of my life I think nothing will ever compare to the magic of Torres del Paine. As we wound down a hilly path past beautiful lake after lake, half a dozen wild horses looked up at us and then went back to grazing on the tender grass sprouts newly brought by the rain.

We took pictures by the *"Fin del Mundo"* sign and followed the trail along the Beagle Channel into the nature reserve, attending to the overwhelming sensation that in just a few more steps we would fall off the earth. Illusive Cape Horn loomed just beyond the clouds. It all felt so absolute. Like somehow, I had finally arrived somewhere. At the end of the road, the End of the World, where more is there for a traveler to go?

We found a clearing in the dry grass and set up our picnic. Suddenly, Simon stood up and ripped off his jacket without a word. Then quickly his sweater, his shirt, his shoes, his socks, his pants! *What is this crazy man doing?* He ran down the hill in his boxers yelling "Take a picture!" as he jumped into the freezing water with a huge ungraceful splash. While toweling off, he told me that he had a dream to jump off the six corners of the earth. I was unaware that the planet had corners, but who was I to argue with a dream?

There must have been a hundred times that day that I'd wanted to kiss him. Not knock-him-down-and-go-crazy kiss him, but let the joy, the beauty, the magic around us escape through my lips. It was just that kind of a place.

***

When we returned to the *hospedaje*, the Dutch Brothers had left for their next train journey. All alone. *Amy, control yourself. He's sweet, and considerate, and warm, and look in his eyes. Stop it, now.* But travel brings you close with people (on all levels) whom you find fascinating. With whom you connect. It's that simple.

Simon pulled back the thick curtains by his bed to look at the night sky. The moon was a half disk beamingly brightly, the sky as clear and full of stars as the nights on the deck of the Navimag. I hopped over him to get a better view. His olive eyes filled mine, and I put my hand on his warm neck. Touch turned to hypnosis, hypnosis to lying side by side barely breathing, barely touching, looking into each others' eyes. Landslide. Timid. Beautiful. Warmth and one beautiful kiss at the End of the World. *Cold, wet and alone?* I don't think so.

We drifted off into sleep in the moonlight streaming through the uncurtained window. When we awoke, we broke into words, into confessions.

"Do you know how long I've been wanting to kiss you?" he asked in a whisper. "How long I've been thinking about that?"

I almost responded with "for the last two days" when he said, "Since I met you."

His voice was shaking. I could feel the tremble in his body. He pulled the covers up over us and accidentally grabbed the bottom edge of my T-shirt along with it, yanking it up over my head, which sent him into a beet-red barrage of apologies for being so forward, and me into fits of laughter.

***

The alarm rang much too early, and I awoke to what I thought was rain.

"It's better than that," he said as he opened the curtains.

Magic. Six inches of fresh snow covered the white wonderland outside the hostel. And it was still snowing... I ran outside and made snow angels in my pajamas, dancing, glowing, the snow turning to steam all around my charged body.

Simon and I arrived uncharacteristically early to the airport for our scheduled 10:30 a.m. flight with LADE, the cheapest tiniest airline in Argentina to fly to Rio Gallegos. The roads out of Ushuaia were now closed for winter, and airplane was the only way out if I didn't want to backtrack. From Rio Gallegos, I planned to take a bus to El Calafate to visit the National Glacier Park Perito Moreno.

The airport was snowed in, and we waited in our 15-person plane on the runway for three hours. Finally when we took off, we bumped, wind howled, it kept snowing, and I took a Dramamine. We lifted off in a white-out, but it cleared suddenly to expose the panoramic of Cape Horn and Antarctica that I had been waiting for. Simon put his warm hand on mine and smiled as if the universe had conspired just for us.

***

"Imagine the universe beautiful and just and perfect," the handbook said to me once. 'Then be sure of one thing: the Is has imagined it quite a bit better than you have.'" <u>Illusions: Adventures of a Reluctant Messiah,</u> by Richard Bach

Moment after moment of gulping life, traveling and journeys, I stood in front of El Glaciar Perito Moreno, mesmerized. The world's fastest advancing glacier at two meters per day, the glacier blankets 250 square kilometers of Argentina's Parque Nacional de los Glaciares. Due to its almost-unthinkably rapid advancement, the ice is being constantly pushed forward from behind, putting the entire structure in a constant state of cracking, breaking, falling, and reshaping itself, causing some of the most dramatic sights and sounds I have ever felt in its daily rebirth.

As I stood atop the viewing platform, I watched the world move beneath me. *Crackle. Crumble.* Sounds of stepping on twigs, of gunfire, of thunder. Blocks of ice tumbled from hundreds of feet above into the blue lagoon, its ripples traveling on their own journeys. *What must it sound like from inside?*

From the top, the glacier was an endless expanse of ice-cream sundae covered in *chantilly* stretching as far as the eye could see. But when I climbed down the hillside staircase to its base, I looked straight up into blue towers, icy chards of glass, a magical castle in the clouds whose caves and crevices sheltered wizards peeking out at me as I gazed into their hideaways.

Another rumble. Another crack. The world moves below me. Above me. *I could be sitting in a cubicle right now. Travels, destinations, journeys. How could I live life without knowing this? The absolute magic of Patagonia. The feeling in my heart.* It sped up its beats. *The excitement. The anticipation. The needing to take a step back and realize, I am really here. This is a land of billions of years. I am twenty-five. Perhaps it's wisdom that's locked inside this glacier, bursting and cracking and speaking to me. I want to listen. To absorb.* My fingers had gone numb in my purple llama-wool mittens. A thunder. A landslide. A great chunk of ice broke loose before my eyes and cannon-balled into the icy water. I wanted to scream. To cry in the presence of this power. Unknowable. And then complete silence. Not another human voice. Not a bird. I heard only the crackling of millions of years advancing, advancing towards me at two meters a day. All I could do was breathe and let the water in my eyes burn. The sun had disappeared long ago behind the mountains as I stood absorbing all I could of this majesty.

***

When Simon and I arrived in Buenos Aires, we made our way toward the theater district. We hadn't spoken much about the romantic turn in our relationship. It just was... But we had our first chance at awkwardness when the hotel clerk asked, "Sencillo o matrimonio?" *Single or double bed?* We looked at each other smiling like two kids caught at their secret game. *Do we go on pretending in public for the sake of properness?   Do we just live in the moment and screw the rest?*

After a short pause Simon said decisively, "Matrimonio" and trailed off into a giggle when the clerk turned his back to get the key.   Our room welcomed us with the smell of antiques and dust and decades of cigarette smoke and fresh soap.   I thrust open the wooden shutters to the tiny balcony and burst out with songs from *Evita*.   I just couldn't help it…   Buenos Aires.   One of the most romantic cities in the world.   *Sola* or *matrimonio*, it was a dream.

We finished the day with a bottle of Valentin Bianchi *vino tinto* and began the next with a strong *cortado* coffee, boarding the city-bus to the place I most wanted to visit: La Boca, Buenos Aires' most colorful neighborhood.   Once a meatpacking industry for Italian immigrants, La Boca gave birth to the Tango and is now famous for its brightly-painted houses on the street of Caminito.   Simon and I got off the bus at the famous soccer stadium to view the historical murals.   We walked a few blocks and turned the corner to stumble upon the most amazing spectacle.   When we heard the unmistakable accordion of Tango music bursting from a café, we quietly peeked our heads in to see a couple in costume dancing passionately.   We watched until the music stopped, and then the male dancer came over to us at the door and invited us in for a lunch of homemade cannellonis ($5) and free admission to the show.

I walked in and fell in love.   It was called *Los Gigantos*, a small restaurant owned by the waiter and his family.   The servers, all in full costume, were the dancers.   The waiter's dance partner was his wife, and the singers and two guitar players were cousins, brothers, and uncles.   The walls were covered in Tango murals painted in vibrant primary colors.   On ten tiny tables lay tablecloths and napkins of bright red, blue, yellow and green. The walls held memorabilia from the history of Tango, and in front of our table was a small stage.

My mind began to race.   *I could live here.   I should live here.*   My eyes filled with romance as I watched the dancing and live music and singing while eating pasta which melted in my mouth.   When the show finished, we drank mate tea and talked with our waiter and host.   I promised to be back for a dance lesson.

Simon and I walked outside to find yet another La Boca spectacle, the street of Caminito itself. From inside brightly-colored houses, people peeked out from doors and shutters and roofs, blue and yellow and orange and red. The cobblestone street was flooded with artists, their oil paintings of scenes from the local *barrio* proudly displayed. Old men wearing dapper suits and felt hats sat in folding chairs playing accordions, and passersby danced in the street. So passionate. On a Tuesday. It was like a dream.

Simon and I spent mornings wandering through the antique market in San Telmo, the Bohemian artist quarters of historical homes. We drank cappuccinos and ate *media lunas*. We listened to musicians in the square, acoustic guitars, singing, drumming. Tumbling, comedy, juggling, fire-throwing, living statues in the park. The smell of hot caramelized almonds. The Museo Nacional de Bellas Artes. Dali, Rodin, Monet, famous Argentine painters. Pizza and beer in bed. And then it all came to a close…

***

Green eyes. Looking into those green eyes straight into his soul. Golden flecks dancing. The innocence, the intensity, the reaching out. I could feel it. I don't know when I got to like him so much. It kind of surprised me. He was many different people all wrapped into one, and I got along better with some than with others. My favorite: the boy in the café. The one I could talk with for hours and hours. Sophisticated in his crinkled button-down purple shirt having been recently released from the depths of his backpack. He brought up ways of looking at things I had never thought of before. Gazing across the table. Knowing looks. The boy who had seen more than his share of the world.

"I don't really try to keep secrets," he said, "But I let things out little by little. Some things you just can't explain. Like if I were to try to explain to someone at home what has happened with you and me over the last few weeks, it sounds too magical. Unreal."

You can't. You just can't explain. It was mine and his and ours. I could write it in my journal, guard it in my head, talk with him about it. But I couldn't expect anyone else to understand.

I found myself falling in love over and over again. In love with love. In love with romance. With adventure. With Buenos Aires. With a tropical paradise. Or at the End of the Earth. The best and worst part of the journey was that you met amazing people and then you said goodbye.

Tiny orange lights glowed from the Presidential Palace across the square as we sat on a park bench at midnight. My face in his hands. Drinking life. *Don't cry for me, Argentina; my tears are for the Englishman.* Tomorrow we go our separate ways -- he back to England, me further on with my journey.

On our last morning, he overslept (as usual) and had an hour to get to the airport before his plane left. Stealing one last kiss, he ran out of the room saying little. *What was there to say?* I may never see him again. Actually, I knew I probably never would, but I also knew that when he talked to himself, alone on cold mornings, he'd know I was out there somewhere, listening.

Passionate about passion. In love with love. Life is a series of brief encounters. Hellos and goodbyes. Loves and losses and learnings. I feel grateful for it all. And I have to believe that from within all this sadness, it can only make me stronger.

***

I returned alone the next day to La Boca and bought a canvas oil painting of a swirly starry sky which the artist rolled up for me and stuffed into a cardboard paper-towel tube. Couples kissed on the Costenera. A professional dog walker passed by walking twelve dogs on twelve leashes, all of different shapes, sizes, breeds, and outfits.

I made my way to *Los Gigantos* as promised to take a Tango lesson which seemed like just the thing to cheer me up. I am far from the most graceful dancer, but my 5'3" teacher wrestled effectively with his towering pupil, twisting and bending me into Latin origami. Dramatic shapes, dips and flourishes. It is hard to point your toes in hiking boots. But as I closed my eyes, I heard the music, and felt the grace, the passion of Tango, the passion of the echoes in my life.

I wandered over to Plaza de Mayo where Las Madres de Plaza de Mayo silently march in front of Casa Rosas every Thursday as they have for the last 25 years. They gather to peacefully demonstrate and demand the government's accountability for their "disappeared" sons and husbands who were killed during Argentina's Dirty War.

I arrived to find Las Madres walking quietly around the plaza circle -- some quiet, some talking softly with friends or visitors, all wearing their signature white scarves covering their heads. Students, grandmothers, young and old joined in. Within fifteen minutes, the crowd had built to about thirty Madres and about seventy others. The lines in their faces. To wonder for so long, maybe forever, *Where is my son? Where is my husband?* To know the atrocities of war. At the end of their speech, the crowd broke into applause and tears. *My heart is heavy today.*

***

I boarded the bus for the 20-hour journey to Iguazú Falls, knowing that in a day's time I would be in the arms of my best friend, Kree, who had recently moved to Paraguay. The radio on the bus played Spanish love songs, and I broke down and cried at someone else's bus-stop goodbye. My emotions were a roller coaster. Up, down. Up. Down. It reminded me in a way of walking the hills in Torres del Paine, and that made me smile. Then I had the overwhelming urge to listen to Brandy. I missed Simon. Love and loss -- again. I'm coming, Kree… Looking for just a little bit of home.

PART III:
PARAGUAY & BRAZIL

IGUAZÚ FALLS

"Oh, the comfort, the inexpressible comfort of feeling safe with a person, having neither to weigh thoughts or measure words, but pouring them all right out, just as they are, chaff and grain together; certain that the faithful hand will take and sift them, keep what is worth keeping, and then with the breath of kindness blow the rest away." Dinah Maria Mullock Craik

Months before when I had been living in Playa Grande, Kree had emailed to tell me that she was quitting her teaching job in San Francisco, leaving her high-school sweetheart whom she'd dated for seven years, and moving to Paraguay. It shocked everyone but me.

It wasn't something she could really put into words, she said. It was a feeling. A feeling she had to go.

I knew that feeling. For me, it had gone discounted, ignored, unloved, for too long, and since I had started listening, it had brought me nothing but joy and fulfillment. *I may not know why, but I know I must... Now all I need is the strength to move forward.*

Kree had accepted a kindergarten teaching position in Paraguay which she had begun only three weeks before, but now that we were so "close" (everything is relative in the grand distances in South America), she came out to meet me for a long weekend at Iguazú Falls.

I spotted her right away as I stepped off the bus. She was beautiful. Independence and confidence sparkled from her hazel eyes to her lipsticked smile. My Amazon sister. Same Kree, dramatically different place. She was probably one of the only people traveling South America who was more conspicuous than I was. She is taller, she is blonder, she is paler. We must have looked like clones recently arrived from a distant planet together in the busy bus terminal. She opened her arms, and I let her warmth and love surround me.

When everything in the world had been so new, every day, for so long, it was the most tremendous relief to feel such familiarity, to be with someone to whom I could tell everything and didn't have to explain anything. We now found ourselves living in parallel, both moving away from the familiar, risking, and finding a life that was bigger and brighter than anything we could have ever envisioned. And for this brief moment in time, we were doing it together. An ex-pat I once met on the road summed it up best: "I like being here and all, but sometimes you just need peanut butter and baseball."

We settled into a hostel, and I refilled my emotional reservoirs over pizza, giant slices of chocolate cake and hours and hours of catching up. Kree glowed with the beauty of taking destiny into her own hands. Like me, she was high on life and reveling in her freedom. Succulent wild women were we, hitting our stride. And the next day, the falls draped us in their majesty.

***

As Kree and I arrived at the Brazilian entrance to the 55-hectare park, an *arco iris* hung in the sky. It disappeared just as quickly, and another rainbow appeared in the mist. Three dark sparrows flew in triangulation, offset by the rushing white backdrop of *Salto Bossetti*. I stood still, eyes widening, futile hopes of taking it all in. Soft strings of moss dripped onto pink wildflowers dotting sheer cliffs. *Cascada* after *cascada*. Ten, twenty, thirty, standing playfully like schoolchildren in line, jumping out of place, pulling at each other's hair, kicking at each other's feet.

Iguazú Falls took my breath away. A world of wonder made of mist and rainbows, water rushing everywhere, from rapid cascades dropping into charismatic whirlpools, to perfect single droplets sparkling and falling onto bright green leaves. Different trails, different angles, different views, different falls. I don't know what I had been expecting. While traveling I had worked on learning to put my expectations away, knowing you cannot be disappointed if you have no preconceived notions. Maybe I thought there would be one, two, maybe three waterfalls -- not hundreds. Not water everywhere, from every side, from every angle, traveling up, down, blowing sideways, swirling, churning, living. Each drop plunging breathlessly. Fearlessly. Saltwater tears and freshwater falls. *Emocionante.*

Kree and I made our way to the footbridge as vapor blew horizontally past us, and the brilliant sun shone into rainbow after rainbow arcing into circles. Taking my eyes in and out of focus, following a singular rushing patch of water downward, my peripheral vision blurred, and suddenly the world was turning. As the mist blew against my face, I looked over at Kree. She was soaked. Soaked in water, soaked in wonder, watching each other open our arms to the world.

At the end of the day, we walked back to the hostel, vibrating with newfound energy. Kree used the hostel's computer to check her email and confirm everything in her new classroom was OK in her absence. Instead what we got was a serendipitous email from our other college roommate J.B. Sloan -- yes, the very same J.B. Sloan who had said he would come down to join me on my South American journey and then didn't, setting off (fortunately for me) a whole separate chain of events. The email was called *"Shadow Dancing."*

Dear Amy and Kree,

Hey there WonderWomen!! It is your old friend J.B. who misses you both very much. This weekend, I had some thoughts that I was excited to share with the both of you. You both are always on my mind.

I was thinking about this thing Carl Jung calls your personal shadow. The idea that everyone has a dark side which is hidden through most of your maturing in order for you to get by. For example, let's say you decide not to shout out in crowds and instead become a quiet person because you have found that to be socially acceptable. One person's shadow may be another person's personality... For example, let's say just the opposite. You learn that you need to shout out in crowds in order to get by, so you generally avoid being quiet.

The problem is that your shadow is still there with you, and it will remain a part of you that you are essentially uncomfortable with until you come to terms with it. Until you dance with it. It seems to me that we are all desperately searching in our shadows right now. Kree, you have left what you grew up with, where you grew up, the relationship you have spent most of your life in, in order to seek out something different. I don't know if I know exactly what you would say you were seeking… I don't know if you know, but there you are dancing with your shadow. Amy has gone to the extreme in searching out her shadow and is probably right there among it, swimming around in it. It is almost like a flip into another personality (or so it seems), but it was really something she has always had with her but just learned to turn off at an early age. I started to think about why I am not with you two out there shadow dancing… The only thing I came up with is that my shadow is different in the sense that my biggest fears and my hardest issues were around commitment. Here I am in a serious relationship, in a job with a commitment to so many people, and you know sometimes in all of the commitment and the chains, it does feel a bit liberating. It is as if my shadow is this… and here I am doing a slow dance with it.

I think it is about facing your fears and moving away from comfort. It is about learning about the other side of your soul in order to fill in the missing pieces to the circle. Once we get all of the pieces together, maybe after we dive off to one extreme or the other, we can eventually find a balance that will allow us to feel comfortable with all of ourselves, and lead to us feeling completely comfortable in our culture. What I am hoping anyway, is that this shadow dancing of mine (which I feel may have gone off the deep end into overworking and no playing) may be balanced out sometime soon. And I am also excited to have you both share your dances with me… be it slow or fast, intimate or a Bible's distance between bodies. Keep me in mind. Once we have brought our shadows into our selves, we can bring ourselves together.

I love you both.

JB

Over the next few days the precious shared moments between Kree and I ran their course and drip-dropped off the edge of time's precipice, falling into deep misty pools below. By mid-weekend some of the teachers from Kree's school in Paraguay had come to visit Iguazú via rented minibus, and Kree now slowly gathered her things to return with them to Asuncion the next morning.

I talked with the teachers a bit, and their reactions to my future travel plans took me by surprise. Here were thirteen people, having just transplanted themselves in Paraguay, and *they* thought *I* was the crazy one for going off and traveling by myself. I got two "*Aren't you scared's*" and five "*Be safe and be careful's.*" As I listened to them praise my so-called "bravery" for traveling *sola*, I wondered if they didn't notice that when you travel -- no matter how many companions you've brought along to supposedly shield you from the elements -- we all face the same challenges. Traveling in a group is a myth, a safety blanket made of Emperor's Clothing. You may think that when the going gets rough, you'll have someone else to lean on, but if they're thinking the same thing, then who will lean on whom? We are all ultimately alone, and the sooner we feel comfortable with that, feel confident to stand independently, the sooner we can open ourselves up to all the opportunities that come with presenting ourselves naked to the world.

Kree and I stayed up late sitting on our beds, talking in the still warm night. Our paths had crossed in the most splendid way -- in a far-off country, in an exotic land. And now it was time to go. Time for the next chapter in my life. In hers. My eyes filled with tears at the thought of saying goodbye... I felt something stretching inside me, something old breaking, something new growing. And it hurt and at the same time felt right.

The next morning we gave a hug and I kissed her cheek, and she waved goodbye as the van pulled away, driving us both toward our newly-made lives.

***

As I took the brief bus trip back towards Argentina and crossed the border to view the other side of the falls, I listened to Tom Petty's *Learning to Fly* on my walkman, and visions of travels flashed through my mind as he sung:

"Well I started out, Down a dirty road, Started out, All alone.
And the sun went down, Across the hill, And the town lit up,
*   And the world got still.*
I'm learning to fly, But I ain't got wings, Coming down, Is the hardest thing.
The good ole' days, May not return, And the rocks might melt,
*   And the sea may burn...*

So I started out, For God knows where, I guess I'll know,
    When I get there..."

As I hummed my way to the Argentine entrance to the park, I
stopped to read the ancient Guaraní Indian legend of how the
falls were born: Iguazú Falls was formed when a jealous forest
god became enraged by a warrior escaping downriver by canoe
with a young woman. The forest god caused the riverbed to
collapse in front of the lovers, producing a precipitous falls over
which the girl fell. At their base, she was turned into a rock, and
the warrior became a tree overlooking his fallen lover.

   Amazingly, the Argentine side of the falls was even more
breathtaking than the Brazilian side because the trails allowed me
to get so close to the water. I first walked the *Circuito Superior*
overlooking dozens of falls from catwalks above, then down
through the lower circuit to stand right in amongst them, ferns
bathing in the mist, fuchsia bromeliads dripping. An entire world
of magic living there. Dragonflies darted by, and *mariposas*
flashed their colors like Halloween night in San Francisco's
Castro.

Plummeting
Crushing volume
One step
And then another free fall
Seconds in all
To the base of El Rio Iguazú.

Free Fall in an explosion
Of nuclear proportion
Bouncing back up again, 50 meters in the air,
Like a giant blowing at a plop of whipped cream through a straw.
Its vapors cool my skin in the Argentine sun,
And all I can wonder is,
What made this thing?
Where does it all come from?

Nature is Hollywood's only rival.

***

I awoke the next morning, bursting with joy and possibilities. *What is it about water that energizes me so?* Since living in Playa Grande, the ocean held every possibility, calming me in its soothing womb. Sitting, watching, meditating. And now at the falls with their magnificent rushes of water full with power and beauty, inspiration exploded like fireworks, ideas glittering down from the sky. I had planned on catching the 9 a.m. bus out of town, but with no job demanding my timely return and no traveling companion to consult, I realized that I could stay as long as I wanted. I could stay without asking anyone or negotiating around anyone's feelings -- all because I was alone. It is completely shocking to wake up and realize that you are in control of your own life. I wonder who I thought was in control before that.

Standing in front of Iguazú, the romance of Argentina's Tango mixed with the exoticism of Brazil's jungles in the mysticism of the world's most voluminous waterfalls. I climbed to the tallest footbridge in the park to look out over *La Garganta del Diablo*, the Devil's Throat, the most magnificent single falls at Iguazú. Nearby rivers of Rio Iguazú and Rio Panará converge here to cover the entire basalt plateau with water, and as the *terra firma* suddenly ends, it sends that unbelievable amount of water plummeting all at once to the depths below. Looking over the edge of the footbridge, I wondered if Columbus' crew might have imagined it this way -- calm clear flat water, and then nothing. The horizon disappeared, and nothing but edge and sky looked eerily back.

I wanted ferociously to stand on top of that guardrail. To spread my arms wide, and push off with my bare toes, and feel… To swandive -- mist rushing against my face -- into the Devil's Throat. And follow every tiny water droplet that had once passed so quietly in the river above, now reaching the edge and peeking over. Falling into nothingness. Flying, if only for a moment. Complete weightlessness, freedom from gravity. Plunging down, deeper and deeper, into a world of a thousand rainbows.

***

The night before I left Iguazú, I sat up late talking with the hostel owner and a group of other travelers. It's funny when you tell people that you're moving on, going somewhere else. Everyone thinks *somewhere else* is scary, no matter where that *somewhere else* is. People in the U.S. tell you how dangerous Latin America is. People in Costa Rica tell you how dangerous Panama is. People in Panama tell you how dangerous South America is. People in Chile tell you how dangerous Argentina is, and people in Argentina tell you how dangerous Brazil is, and I'm sure people in Brazil will tell you how dangerous somewhere else is.

"Be careful," they say.

I am always careful. But I must live.

"The world is a scary place," they say. "Don't go *there*. *Here* is much safer. Something might happen to you *there*."

Why are people so afraid of *there*? Of *them*? I know something will happen. And I know it will be wonderful.

***

The next morning, darkness held the 6 a.m. sky, and streetlights flickered as I tripped my way down the brick road, the shifting weight of my pack accentuating my sleepy stumbling. The quiet night air had trapped the pungent smell of orchids in its narrow streets. Not one breeze. Not one movement in the humid jungle that surrounded me. Dogs crowed and roosters barked in the distance. As I approached the bus station, the smell of fresh bread wafted from the nearby bakery melting in my mouth. I felt the newness in my life gathering strength, and I was ready for my next journey.

Hours later I arrived at the Jesuit Missions and settled down with my journal under a shade tree in the hazy sun just inside the perimeter wall. After a few minutes of writing, I noticed that the whole ground was moving -- thousands of giant ants marched by with crackling sounds, carrying green leaves on their backs.

I didn't startle when I heard a friendly drawn-out *hello*. The young man wore a tour guide's shirt, and without hesitation I invited him to sit with me.

"This place is magic… at least to me," he began.

He stared, eyes forward, at the imposing cathedral. The Jesuit Missions of San Ignacio built in the 17th century still stood, only months before the turn of the millennium. Julio said he had grown up here; his grandfather was Guaraní Indian, his grandmother Spanish. He had been a tour guide at San Ignacio between the ages of ten and thirteen. After that he became a tour guide at Iguazú Falls. He was twenty-nine. By the time he turned forty, his goals were to improve his language skills, speak fluent English, Italian and French, and do something different with his life.

Julio drew my attention to the highest standing piece of architecture and keystone to the ruins: the bilateral columns which formed the entrance to the cathedral.

"Look," he said. "Three Jesuit priests built the right column, and 5000 Indians copied it to make the left. The Jesuit priests made an angel on the right. The Indians made an angel on the left. The priests made a flag on the right. The Indians made a *yerba mate* (powerful local tea) plantation on the left. The priests carved fire to symbolize the Spirit. The Indians carved the *yerba mate* to symbolize the Spirit."

In Julio's version of the story, the Jesuits came over from Spain to protect the Indians from slavery by Portuguese and Spanish *hacienda* owners. Together, three Jesuit priests and one hundred tribes of fifty Guaraní Indians each, built San Ignacio which is only one of the thirty missions in the borderland between Argentina, Paraguay and Brazil. The Mission had a strict organized government as well as daily schedule. The Guaraní learned how to make musical instruments and tools, how to build structures, and how to care for the sick in new ways. The priests spoke directly to the chiefs, who in turn relayed the messages to their people.

Julio asked if I would like to walk with him. *Yes, tell me the story.* I asked if he was sure he wanted to work on his time off (his group from Iguazú was on a tour), but he told me how much he loved sharing his country with others.

We walked to the entrance to the cathedral, and he said, "Listen to the sound." He clapped four times, and indeed, the acoustics were phenomenal.

We stood there quietly for a while, just imagining the 75-meter long, 15-meter high church, full of the Mission's inhabitants, praying and singing every morning. He told me about the other missions, about how writing was first introduced in the Mission Nuestra Señora del Loreto, about how the Jesuits were expelled in 1767 because their organized society posed a threat to Spanish and Portuguese authority. Then Julio's tour group returned, I thanked him, and he left.

Sitting there in the plaza at dusk after Julio had gone, I knew he had opened my eyes, and I could feel the magic there. I could imagine it all. Living here then. History has as many versions as it has individuals who lived it. Julio had told me his version. But this place fascinated me just enough to venture on, to see if others like it could tell their own story through their own words. I decided to visit the mission of Trinidad in Paraguay the next day. I was fascinated. And I wanted more.

   ***

I had to take four buses to get there, including a stop in the Encarnación bus station, a border town which was one of those put-it-down-and-lose-it kinds of places. I stood wearing my backpack, my back pressed firmly against the ticket office wall waiting for my bus when I noticed an interesting sign for a possible (and potentially stinky) destination: I-T-A-P-U-A   P-O-T-Y, 12:45.

It made me laugh deliriously and forget that I was hot and tired and overwhelmed by the swarming vendors. *How does that little girl make a living selling Chicklets gum?* I wondered, as I then watched her unzip the bag of an unsuspecting man and slide her tiny hand in. Luckily she came up with nothing. I debated about telling him but had been threatened by pickpockets before for tattling. Finally I boarded the bus, and from the safety of my seat said goodbye to the hoards on the stage below.

When I finally arrived at the Trinidad ruins, the crowds had long faded. It was just me -- me and the spirits of the Jesuit priests and Guaraní people of long ago. I climbed up and sat atop the remains of the bell tower, a warm firm breeze flitting at my legs which dangled above the roofless cathedral meters below. Not a voice. Not a camera clicking. Then, I thought I heard something. A low hum. *A mosquito? Chanting maybe?* As I walked down the worn steps to the dark cavernous space underneath the church, I felt sure what I was hearing were the haunting voices of the past, souls of the Mission of long ago. *What was it like back then?* I wondered. They seemed to speak from the walls. From the hands that had carved the statues. From the backs that had carried the stones. Red sandstone figures looked down upon me, their smoothed features softened from hundreds of years of wind. I could feel it. See it. Three Jesuit priests and thousands of Guaraní gathered here in this meeting place of the souls where animism met Christianity. A Mission built in the middle of the jungle, in a place that was not yet Paraguay. Suddenly, one lifetime seemed so little to soak it all up.

LUMINOUS FLUX...

"So do not be frightened... if a sadness rises up before you larger than any you have ever seen; if a restiveness, like light and cloud-shadows, passes over your hands and over all you do. You must think that something is happening with you that life has not forgotten you, that it holds you up in its hand; it will not let you fall. Why do you want to shut out of your life any agitation, any pain, any melancholy, since you really do not know what these states are working upon you... since you know that you are in the mids of transitions and wished for nothing so much as to change." Letters to a Young Poet, *by Rainer Maria Rilke*

Once freed of my travel commitments to J.B., there was no real reason to stay in Playa Grande. My self-imposed waiting period for moving on to South America had evaporated, the dry season had begun to spin itself into the humid warmth of waiting for the rains, and yet I just couldn't bring myself to uproot. I was stuck. In love and fascination with the people around me. Week after week, intriguing guests from all over the world arrived to tell me exactly what I needed to hear. And then there was Louis of course, who offered more insight, challenge and frustration in one conversation than most people do in a lifetime.

Louis was full of contradictions. One minute he'd be complaining about his relationship with Marianela, and the next he'd be waxing sentimental on love. One minute he'd be egotistical about his place in the world and how much he knew, and the next he'd be asking me what I thought. But whether he was a multidimensional savant or a just bit schizophrenic was hard for me determine until I gave up trying so hard to box him in, pin him down, figure him out. And as I learned to live with that lack of categorization, some clarity began to emerge. He was all those things, and much of the disjointedness came from his playing a ringmaster role at the hotel and then turning inward to an introverted, introspective private life. I suppose we all have multi-faceted personalities, but Louis', like many other things about him, came out in the extreme.

Louis was not easy to live with, but that in itself seemed important. He questioned me about the morals I held dear and assumptions I had grown up with. And he challenged and teased and taunted to within a thread's width of snapping. Then, just when I was about ready to scream *Enough!* and stomp out of there, he'd tell me how much he appreciated me, admired me, how he couldn't do it without me. And I would stay. He needed me for his freedom (I relieved him of many of his hotel duties). I needed him to model what freedom was.

In a twisted way, I knew it was all kinda good for me. Maybe not good exactly, but at least important to experience. And maybe that's why living there felt so hard. Playa Grande was peeling the onion. Stretching, growing, shaping, changing. The Spanish language hurt my brain. The surfing hurt my body. Louis managed to unravel the identity I had *thought* was me, the one I had come with. And that left me bare and true and raw with emotion. And that felt good. And terrifying. And poised at the brink of making something new.

And for all the headaches Louis gave me, I really did grow to love him. After all, he showed me I could fly... He modeled how the universe *could* be -- and I'm not sure that I would have gone on to do the things I did if I had never met him.

***

The wind began to turn around earlier in the day as ripping *Papagayos* were replaced with onshore breezes. Sitting midmorning out in the glassy break, suddenly the air would become completely still, and then I'd hear *pop-pop-pop*. The barometer plummeted like the bean-pods high in the trees bursting in the humidity, raining their seeds down to earth. The breeze would start to blow softly against my face as I looked out to sea, a warm wet onshore wind knocking down the surf into a sloshing mess within minutes. The changing of the seasons.

But even as the rainy season began to tease us, characters continued to flow through the hotel like the tides, moving in and out, bringing humor and friendship and occasional clarity. And all I had to do was be there -- and listen for wisdom and opportunities.

One day a crew of scientists and television producers from the Discovery Channel (back when it was little more than a series of documentaries for nature lovers) arrived at the hotel to film a special on Leatherback Sea Turtles. They brought with them *The Critter Cam*. This mini waterproof video-camera attached by suction-cup to the turtle's shell and would record live-feed streaming images of "a day in the life of a turtle:" how deep it dove, how long it spent on the surface, what the world looked like from its eyes. After three days of information gathering, the suction cup would simply let go, and the camera would fall to the bottom of the sea where the crew would retrieve it via radio signal. The technology was mind-blowing, and that night would be *Critter Cam's* maiden voyage.

I wrangled an invitation to tag along, and by midnight we were waiting silently under the bright round moon for a turtle to climb the sandy bank to lay her eggs. The scientist would attach the *Critter Cam* while the nesting female was in her trance-like state.

My job was very simple yet very important: *Hold the flashlight.* We used dim red-tinted lights to minimize disturbing the turtle, and I was to hold it so the crew could see to attach the suction-cup.

"Closer, closer," they whispered as I neared the nesting mama stalk-still in her concentration, her laying almost complete.

"Closer," they coaxed.

I stepped, I leaned, I stretched that faint little light as close as I could reach... And then, just at that moment, the turtle decided she was finished laying and began to push sand back over the hole she had dug with her enormous flippers. I had gotten so close that at the first surprising stroke of her long, broad, dinosaur-like flipper, she stepped right on my foot. My flip-flopped foot. *Oooh...* I winced and took a step back as she released me. I felt broken, but I didn't cry out so as not to ruin the project, not that the scientists were focused on me anyway. And although I couldn't surf for a few days, it eventually healed, and I spent the rest of the week watching live-streaming video of the life and times of the mama who crushed my big toe.

Three months later as I walked down the wet cool sand for dawn-patrol surf, I watched her little babies hatch from their nest high up on the sand, scurrying with tiny pushes to the water below as the ghost crabs scuttled out of their way.

***

We got a lot of really interesting guests at Hotel Las Tortugas. It was what Playa Grande was about. And I was always trying to tease out people's secrets to life, particularly those who had successfully struck a balance between a career where they felt successful and a life where they could still travel.

Emma had the coolest job in the world. She did advance work for nature film documentaries with a well-known British host and crew. Her job was to do the research necessary to get a project set up for filming in a foreign country, such as researching where the animals lived, how the film crew would travel around, where they would stay, and what they would try to get on film. And once she set it all up, she just went along to make sure everything went OK. It sounded perfect to me. In the last year alone, she had traveled with the crew to Uganda to film the Mountain Gorillas, to Capetown to film Great White Sharks, and now to Costa Rica to film the Leatherback Sea Turtles.

I met people for whom it took much of their lives to find the job that was right for them. Michael was in his late thirties working as a successful banker in the financial district of San Francisco when he literally turned his life around. He had had a well-paying job with lots of room for advancement, a fancy car, a nice apartment. But Michael was unhappy. Actually, as he tells it, he didn't even realize he was unhappy. But one day, Michael was driving south to work as he always did, and something inside him snapped -- or clicked -- but undeniably, something happened... And when Michel got to the next light, he made a U-Turn. And when he started driving north away from work, he just kept on going -- until he found himself in Seattle. He called the office and told them he wasn't coming in (ever), and as he stood and looked out at the great Pacific Ocean, his childhood dream of being at sea washed over him with a tranquility he hadn't known since he was a boy. Michael became a tug boat driver. He still makes great money. He has as much time off as he chooses. He is on the ocean every day. He's never been happier. And he has never looked back...

I often met people at the top of their fields -- CEOs, business women who traveled internationally for work, all the things I thought I aspired to do (primarily because they would get me out traveling in the world). And these people would sit patiently with me for hours as I probed into their personal and working lives, trying to assess if what they did would be a good fit for me. They would talk about their busy schedules and their powerful positions and then say that although their jobs sounded glamorous, they really never had any time to actually explore the country they were visiting since their hosts kept them chaperoned and their home-offices kept them saddled with cell-phones and laptops. And after I'd finished grilling them, they'd say the same thing: "I wish I was doing what *you're* doing."

People said this to me time after time. Smart people. Experienced people. Respectable stable people. Here I was, eyes and heart open, listening for a sign, searching for a direction, and now people were telling me that I was already there. I *was* traveling. I *was* learning. I *was* gaining first-hand experience in a field that I thought I had to go home and study in school: running a small business abroad. *You are already there. You just skipped some steps.*

This was mind-boggling. And not easy to accept. It was all too easy, yet at the same time, living in Playa Grande -- in the now -- was sometimes all too hard.

***

I met person after person who dropped gems of wisdom and courage and validation into my lap. They came at a time so poignant that they found their way in with a click and latched into my soul. Charlene was an artist who had found happiness with a microbiologist. They were both travelers. She had lived in Turkey and the Middle East throughout her twenties, and he had conducted research all over the world as a professor.

Now in her late fifties, Charlene reassured me, "You always can find a way to keep on traveling. It becomes a way of life. And if you decide you want a partner, you have to make sure they want the same thing."

She told me how they used to take their young kids everywhere during their years of research -- Africa, East Asia. And when I asked what their grown children now thought about their experiences, she responded, "They turned out O.K., surprisingly. They missed a lot of school. But it turns out kids don't need as much school as most people think."

As the pair walked hand-in-hand down the beach, I leaned against the restaurant balcony railing, and my attention turned toward a tired-looking couple in their early-40s sitting poolside, half-reading, half-occupied in subduing their five daughters engaged in open combat. Ages toddler to 12 whined and shouted and screamed, drowning out the sound of the lapping sea.

Poor working souls, I sighed. *Here are their ten days of "freedom" a year. Ten days out of 365. Here with their family. Hoping for stolen moments of relaxation between the "no's" and the "stop that's."*

I had always known I was different, but by then I had begun to recognize and embrace those differences and find a small pocket of people who understood them, too. And as I looked at that family in what seemed to me like chaos, I gave myself a gift. I told myself that if that was not the life I wanted, than I didn't have to make that kind of life. *I* guide my destiny. I just have to remain vigilant at all times, asking myself *why* in addition to *why-not.* I have to resist becoming so tired, so worn-down, so automated that I give in because it's easier to go with the flow of a predominant culture. It is a lot of work to live with constant vigilance, but it is worth my happiness.

I have come to truly believe in my heart that *anything* is possible. As women, but especially as young women, we are led down a path by society. It is wider than the path our mothers and our grandmothers knew, but it is deep and well-trodden nevertheless. It is lined with fairytales of Prince Charming, of super career women who "have it all." But I want to scream out: *You don't have to get married if you don't want to! You don't have to have kids if you don't want to! You don't have to rise to the top of your field to feel a sense of achievement! You don't have to live someone else's dream!*

Why do we so shun the importance of making our own tailor-made happiness? We say it's because we don't know how to get there, but I think we really do. We are just afraid of what change might mean. Leaving a job. Leaving a boyfriend or a spouse. Financial instability. Leaving what we know, what we've always done, what's been prescribed for us, who we've always been, in pursuit of something bigger, more genuine, more us. And it is scary to step off into the void, into the nothingness...

But finding women who *have* stepped off and thrived makes it not so scary. And during my time in Playa Grande, I was fortunate to meet so many people who had gone off the path, but really I think I found them because I finally opened my eyes to them. Unlikely characters who had found their own way, grappling along *sola* in the dark, finding strength in themselves, in each other's braveries, and in the indisputable results of knowing that you're living your life *just* as you know it was meant to be.

***

After that, it became harder to stay in Playa Grande. It became harder to put up with Louis's oscillating moods. It became harder simply to be in one place -- knowing that the whole continent of South America lay out there in front of me, its deep Amazon jungles and its Patagonian glacial peaks just out of reach until I stretched my hand just a little farther and began to venture out from this challenging yet secure world I had made for myself. Louis would say, *"You'll never find anything as good as this"* -- and I knew he was probably right. But soon the drive for something new outweighed the comfort of something known, and the balance tipped.

And with that, I began to make small forays out into the world...

AMAZON SYMPHONY

After a three-hour bus ride from the city of Manaus, two more hours in a motorboat stacked high with bananas, and an hour paddling a leaky dugout canoe made from a *sucupira* tree, I found myself on the Rio Urubu, a tributary of the Rio Negro in the Amazon region of Brazil with Adoni, a young man of twenty who had agreed to be my guide. No one knew the Amazon jungle like Adoni; he had grown up on the land now set aside as a nature preserve inside the Basin, and he knew every plant, every flower, every waterway, every bird. What Adoni did not know was English. Nor Spanish. He spoke a bit of Portuguese (which is nothing like Spanish, contrary to what I had been deluded into believing). But somehow, in the five days I spent with him, we nurtured a friendship inspired by the wordless harmony of the environment around us. They were days I will never forget.

I had arrived in Manaus, the jumping-off point for trips into the Amazon and home of the nineteenth-century rubber boom, seeking a trip that would accommodate my backpacker budget. I faithfully followed my guidebook out of the airport, past the tour touts, into the rain, into a taxi, and finally onto the doorstep of Mr. Pessoa. I explained my situation and my budget and told him I was looking forward to joining one of his tour groups which I'd read so much about. Quite surprisingly, he confided that his small business had had no tourists in almost two weeks, but he would be happy to arrange something for me.

Did that mean -- gulp -- I'd be going all alone?

He would need to, of course, make some adjustments to make my trip economically feasible for just one person.

Into the Amazon alone? Traveling from town to town in South America was one thing, but into the jungle?

He told me I'd have to rely on public transportation to get me as close as possible to the site of the small camp. Yes, he proudly guaranteed, it would be a very isolated experience where there would be no other tourists to bother me.

Was that a good thing?

And he had the perfect guide for me -- someone who had not been with his company long, someone who was quite young, and well, someone with whom I did not share a language, but he was sure that wouldn't be a problem...

Before I knew it, I was signing on to go into the world's most infamous jungle with a kid I didn't know, whom I couldn't talk to, for five days, and the only one who knew exactly where I'd be was the man in the tour office. I found a small hotel near the center of town, flipped on the slow-moving ceiling fan, and took off my rain-soaked boots as the sweat poured from my face. I sat down and sunk deeply into the single bed, wondering when in the last year I had lost any sense of good judgment. Good judgment had been -- well -- good to me in the past, but I knew now there were places it could never take me.

I took in a long breath, sighed deeply, and packed a small bag with things I thought one might need in the Amazon.

***

When Adoni and I arrived at camp, Doña Sonia came out to greet us. She was the cook and the only one who lived at this remote site, hours from the nearest town or village. She was maybe forty, maybe older. Tawny, wiry and tough, with long flowing dark hair and sharp eyes. I thought of fifth grade history class where I had learned the word, "sinew"; Sonia was the definition personified. And I adored her instantly.

I settled into camp, a small clearing between river and jungle which had three structures: the sleeping quarters (made of six vertical wooden poles supporting a thatched roof where Adoni helped me string up my hammock), the kitchen (a structure identical to the sleeping quarters but with a table, benches and a wood stove; this was Sonia's domain), and the bathroom (a 4'x4' bamboo shack straight out of Gilligan's Island with not much more than a stinky hole in the ground but better than stepping on a snake in the middle of the night while looking for a place to squat).

It was already mid-afternoon when we settled into camp, and Adoni was quick to offer to take me canoeing in the swamp. *The swamp.* The idea conjured up visions of tiny eyes peering out from behind every gnarled tree-branch, and I jumped excitedly back into the dugout. I anxiously grabbed one of the heavy wooden paddles but in the heat was soon exhausted. Although the mangroves provided shade, the swamp was the hottest, most humid place I had ever been in my life. Adoni told me to relax and leave the paddling to him -- after all, he'd been doing it since he was *this* high. I sat back and watched the world glide silently by. It really was what I imagined the Amazon would be. A low canopy of spooky jungle trees hung above the shallow corridor through which we paddled; Adoni told me it would be dry in this very spot in less than a month as the rainy season came to an end. Termite-eaten branches plunged into the water, and pollen and dead leaves floated on the surface. Where the sunlight filtered through the branches, a reddish color glowed in the crystal-clear water stained by the leaves and mangrove roots. But what was most amazing was the stillness. Trees above the surface reflected in the water below and formed a perfect mirror. Branches jutted out from the watery depths and reflected their twin, creating a parallel universe as I floated between the two.

Next we paddled into the *igarapé*, a tributary of the main river that gradually narrowed until it ended in the middle of the jungle at a plentiful pool of fish. Like the swamps, the *igarapés* dry up and disappear in the dry season, and when we got out of the canoe to explore on land (and rest my aching butt from the wooden seat), I was surprised that beneath the deep layer of dry leaves, I sank quickly into the spongy ground. Adoni said this bank was underwater only a few weeks ago.

It was nearly sunset by the time we paddled back out onto the main Rio Urubu. The air blazed as hot and humid as a furnace, yet nothing disturbed the perfect stillness of the watery mirror. The symphony had begun. Two pairs of scarlet macaws screeched their evening calls as they flew overhead in fiery rainbows that mate for life. *Papagayos*, the green macaws, cried out in flight like tiny emerald explosions. Doves cooed somberly, and toucans called from high in the jungle canopy. The cicadas joined in. Then high-pitched chirping of *ranas*, and the deep croaks of the giant bullfrogs in three-part harmony. An unnerving sound broke the arrangement when a night bird cried out like a child in pain. As the orchestra rose to crescendo, I closed my eyes and listened to night fall on the Amazon.

When we arrived back at camp, Doña Sonia was nearly finished preparing the dinner of rice and fish. We sat down at the table in the kitchen, and I watched her tend the huge cooking fire. Francisco, a migrant laborer who had spent the day repairing the kitchen's thatched roof, joined us for dinner. He was from the Tucan tribe of Guyana, a country in the northeast of South America which had been a British colony until 1966. Francisco explained that there was often tension in this region with Guyanese immigrants since as native English speakers they had run many Brazilians out of their tour-guide jobs. But Francisco preferred to work with his hands. He was a joy to visit with that night as he told stories of jaguars and snakes and what it means if a boa constrictor crosses your path. He explained how you could ask it questions, and how it can heal you, and how you should respect it.

After dinner, I set up my mosquito-net by candlelight, and Adoni went down to the river to get water for me to wash my face. I wrapped up in my hammock and listened to the jungle sounds, mysterious and haunting and beautiful, and wondered how many hundreds of living creatures were watching me in the moonlight shadows at that moment.

Adoni showed me how to lie diagonally in my hammock so my feet wouldn't stick up in the air and go numb, but I didn't sleep right away. Instead, I got up and walked out from under the palm roof and looked up -- and it took my breath away. I had never, in all the places I had visited, seen so many stars glimmering so brilliantly. Diamonds flashing their whites, their yellows, their blues and reds like magical jewels. Billions of curious twinkling eyes gazing out from their hiding places in an undiscovered universe.

***

I awoke from the most peaceful sleep I could ever remember to the sound of the only three human voices in the world. Adoni, Francisco and Doña Sonia whispered in the kitchen, their voices muffled by the soft calls of a *pareja* of macaws, so different from the disquieting nightsounds. Swaddled in my hammock, a light breeze caressed my face and I returned to what I knew as infanthood. Contentedness. Peace. Amazonas, the heart of the world.

I slipped on my fleece sweater in the cool morning air and stood out by the river to watch the sky change from midnight blue to pink and orange. As the sun crawled up the sky, Doña Sonia's voice startled me. "Coffee?" she asked. I went to the table to find homemade *bolo de trigo*, a floury flat-cake with sugar that was the closest thing to a pancake I thought I'd ever see this deep in the wilderness.

After breakfast, Adoni, Francisco and I hiked into the jungle. As I sank like an elephant into the spongy ground, the two men showed me dozens of plants and their medicinal and practical uses.

Adoni spoke as Francisco translated, "The jungle is perfect. For everything the jungle has that can do you harm, it also has an antidote, a medicine growing right beside it."

Like life, I suppose. It's all there, right in front of you. Things that can do you harm, things that can do you good, but you must move fearlessly forward in order to discover them.

As we walked through the jungle classroom, Adoni pointed out the *burracha*, or rubber tree plant, good for mending many things like water-jugs and boats. The *bengue* plant can be boiled to make tea to cure colds, and *muruxirana* can be used as a wash to clean infections.

Adoni wove me a bracelet from *envira* plant and carefully twisted a whistle out of a palm leaf that we could use for emergency communication. Gifts everywhere. After seeing the bounty here, it is not surprising that a greedy few have exploited these great treasures, over-harvesting the natural resources of the Amazon for financial gain in the global economy.

By the time we returned to camp, my clothes were soaked with sweat which streamed down my body and dripped from the

tip of my nose. I lay down in a hammock and stared up at the
ceiling of the rancho where the shed skins of giant spiders lay
vacant, wedged between the wooden poles. I was fascinated. I
vigilantly extracted them, careful to keep all the legs intact, and
proceeded to glue them onto postcards which I later sent to my
closest friends. Fortunately, Adoni interrupted this gruesome
activity to ask if I'd like to go fishing -- for piranha!

A few minutes later, there I was, paddling out to his secret
spot, sitting with a hand line, baiting my hook with raw chicken
skin. I lowered the line five meters off the edge of the canoe,
and began to feel like I was in a Jaws movie. Old rickety boat,
leaking. A man. A woman. Fishing quietly. Surrounded by
silence. Then the music starts... duh duh, duh duh...

In Manaus, I had visited the fish market, fascinated by
wonder-stories of man-eating fishes in the wild Amazon. Inside
a metal airport hanger was one of the biggest and most varied
fish markets in the world. In fact, the Amazon is said to be so
unexplored that biologists are discovering new endemic fish
species at the rate of over a dozen a year. Inside the market I saw
creatures I could not believe, creatures which had fallen straight
out of Dr. Seuss' imagination. Some had the teeth of a dog.
Some had flippers like a dolphin. Spotted like seals. Striped like
zebras. Every color and size from the length of my finger to the
length of the table. One vendor proudly displayed a six-foot
pirarara, the infamous fish known to grow up to five meters and
weigh up to 150 kilos and whose toothless mouth is so big, it has
been said to swallow people whole!

As Adoni and I sat in the tiny canoe, my mind raced back to
what I had seen there and the wondrous unknown of the deep.

"What would happen if I fell in the water right now?" I
asked.

Nothing, he seemed to say. He mimed that the piranha are
afraid if you're moving, but if you're dead and fall into the river,
there will be nothing left but your bones.

Gulp. So Hollywood doesn't make this stuff up?

The fishing trips *I* knew were a multi-hour process, all about
the art of waiting, and if you got a nibble, it was a near miracle.
But when you lower raw meat fifteen feet down into the Amazon
River, results are immediate!

A nibble, a bite, a tug, a PULL! Adoni pulled out a piranha the moment his line hit the water, wiggling and snapping and making all sorts of terrible noises. He held it in his hand, up to his ear.

"Hello? It's a cellular," he said.

He giggled, but I was terrified it would take his ear off. I couldn't believe how small it was (only about six inches long), and it didn't look nearly as menacing as I had expected until he pulled down its lip with a hook to show me those teeth! Tiny razors gnashing on powerful jaws. He tossed it into the bottom of the boat where it struggled and chattered and flipped around in the water that had leaked in. I pulled my sandaled toes up on the bench with me.

Adoni pulled up another fish, and another and another. I got plenty of bites but just couldn't hook one. They were so fast! Finally, a nibble, a stronger bite...

Pull, Amy, pull!

Up it came. It snapped around on the line, hanging in mid-air. *A piranha all my own!* We finished the night with a total of ten (including my one), and Adoni cleaned them with his machete, Sonia cooked them up, and we sucked the bones dry. Adoni cut the teeth out after we'd finished eating so I could make a repulsively impressive necklace. Strange jewelry for a former vegetarian, but maybe that's why I wore it for so long.

After dinner, we decided to go out in the canoe again, this time by the light of the brilliant waxing moon that had risen high in the sky. As we walked toward the boat, a figure moved out of the shadows. Sonia stood on the shore, bathed in moonlight, her hair long and wild, her hard body stiff, a spear in her hand. A moon goddess on the hunt, she seemed almost to glow. Two fish about 9 inches long were stuck on the end of her spear as she held it high above the water. Poised, waiting, ready.

The Amazon swamp at night. Come ride through dead trees and shadows. Spooky croaking and chirping echoes. Howls and screams that made my skin crawl. As we glided along silently on the moonlit water, we looked for caiman, searching with our flashlights under the tree roots and branches for the glowing orange reflection of their eyes. Adoni told me to keep searching as he stood up in the bow of the canoe to bail. With him obstructing the front view, I didn't see the stump sticking out of the water up ahead as we continued to drift along, and BAM! The boat stopped suddenly, and I looked up just in time to see Adoni stumbling to catch his balance, standing straight up in the front of the canoe, arms whirling backward in circles like a cartoon.

"Woah! I almost fell out! See, I'm the best guide ever!" he seemed to say in Portuguese.

We laughed hysterically, but only because it was so terrifying. Imagine floating through the Amazon swamp at midnight when your guide falls into the water and gets eaten by a crocodile. That would make quite a different story… I wasn't too disappointed when we didn't see a caiman that night, and I nestled down into my hammock safe and dry.

***

On a foggy dawn, parrots screeched in the distance. My eyes contentedly drooping, Adoni and I again paddled our canoe into the river's misty water-forest, life all around us. The chirping of small birds, the whizzing of insect wings, and the occasional shrill scream of an animal unknown. The sun rose white over the trees through the cloudy filter, and its diffused light created the most perfect mirror yet on a river made of glass. We floated silently among the trees, so close that I could have reached out and touched the wild birds.

SPLASH! Not ten meters from the boat.

"What was that?!" It sounded big.

"A pink dolphin," said Adoni.

Another funny trick on the tourist, right? Pink dolphins? Dolphins in a river?

And then I remembered hearing something about the elusive pink dolphin of the Amazon, but I had thought it was a myth.

SPLASH, SPLASH.

Now there were two, right before my eyes, jumping out of the water in front of the canoe in this magical place.

In the dimly-lit dawn I could see humps on their backs, and asked Adoni, "Are they really pink?"

He explained that near Manaus there is a famous place called *The Meeting of the Waters*, where the Rio Negro (literally a black river) meets the yellow-colored waters of the Rio Amazonas/Rio Solimões. If you go out in a boat, you can see these rivers come together; amazingly, they meet but do not blend. In the yellow water, the pink dolphins look even pinker, and that is where they got their name. On that morning I sat in the stillness, transfixed on the beauty of these pink playmates of the imagination.

When we returned to camp, I followed the sweet smell of sugar and oil toward the kitchen hut and timidly peeked in. Doña Sonia was making *bolinho*, small balls of flour, sugar and water and deep-fried in oil; they smelled like donuts. She called me inside to turn them over by poking them with a wooden stick.

After breakfast, black clouds glided in, gusty winds came out of nowhere, and sheets of rain pounded down on the rancho. The storm finished as quickly as it had started, and Adoni and I waited for the leaves to stop dripping before taking a jungle walk.

Adoni had told me that his family made their living by making handicrafts to sell to tourists, and when I asked if he would teach me, we began looking for the infamous *Sao Brazil* wood. Deep beautiful red in color, we found a tree that had fallen two days ago and took turns cutting off dead pieces with the machete. Then we searched for a piece of bamboo to make a blowpipe.

We spent a buggy afternoon at camp sitting on a wooden bench making handicrafts. So quiet. Sonia sang as she painted her toenails, talked to her *loros*, and watched me nearly cut my leg off with a machete. Adoni said no one would love me if I only had one leg so I should be more careful. He took the machete away and cut a section of bamboo for my blowpipe. I used palm leaves to clean out the inside and my pocket knife to whittle it into shape. He showed me how to make darts out of sharp sticks and put a little puff of dandelion-like weed on the end. And then I blew -- it really worked, as the dart lodged in a nearby tree.

Adoni used his machete as gracefully as a sculptor to carve the *Sao Brazil* wood into a beautiful red hairpin. He made one for me and one for Sonia. I tried to make one too, but it just kept getting smaller and smaller as I tried to get it just right.

That evening, I looked out to see Adoni walking into the river with a bar of soap. Pretty soon, his hair was thoroughly sudsy, and he was singing. I asked him if he was worried about taking a bath in a piranha-filled river, and he responded as he often did, "No problem."

When he was done, I grabbed my soap (for the first time since arriving) and headed in. It felt glorious, especially after constantly sweating for days, but I remained vigilant and continually moved my feet around, just so the piranhas wouldn't have to wonder if I was alive and wanted to stay that way.

***

Although my sleeping quarters were no more than a palm roof, I still wondered what it would be like to sleep under the jungle canopy, a hammock tied between two trees. *It doesn't hurt to ask...*

Minutes later, Adoni and I had packed up and were bush-whacking (in the dark) walking for an hour out into the middle of the jungle. There was no path, but with my flashlight mounted on my head and my hammock tied around shoulders, I trailed quickly behind Adoni, stepping where he stepped, walking where he walked. After about ten heart-stopping minutes of thinking every stick in my path was a snake, I began to wonder if this might not have been such a good idea. I knew there was no way that I, queen of the directionally-impaired, could find my way back to camp if something happened to Adoni. I tried to push the doubts and questions to the back of my mind and focus my energy on my excitement.

When Adoni finally stopped, I sighed with relief.

"We're here," he said.

I wondered how he knew where *here* was. I asked him if this was where he always camped, and he said that this was his first time here. A little disconcerting, but if sleeping in the virgin jungle was what I had wanted than sleeping in the virgin jungle was what I got.

I strung up my hammock and fixed my mosquito net around it tightly. I hung my boots from the strings, wondering which of the world's deadliest creatures would make a bed in them tonight. The eerie sounds of the night-jungle had intensified as we'd moved farther from the river camp. Frog croaks reverberated inside my chest, and bat wings swished, brushing closely by my head. I looked up into the treetops whose two trunks held my hammock. They stretched thirty meters straight up into the air, and the moon peeked out from behind their high branches. I imagined the yellow eyelash vipers that might be slithering down as I laid there, sliding across my hammock strings, looking for a little crack to creep into and snuggle up next to my warmth.

My mind kept me awake most of the night, and when I finally did sleep, I slept terribly. I had horrible nightmares, and each time I woke up, I was frightened -- and desperate to pee, but absolutely dead-set against setting foot on the ground. In a never-before-achieved acrobatic maneuver with no witnesses, I propped both hands on my hammock in a handstand, and balanced one leg against a tree, ultimately resulting in a slightly damp but relieved hammocker.

To awaken under the jungle canopy can be startling, eyes opening to the treetops far far above. Sunrise means only enough light to reflect the fog, enough to know you're deep in the heart of somewhere strange and unfamiliar. I lay awake watching Adoni, waiting for him to stir, and when he finally moved, I hurriedly told him about my strange dreams and restless sleep. He said that it must have been the Spirits that live in the jungle. They did not know us. We were not invited here.

I got the chills as he said it -- because it felt real. And I never again doubted that the forest has a Soul.

We walked slowly back to camp, and after breakfast Sonia gave me her address and asked me to send her a copy of the photo we had taken together. She showed me her photo album. A daughter with a new baby. Another who had died. She asked if I had any photos of my family, and I showed her the little album I kept for just those occasions. Adoni said he had a picture of ten of the people in his family, but that wasn't everyone since they're never around at the same time. I started to feel the tummy pangs of homesickness. Grateful to have a happy healthy family. Sad I could not be with them, but glad I was here. Since seeing Kree, I felt those pangs more often, the craving of close connection, someone beyond kind strangers.

Sonia and I hugged and said our goodbyes, and Adoni and I loaded the canoe and paddled back out toward the Rio Negro. My last day in the Amazon was to be spent with him and his family.

***

Adoni had invited me to his mother's house which was located on a small tributary of Rio Negro, called Rio Janauary inside the

Amazonas National Park. After paddling our way back to the main river from camp, we met up with the speedboat, and after a few hours it dropped us off at a place where I was surprised to *not* see Adoni's village. Just jungle. More jungle.

I followed behind Adoni as I had learned to do without question, but when you don't know where you're going, and you don't know how long it will take to get there, you seem to wonder *Are we there yet?* over every bend.

We walked for at least an hour, uphill and down, along narrow paths, through mud and knee-deep swamp. We passed through a small village where we talked with some of Adoni's relatives and friends. He had not been home in over four months. As we chatted, his cousins decorated an extravagant mask three feet tall which wore a headdress of reddish-orange seeds and giant scales from the *pirarcu* fish. It still hangs in a place of distinction on my bedroom wall today.

We continued walking down the dirt path and came to a stream. Adoni untied a small flat-bottomed boat, and as he pushed off and began paddling, a woman appeared on the other side of the bank. She had deep-worn lines across her leathery face, but her hair was dark black. As we approached, she remained completely stoic.

A potential member of Doña Sonia's sinew clan, I thought. The woman carried in her right hand a rusty machete with a pale wooden handle, and on her back a rice sack loaded with something lumpy and heavy. As she stepped into the dark water and started to wade across, Adoni said, "That's my mother."

No smile. No shout of greetings. No sign (that I could see) of recognition. When we reached her, Adoni's mother was chest-deep in the stream. They spoke five or six words in a low tone, Adoni took the sack from her, and they continued on their separate and opposite paths.

I was confused. *How could a mother who had not seen her child in four months not yip with joy?* I was never surprised at how surprised I was while traveling.

On the other side of the water, we reached Adoni's community. Shirtless children played under palms in the warmth of mid-day, and as we approached, faces began to peek out from the four houses built on stilts.

All Adoni's family lived here: his ten brothers and sisters, and their husbands and wives, and their children. They came running out of their houses, excited to see him, excited to see me. I was taken by the hand and led around the grounds and into homes, spoken to in quick energetic tones. Everyone smiled and laughed. The women wanted to show me jewelry they had been making, and naked babies were thrust into my arms as the women sorted through piles to show me their best.

Adoni's mother returned. She had changed her clothes and was now wearing a blue floral skirt that fell below her knee. I never saw her crack a smile, but now she looked regal. The matron. She put her hand in Adoni's and spoke in his ear. He laughed.

The sound of thunder shook the house in which a dozen of us stood. There hadn't been a cloud in the sky when we had gone inside, but as the colossal raindrops drummed against the corrugated tin roof, it felt as if I was trapped inside a giant timpani. There was no way to be heard over the deafening roar. We stood quietly, listening, smiling, eyes raised -- moments of human silence amongst nature's reverberating rhythms -- until the storm became clittery-clanks from dripping trees. We all went outside, and I suggested gathering for a photo. And although there were some members who were not present that day, fate allowed me to capture Adoni and seventeen family members on film. When I arrived in a metropolitan city later that month, I sent that photo to the address Adoni had given me. And I never heard from him again...

SALVADOR

The afternoon rain pounded on the roof of the hostel in the vibrant neighborhood of Pelourinho in Salvador de Bahia, Brazil. I had arrived a few days before to share a dorm room with a missing occupant whose belongings had been strewn from floor to ceiling. Her name was Monica, Monica from Italy. Friendly and beautiful, Monica managed to maintain an impeccable sense of fashion despite being on the backpacker circuit. Although her vocabulary was limited to survival-English, we enjoyed short conversations, and she was a lovely person to bunk with. It was amazing how many people I met during those days who didn't know much English and yet knew just what to say.

On my fourth day in town, I returned from a day of museum-wanderings to an empty room where I stripped off my wet clothes, crawled into my sleeping bag, and snuggled in for a nap against the cold soggy day. I dozed on and off, listening to the rain tap against the window, until I was awakened by the sound of voices. Girls' voices. Girls' voices speaking English. North-American English. In that half-dreamy state, I thought I was home. There had never been a sound so sweet. The next day was my 25th birthday, and I suppose some part of me craved familiarity, an accent-free flowing conversation, chocolate cake, girlfriends, talks about everything and nothing.

I gathered my stranger-meeting courage and walked toward the open door of next room to meet Stefanie and Caroline, both smiling and both sopping wet, best friends from Canada. Stefanie was a redhead with big brown eyes and a shy smile. Caroline was a short brunette with a 7-foot-tall personality whose wavy hair was tied up backpacker-style in a navy-blue bandana. I immediately felt at home with them.

They had just arrived from points far north via a two-day, got-stuck-in-the-mud-and-had-to-push bus ride.   And they looked it. Caroline was ready for some beach time "to chill," as she put it. They invited me out to the white sands of Arembepe the next day, and when I admitted it would be my birthday, Caroline said she would invite some of the other girls from the dorm to join us. We agreed to meet in the morning. I hoped for sun, smiling warmly as I dove back into my sleeping bag. Girlfriends are important.

***

I had spent my first few days in Salvador alone, exploring the historic city, walking up and down the hilly cobblestone streets lined with brightly-painted restored buildings and old churches that mark the neighborhood of Pelourinho. Salvador de Bahia is northeast Brazil's largest city and perhaps one of its most fascinating.   It is said to have the best-preserved African traditions in all of the Americas, and its unique culture shines through in its food, music, art, and religions.

Music meets you at every corner.   Block after block, musicians stand under awnings filling the air with beats and time, different performers' songs blurring from one into another like a radio-dial stuck between two stations as you make your way down the long streets.   The deep rich sounds of the *djembe* explode from innocent storefronts, and stringed instruments twang brightly from behind closed doors.

Olodum, a local drumming group hundreds of members strong, addresses racial discrimination and socioeconomic inequality through music. I stopped to witness them marching together down the street as the vibration of their percussion reverberated deep in my chest, their parade so long that some members were rounding corners as others were still streaming from their practice-hall blocks away. The next night I sought out their performance in Pelourinho Square, the sight of Salvador's former slave auction, a powerful location which only deepened the group's wordless message.

After the music, it was the food that made its deep impression. I loved to eat at the stalls run by Bahian women wearing white cotton flowing dresses with white cotton headwraps. My favorite food at the stalls was *acaraje*, fried cakes stuffed with shrimp and peppers, but you couldn't go wrong if you loved all that was good and spicy. The other option was a buffet where you paid for food by weight. Really. You could put bits of any local delicacy you wanted to try on your plate, and just put it up on the scale at the cash register for 70 centimes a quilo. The what-you-see-is-what-you-get approach to food was a reassuring alternative to ordering off a menu in a language I didn't understand.

I walked down to one of the waterfront's two-story buildings which housed paintings, sculptures and jewelry for sale made by hundreds of local artists. After browsing up and down the aisles for hours (being both decisionally-challenged and financially-strapped), I finally chose a small acrylic painting of a dozen Bahian women washing their laundry on the bank of the bay. You can't see the facial details of any of the women, but I loved their strong arms and generous curves. On the back was scratched in pencil the word "*lavandería*," and the painting burst with orange and green headscarves, yellow and pink petticoats, all of which reminded me of the vibrance of the city.

One evening, I attended a folklore dance performance and demonstration of *candomblé*. It was not a true ceremony, of course, which is a deeply-guarded spiritual practice, but it was my first exposure to this traditional religion carried to northeastern Brazil by African priests brought as slaves. During ceremonies, believers try to channel any number of gods and often go into a trance. Widely misunderstood, many outsiders fear *candomblé* and equate it with voodoo.

My favorite part of the ceremony was when I learned of Yemanjá, Queen of the Ocean and feminine spirit of creation and moonlight. On days in February and December, Salvador's residents pay her homage by leaving offerings of flowers, perfume and lipstick on Yemanja's shrine in Rio Vermelho, and seafarers heed her particular respect. Another beautiful moon goddess. Of mystery, of power, a guardian of journeys. I have only to turn my face upward, the light falling softly on my cheeks, and ask her silently for a moment of strength, a breath of inner-peace, an assurance I'm on the right path.

***

At Museo de Arte de Bahia I walked for hours among photographs and paintings from the last three centuries. In a spectrum of caramels, coffees and midnights, oil paintings revealed portraits of Bahian society. Black-and-white film captured details of everyday life, from a store owner in a felt hat selling a sack of rice, to groups of men laboring to build the roads of a modern city. From women in white dresses stirring bathtub-sized steaming pots, to little boys and scruffy dogs playing in the streets high in the hills of Pelourinho in 1935. Those little boys would be very old now, and yet images of their youth remained untouched, unwrinkled, unhunched in this sanctuary. Three hundred years of time captured in a four-room gallery, a city's unspeakable history of slavery to the proud traditions which emerged from its abolition.

After I had finished touring, I walked into the museum's bathroom to rinse my hands and face with cool water. When I looked up, I stood breathless at what I saw in the mirror. Had I forgotten that I was not just another passenger on the city bus, not just another person walking on the cobblestone streets? I realized it with strange suddenness.

Amy, you're white.

Not black. Not brown.

You are WHITE… as white as they get.

And I looked at my long narrow nose, turning to see its boney high profile. And I looked at my sleek blond hair, shiny and slippery. And I looked at my light blue eyes that so many passersby stare into and smile. And I felt surprised. Different. Completely alien. *How must I look to other people?* And I looked again.

I looked at my thick black headband and my short blond hair that curled up around my chin, and it looked so strange that I reached up to touch it. I saw my long fingers and short fingernails with dirt underneath and a silver band on my middle finger that shone in the fluorescent bathroom lights. And I felt even more alien. It wasn't just that I was different from everyone else I saw here, from the people with whom I shared meals and buses and coffee, from the people with whom I had shared the last year of my life. It was that one day before my 25th birthday, I realized that I was different than *me*. I was not the Rapunzel I had been at sixteen, or the round smiley face of college late-night ice-cream sundaes. I was someone else. I was someone whose beauty and charm no longer came from her long flowing hair and shy demeanor. I was someone who attracted people to her -- lots of people -- because she was different. Because she was true. Because she was joyful. Because her emotions had caught up with her intellect? Had what she thinks finally aligned with what she feels?

A trekker? A surfer? A succulent wild woman who saw a glimmer in fresh travelers' eyes when she told stories of her adventures? Maybe she didn't know who she was to others, and maybe she could be anyone she wanted to be on any given day. And maybe her identity was all those things together, ever-changing. Maybe she was just beginning to learn who she was to *herself*. But she knew at that moment that she was different. Not just different in the way she looked from the people around her, the people who looked into her eyes with concerned questions. *Is she lost? Why is she alone?* Those eyes had seen many miles, and she was different now -- different than she used to be.

***

Blue sky, sunshine on my shoulder, ocean waves and white sand. I could have been anywhere on my 25th birthday, but I wasn't. I was in Arembepe, Brazil. Goosebumps covered my warm body on the first sunny day of the week. Tom Petty whispered to me through my walkman headphones, and faces of my recent past leapt through my mind at light-speed. Quartz crystals stuck to the soles of my feet, hearts stuck to the soles of my soul. I thought of Louis and Daisy and Simon and Eveline and Carmen and Alex and Marianela and gritty Nescafe and muddy cargo pants and moonlit canoe rides and ripe mangos and flying across ocean waves. Excitement grew inside my stomach. *I'm getting there.* One year older. Many hearts later. Zillions of synapses connected. Stronger.

I looked at my company across the mounds of sand and sarongs: Monica from Italy, Stefanie, Caroline, and three other girls who thought that a sunny day lying on the beaches of Arembepe was the perfect way to spend anyone's birthday. We dipped our toes in the freezing ocean, ran squealing from the encroaching tide, and soaked up as much warmth as we could endure (which meant Stefanie and her redhead complexion spent the next three days slathered in aloe).

As the sun sunk lower in the sky, I pulled on an orange tie-died dress I had bought myself for my birthday, slid on my jungle jewelry, and bounced my sassy self (new-found friends in tow) back to the bus stop for Salvador. It might seem strange that I found so much joy with these somewhat-strangers. But women in the traveling world are so rare, and a friendship on the road can be made instantly on almost nothing. I may have known them for just days, and we would probably never see each other again, but life is made up of just moments.

Back in town, we stopped to watch the acrobatic swing-kicking and mid-air-whirling of *capoeira*, a martial art developed in Brazil as a way for slaves to build strength and quickness against their oppressors. So slave owners would not recognize it as a threat, it was disguised as a dance. In beautiful harmony of graceful movement and skillful athleticism, black skin silhouetted against bright blue sky, and muscles rippled atop white cotton pants. I watched, mesmerized, as bodies pinwheeled in aerials, and the *berimbau* "doii-ng"ed in accompanying time.

The girls and I sat down for a perfect birthday meal, and Stefanie and Caroline bought me a quarter-kilo of fudge in place of a birthday cake. We headed across the main square, and as we weaved through the nightly crowd which gathered to listen to bands play, my hair was stroked, my bare shoulders kissed, and women whispered in friendly tones. We bought *caipirinhas* at a stand in the park where the vendor used a wooden stick to crush fresh limes with sugar and the local *cachaça* alcohol. Now here's a tip: Do NOT drink *caipirinhas* while still on malaria medication. After half a glass, you feel like you've had about six. (It did help save money on alcohol, though...)

I danced and hummed and watched the world around me, fascinated with the expert bootie-wiggling whose equal I had never seen. Brazilian women -- ALL Brazilian women -- can shake their backsides with a hipshaking-hula-buttjiggle that happens so fast you can't really see how it works. It's either a gift or a timeshift into an alternative quantum dimension, and I was absolutely unable to recreate it despite practicing whenever I got a mirror in private.

When I arrived home that night, I dropped into bed and landed on the thick paper envelope which I had laid there before I had left that morning. It was the only birthday present I had carried with me to Brazil. I sighed and slid my finger across the top to open it. Inside was a hand-painted card of watercolor love and these words:

Dearest Amy,

I am so blessed to have a best friend like you and to have this time at Iguazú together... You take my breath away. I am amazed and inspired by your endless sense of adventure, your passion for life, and your ability to really listen to yourself and do what you need. Your spirit has touched me and so many others in such a short time.

So, I want to wish you a very happy 25th birthday. A quarter of a century, and life has given you so much already. Imagine what happiness and adventures lie ahead. Celebrate yourself today and enjoy those happy feelings of being there, traveling, growing, meeting strange people, seeing amazing things, and being 25.

Happy Birthday and many hugs and kisses,
Kree

And I felt full. And I felt empty. And the last thing I remember of being 24 was drifting off, smiling, lying on a tear-stained pillow filled with love.

THE DAY I FELL OFF A HORSE

I knew it was a bad idea the moment I accepted. I had been perfectly happy sitting atop a horse that walked slowly across the hard cracked ground as I gazed out tranquilly, almost hypnotically, out upon the dry floodplains of the Pantanal whose near-endless 230,000 square kilometers stretched from Brazil into Paraguay. But my emboldened attitude of *why not?* had gotten the best of me, and when Bonifacio, my guide, asked, "Do you want to gallop?" something inside me screamed, *I want to do it all!*

I am not a great horse rider. Actually, it would be generous to say that I'm intermediate. And so, with Bonifacio's high-pitched *HeYaw!*, I found myself clutching for dear life my horse's saddle horn, his mane, his neck, anything I could grab, my hands searching wildly, my body bouncing higher and higher off the saddle which had become a springboard. The horse had launched into a full-speed run alongside Bonifacio's horse. Bonifacio had, however, grown up on the Pantanal, grown up on these animals, and rode with velvet grace. But I didn't have much time to watch him. I was watching the blurs of scenery and the ground rushing by at sickening speed as I bounced further and further out of rhythm with the racing horse, now reaching heights of many inches off the saddle.

I'm going to die, I'm going to die, rushed through my head with an impending obviousness, and just when I was sure the next bounce would eject me, Bonifacio pulled his reigns to the side and his horse pivoted to a complete stop. My horse dutifully followed in a tight arc, but my unsuspecting body carried on with straightforward momentum. The laws of physics will not be disobeyed. A full run, a quick turn, and I found myself hanging at a ninety degree angle, left stirrup up in the air, my head down around the horse's belly, looking straight down at the ground which was still many feet below me.

Being an experienced childhood trapeze acrobat on my backyard jungle gym, I thought, *I'll just sling my right foot out of the stirrup, and then my left foot that's hanging up there on top, and then I'll just land on my feet.* Well, when I slung my left foot out, I landed on my head... and my right shoulder, and the right side of my ribs, and my right hipbone, which all managed to hit the unyielding ground at the same time. Somehow, I felt very surprised that gravity had double-crossed me, and I lay there stunned for a moment. I looked up to see that the horse was still moving, stumbling toward me, so I tucked into a ball and rolled away.

Bonifacio came riding back, speechless. He offered down his hand to help me up, but my legs didn't work. I told my body, *Stand up*, but it just stayed there.

Oh my God, I'm paralyzed. I can't move. My parents are going to kill me.

I still don't know why my body wouldn't work when I told it to. Maybe it was the shock. But Bonifacio hopped off his horse, dusted me off, and helped me up as a grunt burst from my chest, my eyes still spiraling like saucers.

Yes, I got back up on that horse -- literally -- and rode back to the ranch where the Señora rubbed some sort of cattle cream all over my body. I popped four aspirin and went to bed, and when she woke me for dinner, I could hardly move. And that's pretty much what I remember about the Pantanal...

***

It wasn't all bad. In fact, it was quite spectacular. I had traveled to the Pantanal because it's considered the best place in South America to see wildlife due to its unique topography. It is the world's largest alluvial floodplain which means that in the rainy season, it is completely underwater. Even the raised road, built for farmers and untraveled by public bus, is often impassable. At that time of year, land animals stand on any small mound of dry land available, making them very easy to see.

But at the time I visited, it was the very end of the dry season. What little water remained was concentrated in small ponds, and all the land animals that would otherwise be dispersed over a much larger area were forced to come to these to drink. As for the fish and amphibious animals, they were wedged into these pools like sardines. As Bonifacio drove me and three other tourists in a VW bus over rotting boards and rickety bridges, we got out of the car to watch a *jabiru*, a huge stork with a red neck and a great wingspan of 2 ½ meters that has become the symbol of the Pantanal. I looked into the nearby waterhole and saw a large caiman about two meters long resting on the opposite bank. Then I saw a set of eyes pop up in the water. Another caiman. Then another and another until I took a step back, refocused my eyes, and realized that every single black bump that was floating in the water was a caiman! There were easily 200 in that one small mud puddle, and Bonifacio said there were many more pools to explore.

The quantity of animals in the Pantanal was overwhelming. I spent the next few days watching *capybara* (the world's largest rodent), river otters, toucans, numerous river birds, monkeys, snakes, and thousands of termite hills which looked like five-foot tall upside-down ice-cream cones made of dirt. But it was also the proximity of the animals that was mind-boggling. We arrived at the farmhouse where we'd be staying and went immediately out to a flat-bottom boat for a sunset ride. A weathered old man in a weathered old cowboy-hat stood at the stern and pushed us along the shallow river with a long pole, but this was no Venice -- not a pigeon, not a cathedral, just light-colored eerie eyes peeking up above water and then disappearing, leaving tiny bubbles which slowly floated to the surface.

The wind was strong and pushed us along as we viewed the magnificent egrets, herons and *jabiru* standing on stilted legs in the shallow water then taking flight, silhouetted against the red ball of fire setting in the sky. The caiman were everywhere. The gunwales of the boat floated low with its five passengers huddled safely away from the edges. At dusk, the caiman got closer to us. Then we got closer to them. Our boatman poled along only one

meter from a sandy island full of them, fifty just laying there in
the day's quickly-disappearing warmth. I gasped and held my
breath so many times I wondered if I'd accidentally pass out.
Each time the thrill got greater. Later we saw just a tail sticking
out of the water on the shore and thought it might be dead. The
boatman touched it with his pole and FLASH! It thrashed
around and sunk into the river, invisible again, beneath the murky
water.

The next day, we went back out and fished for piranha, but I
caught a caiman instead. There I was, in a little metal boat,
bamboo fishing-pole in hand, when I got a bite -- hard. I pulled.
It pulled back. A black bump surfaced and snap! Oh yes, the
one that got away. But it was t—h—i—s big.

At night we sat outside the farmhouse by a campfire, singing
songs with the ranch-hands on an out-of-tune guitar. I wondered
if there was a reason that I ended up in this beautiful wild place
with three young business people about my age who were all on
short vacations. One guy was in business school in California,
and a husband-wife Dutch couple were each consultants for a
high-powered international firm. They talked about work while
watching river otters and spoke in biz-lingo while fishing. I
interviewed them about their paths and choices to try to assess if
I should be doing what they were doing. And you know what I
found out? They all wished they were doing what *I* was doing!
They were as totally clueless about life as I was, but they weren't
even happy. I was. The happiest I'd been in a long, long time.
Maybe since childhood. I thought about what made me happy.
And the answer was *this*! *Right here, right now. Why would I ever want
to go home to that?* How many times can you be completely free?

By the end of the trip, I hurt -- a lot. Whatever cow salve
the Señora was using on me kept my body from bruising too
badly from my fall, but I still couldn't move very fast. With what
felt like fractured ribs, I could barely zip my expanding 20-kilo
backpack. And carrying it, cinching it around my waist, and
steadying it for two days before I got medical help, was my fate
until I could leave the Pantanal.

On the last day of the trip I rode in the bed of the farm
owner's pickup truck back to town as we bumped down a muddy
road dodging cows somewhere in the middle of the *campo*. The
dry grass hills, the large canopied shade trees, the golden light all

reminded me of Louis and Marianela, and between the grunts and "ouch-es," thoughts of Playa Grande made me smile.

When I arrived back in city of Cuiabá, I called my Brazilian friend, Jan, to ask if he knew any doctors in the area. He said I should go see his friend at her dog grooming business.

"Don't worry," he assured me, "She used to be a surgical nurse."

Rosane and Roberta, a darling lesbian couple who owned a pet shop and were crazy about poodles, welcomed me with open arms, squeezed and checked me, and told me that nothing was broken. Then they gave me some lovely pain killers and took me out for lunch. I declined their offer to clip my toenails.

***

When I arrived in Rio, I met Jan at his office. I had always thought of Jan as the Brazilian guy who performed compromising yoga stretches by the pool in his Speedos. I know, I know -- but he was still a really cool guy. Being half-Danish and half-Brazilian, you had to give him a break with the whole banana-hammock thing.

Jan had been a regular at Hotel Las Tortugas for years; in his late forties and in good shape, he had been surfing Costa Rica's hideaways for over a decade. The last time I had seen him, I shared my plans to leave the hotel and explore South America. He said I absolutely must see Brazil. I could stay with him in Rio; he had an extra room, and his cats always needed company while he was at work. The offer was fantastic but didn't surprise me. Jan was a generous amiable guy, the kind of guy who gave rides in his rental car to vehicle-deprived wave-seekers to explore new surf-breaks. The kind of guy who packed hard-to-find car parts into his suitcase and hand-carried them to the hotel for Louis's pickup truck. The kind of guy who liked to surf almost as much as he liked to smoke weed.

So when I got off the bus among the high-rises of downtown Rio in a business district surrounded by the city's signature dramatic hills, I wondered if I was in the right place. It was all so posh. So grown-up. I found the building which matched the address he had given me, and took the elevator up to the 24th floor, cramming in with the returning lunch crowd, trying not to bash their crisp suits and ties with my filth-covered

backpack.   I exited the elevator and walked timidly into a
gorgeous reception area filled with fresh-cut tropical flowers
towering from crystal vases.

"You must be Amy," said the woman behind the desk. "Jan
had to step out for a moment, but he said you could wait in his
office."

She led me down the hall to the corner office whose view
looked out dramatically over the sun-shimmers in the bay.   She
motioned for me to sit down on the white leather couches as I
looked down at my dirty cargo pants, dust imported straight from
the Pantanal. "That's OK, I'll just stand."

Although I was initially taken aback by Jan's executive-by-
day, surfer-by-night identity, it became less disjointed as I got to
know Rio. In Rio, people take time out in the middle of their
workdays to go to the park.   They ride their bikes when they
leave their offices.   They hike in rainforests plunked and
preserved in the middle of the city.   When it's sunny in Rio,
people take the day off.   When the surf comes up, people take
the day off.   When people feel like it, they take the day off.   It
was the greatest city I had ever seen.

Jan made me feel completely at home.   Like his office, his
fifth-floor apartment in Urca had a million-dollar view.   The wind
howled though a small opening in the 50-foot picture window
which offered a panoramic view of the bay.   Clouds sailed by
behind Rio de Janeiro's landmark *Cristo Redentor,* standing with
outstretching arms atop the 700-meter peak of Corcovado as
yachts bobbed up and down on uncharacteristic wave chop.   It
was warm inside the apartment accented with hardwood floors,
sparse modern furniture and new age music. My room lay in the
shadow of the Sugar Loaf, gondola cars whirring up and down
their sky-high cables as I slept into the late morning. I even liked
his cats -- and I don't do cats. Big, fat and furry, tails swishing in
rhythm.

I toured the city while Jan was at work, and in the evenings
we had great talks. On weekends we surfed until our lips turned
blue, we watched Botafogo defeat Flamingo at Maracana soccer
stadium, we even nearly got car-jacked (which didn't seem to
bother him too much -- he just floored it and blew through the
red light). Then we celebrated by sampling 30 flavors of tropical-
fruit ice-cream made from fruits found only in Brazil.

I was anxious to soak up the infamous Brazilian beach culture, anxious to see the stunning places which had inspired and immortalized songs. I walked from Ipanema to Copacabana, singing all the way there. As I ventured out onto the awaiting busy strip of white sand, the beach was packed -- in the winter, on a weekday, in the middle of the afternoon. I looked left, I looked right. Gorgeous tanned bodies lay like scattered golden leaves. Bronzed buns stood out proudly from string bikinis, and I was the only woman on the beach who wasn't wearing a thong.

Well, I can fix that. I am very resourceful. I spread my sarong out on the sand, laid face down, and tucked each side of my bikini bottoms into my butt-crack.

There. Ahh, the warm sun feels so good on my skin. Ahh, it's so peaceful, the waves lapping. Ahh... Hey, what's that? Snickering? I looked up to see two teenage boys walking away from me, laughing, pointing at my big white glaring beacon of a bus-riding pimplebutt. Defeated, I turned over on my back and resolved that one day, when I was rich and famous, I would invest in some quality swimwear.

***

My discoveries in Rio were as much about self as the city around me. Those weeks, all curled up in Jan's cozy apartment, I finally got to stop and rest my road-weary bones. And the less I moved, the more I thought. And not in a good way.

I was going on over a year on the road, and thoughts of home started creeping in. I spent days torturing myself: feeling guilty about what I was missing in my family's lives, feeling pressure to return and do something "responsible," wondering what would happen to all the loose ends I had left, wondering how much longer my travels *should* go on.

I'd always had a problem with decision-making. I was terrified about not getting it right, and I was paralyzed to do *anything* until I was sure. One night over dinner I talked with Jan about it.

He said, "The hardest decisions to make are between two good things. After all, wouldn't the decision be easy if the choice was between something good and something bad? So if the decision is between two good things, then the decision doesn't really matter. Either is OK. Both are OK."

And I found that reassuring.

And that cleared the way for a bigger question: *Amy, maybe the reason you can't make a "decision" about when to go home is because you're hiding behind this journey as a temporary one. When you end it, you're expecting to return to things as you left them while in the meantime you have changed. You are still changing. The people you have met on the road know such a different Amy than people back home. What will happen when who I was and who I am collide? How will it all turn out?*

And I couldn't decide.

So I bought a bus ticket west, and just kept moving...

"Trials never end, of course. Unhappiness and misfortune are bound to occur as long as people live, but there is a feeling now, that was not here before, and is not just on the surface of things, but penetrates all the way through: We've won it. It's going to get better now. You can sort of tell these things." Zen & The Art of Motorcycle Maintenance, *by Robert M. Pirsig*

But the travel impetus that kept me exploring South America alone had only just begun to bud at the end of the first dry season in Playa Grande. And after talking to enough worldly clients and spending enough time reading about all the cool places I still hadn't seen, I began to move away from Playa Grande very slowly, one baby step at a time.

First I went to stay with Drs. Ebe and Phyllis Kronhausen, longtime friends of Louis and Marianela. In their mid-eighties they still practiced psychology, wrote books on health and longevity and grew ornamental and medicinal plants at their farm outside San Jose. In their early life, their adventures included living intimately among the Parisian art scene with friends such as Dalí, exploring Mexico and Central America by rusty VW bus, and becoming renowned as some of the world's foremost erotic art collectors.

I left Playa Grande for the first time in months and spent a cathartic weekend eating hearty homemade vegetarian food, having my psychoanalytic profile examined, and being chased around the house with a syringe filled with vitamin B which Phyllis insisted would make me feel better. "You look terrible, you know," she coaxed. Louis said they probably just wanted to see my butt.

My next break-out from Hotel Las Tortugas came a few weeks later when a guest named David, who had come to Playa Grande to surf away the stresses of living in downtown San Francisco, had a surfing accident. On his first day of vacation he sliced open his heel from one side to the other with his board's skag just missing his Achilles tendon, and ended up with 15 stitches from the "Crack Doctor," an Argentine medical professional in Tamarindo who always seems excessively alert. David was ordered to stay out of the water for the rest of his trip, but instead of sulking, he rented a Suzuki and started touring the rest of Costa Rica, using Playa Grande as a base. He sought out the things he would have otherwise missed had he spent the week surfing. Hungry for company, he invited me along. Hungry for a change of scenery, I gratefully accepted.

And the scenery was exquisite as we drove towards Volcán Arenal, one of the most active volcanoes in the world. Along the road giant elephant-ear leaves dripped near waterfalls soaring down rocky mountainsides. Dozens of *pisotes*, cousins of the raccoon with pointed snouts and ringed tails, ran alongside the cars, hungry for handouts. As we rounded a bend, Arenal's deep cold emerald lake seemed to appear out of thin air, and soaring from its waters stood the most perfect gray cinder-cone, rising up through the rainforest canopy into a sky scattered with white puffy clouds. It was like a dream.

Before I knew it, I was soaking in the volcanic hot springs among vibrant orange and purple birds-of-paradise. As night fell, the smoke puffs from the volcano turned to liquefied explosions. *Pop, oooh, ahh,* and molten lava burst from the cone into the night sky, scattering rivers of orange glitter which dripped down the mountainside.

Mouth agape, I wondered, *How could I stay in one place, however ideal, when there was all this in the world out there to see?*

***

A few days later, David decided to make one more trip before heading back to San Jose. He was headed for the lush southern tip of the Nicoya peninsula to explore the town of Montezuma, a laid-back hippy destination, complete with gringo-friendly restaurants serving frozen yogurt and screening classic cult films.

By this time, I'd had a taste of what awaited me out there in the world. I felt satiated with Playa Grande and had decided to move on soon to Guatemala, rich in cultural history and an affordable place to re-enroll in language school (my Spanish had gotten lazy in Playa Grande amongst English-speaking hotel guests). I had told Louis about my plans, and although high season had not officially wound down, he hesitantly accepted my decision. *What choice did he have?*

So with the end of my Costa Rican tenure in sight, I asked David if I could join him on his last trip. I planned to stay on alone for a few days in Montezuma after he left and then make my way back to Playa Grande -- somehow. And soon we were following the dry hills out of Guanacaste into the mosquito-ridden jungle of the Nicoya peninsula.

When we arrived in Montezuma that afternoon, David was anxious to make the most of his few daylight hours, and we swapped our flip-flops for hiking boots and headed up the slippery boulder trail toward the town's well-known waterfall. As we sat dangling our feet into the cold green pool below, local teens bursting with testosterone climbed the cliffs and soared in swan dives from midway up the falls with shouts of joy and terror followed by the immense displacement of water.

I watched the yellow moon rise over the sea that night as David drove away, and suddenly there I was, standing alone at the first moments of another beginning, poised to embark upon my next story... The story of my first Latin lover.

FULL MOON...

[The] "boys lived on a diet of perpetual sex, entertaining the unchaperoned and romantic foreign girls who arrived on the island in search of true love and multiple orgasms in the arms of any latter-day Adonis who agreed to sweep them off their feet. They considered themselves so indispensable to the tourist industry that there was even talk of forming a union to represent their interests." <u>Corelli's Mandolin</u>, by Louis DeBernieres

I became sort of a loner in Montezuma. I hung out in all the guidebook hotspots hoping to meet other travelers. Actually, I hung out to see if they would meet me. *Just sit back, observe, and see what happens. See who you meet.* I wondered if I might meet someone who was headed where I was headed, who wanted to experience what I sought to experience. *That's how this works, right?*

Without Daisy, without Evelyn, without Louis, I felt really alone. Not lonely. Just alone. It was funny really. I felt excited all the time for no more reason than simply believing the world was open to me, a beautiful mystery waiting to reveal itself. Wondering when the next wonderful surprise would come around the corner, feeling I could do anything I wanted, meet anyone I wanted. Someone with whom to explore the wilds of Peninsula de Osa, land of jaguars and toucans. Someone with whom to join me in Guatemalan language school. But I was still looking outward, toward others, toward the future, having not yet arrived at the quiet joys of being alone in the present.

As I watched people walk down the main drag from my safe perch on a café terrace, I started to see the same faces. But they were always with someone else. And so I was quiet. And I watched. And sometimes I smiled. And sometimes they smiled back. But mostly the boys. And at night I returned to Pensión Lucy's Room 6, a former broom closet with a single bed and ocean view, breezes blowing pink-and-white gingham curtains to horizontal and waves crashing below.

The next day no one came. Again. No one came and talked to the strange quiet girl sitting by herself in the café, walking along the waterfall, writing in her journal under the *almendra* tree. I focused my search on what I missed most: female companionship. Women like me. I mean, I guess I wanted to meet *me*. Figure out what I was up to. Where I was headed. If I was going to be OK. But as I watched women walk by with boyfriends, in groups, with other female friends, I noticed that the feminine creature seemed to travel in packs, stick together, kind of like the way men say we like to go to the bathroom. And it seemed that when you have someone you're happy with, when your social situation is secure, you are not really looking to meet anyone new. And so the women walked by. Didn't smile. Didn't notice me. And I felt like I was part of my own experiment as I discovered that when you travel alone, you are destined to meet other lone travelers, most of whom are male -- most of whom are not the people you seek, are not the trusty companion who connects emotionally without an alternative sexual agenda. I was beginning to understand, despite my feminist and psychological training, that women and men are, at their cores, different. There are guys for being boyfriends. And there are women -- for everything else.

By the third day, I had seen every nook of the town, every used bookstore, every menu featuring a garden burger. I decided my time here was complete, and that I would try to get to the nearby surfing town of Mal Pais to see if I could hitch a ride with some surfers who had a car and who happened to be headed north toward Tamarindo or Playa Grande; the only long-distance buses leaving Montezuma that I knew of went to San Jose, the opposite direction of where I wanted to go.

So I walked down to the main square in search of a minibus or taxi headed toward Mal Pais, and with neither clearly visible, I spotted a little information booth at the center of the plaza featuring "tours, trips and outdoor adventures." There was a long line, and as I waited patiently for the guy behind the counter to get to me, he peeked around the others and gave me a smile and tried to help me out of turn. A great smile. A brilliant smile. A smile that lit up an outdoor adventure booth.

I asked in Spanish how much a taxi to Mal Pais would be. He said about $20.

"Wait," he said suddenly as he called his friend over and asked him something.

The friend who spoke good English said there were fiestas in Playa Manzanilla which he and his friends were heading to. It was on the way to Mal Pais, and if I gave him some gas money, he would drop me off. They were leaving in 30 minutes.

Mucha suerte! I ran up the hill to my pensión, paid my bill, checked out, and ran back down to the main square with my pack. The guy from the adventure booth, his English-speaking friend who was the driver, and three other guys were waiting in the truck for me. And then I had an idea.

"Could you drop me off in Mal Pais *after* the fiestas?" my freshly-ignited adventurous spirit asked. *Here and now.*

"*No problema*," came the reply.

So away I went, feeling the tickle of excitement inside me as we bumped down the rough road.

***

We jerked from side to side down the rutted track, over a mountain pass where a vehicle had stalled out in the middle of the one-lane road. The driver of the car sat serenely inside, singing in slurs and lifting a bottle of *Cuatro Plumas* to his lips. Our pickup truck crawled carefully by, ever so slowly, hugging the outside of the bend, dirt clods dislodging below our tires and falling into the void below.

When we arrived at the fiestas, the usual beer, music and debauchery was already underway. The live marimba band found tempo with DJ remixes over a blown sub-woofer, and as I walked with the boys to the beach, they told me that this fiesta was special -- it featured a sand sculpture contest! When we reached the proposed site, the adventure booth guy plunked down and dug in. His friend told me that he was an artisan wood sculptor; he was just moonlighting as an adventure booth worker. The sculptor must have seen the surprise on my face because he looked up and smiled that beautiful smile at me again. Sergio was his name, and I stood and watched him shovel and mold and pack and smooth, bringing the wet sand quickly to life. First came the head, big and round, three feet in diameter. Then a hand appeared. First the right, then the left. There were no arms, as if they were still trapped beneath the sand waiting to be uncovered, but he sculpted a slightly-bent right knee with a left foot stretching toward the sky. The abstraction was exquisite. Like a man reaching up out of the depths, every muscle fiber beautifully-shaped.

Like most highly-structured academics from repressed suburban family backgrounds, I had always dreamed of dating an artist. As I watched Sergio move his hands lightly, firmly, over the sand, I could almost see them on my body. I felt twitters awaken inside my Playa Grande nunhood as I watched his kind brown eyes undulate from the intensity of his project to his friends and me, boyish laughter freely escaping his lips. He spoke no English, and since my Spanish skills had backslid, I didn't try to speak. Simply staring at his mouth was enough to mesmerize me.

Meanwhile the other four guys took turns entertaining me, showing me salsa dance steps, explaining the rodeo competitions and just generally hitting on me. The biggest macho of them all was a pint-sized fourteen-year-old, presumably the self-appointed PimpDaddy of Montezuma. The other guys in the group warned me to steer clear of this self-made Romeo, but it wasn't hard to see for myself. He tried to entertain me, act cool, flirt with other girls, ask me if I had a boyfriend. I tired of him quickly. When the rodeo and sand castle contest were over, Sergio asked me if I wanted to jump in the ocean with him to wash off. Oh how beautiful his Spanish was. Spoken from a mouth of ear-to-ear smiles. Warm and sincere. We swam and talked then walked over to ask his friend, the driver, if he could get me to Mal Pais before dark. He said that we would leave in an hour.

Sergio and I went to the beach to wait and found a log to sit on as we watched the sun set due west. He said this was his

favorite spot because it set right smack in front of you. His
gentleness put me at ease as we talked. Beautiful flowing foreign
sounds. He was just so unassuming. I noticed that he was slowly
moving closer on the log, moving so slowly that maybe he
thought I wouldn't notice. Then he reached over and kissed me,
softly, sweetly. It didn't really surprise me that he had tried.
What did surprise me was that I'd let him. There was no wow.
No fireworks. No butterflies. Just a feeling of *Hey, this is nice. I
almost forgot what this is like.*

We talked in quiet murmurs and kissed and watched the sky
turn colors until the abrupt shout of teen PimpDaddy severed the
bliss; the driver was ready to leave. And all of a sudden I was
quite embarrassed.

We walked back together towards the fiesta. I tried to act
casual, but I couldn't stop smiling. Sergio tried not to make a big
deal about it in front of his friends.

Then he turned to me and said, "You don't really want to go
to Mal Pais, do you? Come back to Montezuma with us."

Then all the others chimed in. "Yeah! There's more to do.
Hang out with us!"

I smiled and thought about fate, and how when it kisses you,
you can't just go to Mal Pais and leave it there standing
unrecognized, unappreciated. And I looked at Sergio's flushed
face and big brown puppydog eyes and thought, *Why the hell not?!*

"OK, let's go back."

After all, there would be a bus back to San Jose in a few
days…

As we got back in the truck, Sergio's eyes were slightly
closed as if he was floating, and he smiled and smiled that lovely
smile and held my hand the whole way home. They were artist's
hands, soft and beautiful. Everything I had imagined. He traced
my fingers, my bones, my nails so gently as the car bounced back
and forth violently over boulders and tossed up clouds of dust.
It felt wonderful to have him close. His innocent touching and
caressing. When we got back to Montezuma, he carried my pack
up the hill to Pensión Lucy, and I checked in again to still-vacant
Room 6, and we made plans to meet in an hour. I needed a
shower. At the beach, he'd kissed my neck, and I warned him I
was salty and dirty.

"Es natural," he had said almost euphorically. *Why does everything sound so romantic in Spanish?*

***

I showered, shaved my legs, put on my favorite pair of underwear (although I couldn't justify why since I had just met the guy), and headed off to a restaurant where the guys from the fiestas were already drinking beers. We joined them and spent the evening laughing and talking the best we could, which made for more laughing. Sergio asked if he could see me tomorrow. I said of course. The reality was that he worked at the booth in the center of the town's main square, and if I was to go *anywhere* in town, yes, he *would* see me. There was no way to avoid it. We made plans to meet when he got off work.

He walked me home and we stood on the porch and kissed for an hour. His words sounded so beautiful... I can't even remember them, and even if I had known what he was whispering, it couldn't have been any more beautiful than what I imagined. The old saying that *the only way to really learn a language is to get a local boyfriend* is a myth. I didn't listen to a word. My cerebral translator had shut down. But as the hot breathy *r*'s rolled against my ear, and the sea lapped softly on the sand beneath my porch, I drifted off into an other-worldly space in the *now* finally shared by two.

How could I have known that after three dates he would turn into a wolf?

PART IV:
BOLIVIA, PERU & ECUADOR

THE DAY AN EAGLE LANDED ON MY BACK

After hurling myself west across the continent, I arrived in Chile's northern Atacama Desert, a dramatically different landscape than the Brazilian beaches of Rio de Janeiro from where I'd come. I spent a few nippy desert mornings climbing sand dunes scattered with wild llamas, hiking among the towering rock formations of Valle de la Luna, and watching El Tatio's dozen geysers stream simultaneously into the sky. On the fourth day, I began my journey across the Chilean border into Bolivia via the world's most magnificent salt flats, the Salar de Uyuni.

My preparations were minimal. I signed up with a jeep tour since no public buses crossed via that route. I bought a pair of silver bug-eyed sunglasses at the drugstore to protect my eyes against the salt's blinding glare. And then I waited at the town's main crossroads to be joined by my fellow migrants.

There was a problem, of course.

"No problem," said the guy from the tour office.

Our dusty rusty jeep, idling and ready to depart, was already packed with our group of six tourists, one driver, and a cook, to which we would now be unexpectedly adding a testy Australian couple who were shouting at the manager about tour arrangements. You see, they had just arrived *from* the Bolivian salt flats having completed the trip in the opposite direction.

Unfortunately, they had been under the impression that the tour was round-trip. And now they fought like pit-bulls to get themselves back from where they'd come, back to their stuff, back to the hostel that was holding it. So, ten people packed into a jeep which was already maxed out at eight, that is, in addition to our backpacks, food, two spare tires, and three 5-gallon gasoline cans all strapped to the roof, the tails of fraying ropes dangling against the back windows.

Eliseo Abraham gave a sigh. Our soft-spoken guide, after being given the evil-eye by his employer, asked the six original passengers to kindly squish together to make room. For me, it meant moving to the front bucket seat. Good news, right? Not so much. I now shared it with Markus, the English doctor/rugby-player who weighed close to 300 pounds. Big-boned, you know? So I sat on the outside near the window, with my left bun on the seat, and my right bun wedged half-way up the door, and the door-mounted fire extinguisher up my butt. He sat with his right haunch firmly planted on the seat, and his left cheek hanging up in the air precariously blocking the gear shifter which Eliseo Abraham was delicately trying to maneuver without too much embarrassment. It wouldn't have been that bad, except for firstly, the crossing was three days long, and secondly, the roads in Bolivia are not really roads at all. They're sort of impressions of roads. Dirt, if you're lucky. Sand, if you're not. And thus we started out on our journey, united against the elements (and the grouchy Australians, who never stopped complaining) and ready to see what the next few days might bring.

After an hour or so, Eliseo Abraham asked, "Does anyone have a tape?"

My guess was that he was trying to drown out the whining coming from the backseat. As I pulled out Lenny Kravitz from a Ziplock bag in my daypack and handed it to him, he slipped it into the cassette player in the dash whose silver letters gleamed proudly: *High Quality*. Click, click. Click. We strained forward in unison as Eliseo Abraham slowly turned up the volume dial. The tape deck turned and whirred, and out came the garbled sounds of a record player turning at the wrong slow-and-low speed, like stoned snails trying to keep a melody. We all broke into hysterics, singing along all the whole way and marveling at the *High Quality*.

Our first stop was Laguna Verde and Laguna Blanca where we ducked in from the whipping winds to pay our fees to the park ranger who invited me to stay with him (permanently) and drink wine. By lunchtime, we had reached a natural hot springs where we pulled off the road so that the cook, who was hidden somewhere in the back of the jeep beneath a bundle of supplies, could make some lunch. A crazy French girl named Muriel stripped off all her clothes without a word to anyone but herself, skipped down the road through the bone-chilling gusting wind, and jumped in the hot springs for a soak. *How does a person develop that brazen lack of inhibition?* I wanted to find out.

After lunch, we arrived at Laguna Colorada, a lagoon which turns red at a special time each afternoon as the sun's angle reflects onto the lake's billions of algae. Hundreds of flamingos stood stilted on one-foot, taking flight all at once in a blushing flurry when Eliseo Abraham clapped his hands. As the sun went down in Valle de Rocas, the solitary rock formations in the middle of the desert reached into the sky in midnight-black silhouettes against the bright yellows, oranges, and pinks firing in the heavens.

Just a few kilometers away lay the settlement of Alota where we spent the night. We were served what fellow-traveler Fabio referred to as llama piss tea and were shown to our room. Yes, room -- singular. The Australian couple stayed in a private room in another building, and the six of us crammed into a dirt hut with three sets of rickety bunk beds. The stink of backpacks and socks mingled with delirious laughter now free to fill the remainder of room through the cold dry night.

***

The next morning, we dumped the grouchy Australians. As designated translator, I dutifully worked between the parties as the couple forced a morning of negotiations on Eliseo Abraham, a man whom they had just met, a man who had nothing to do with their dispute with the agency, and a man who couldn't do much to remedy it. Finally, it was agreed that Eliseo Abraham would call a truck to come pick them up (although I never saw a phone), and they would stay in Alota until it arrived. I don't know what ever became of them, but I was glad they were out of the jeep and that our compressed buttcheeks had a much-needed opportunity to re-expand.

On that second day, we passed through the tiny town of San Agustín where little boys ran up to the truck to get their picture taken. We walked around the modest cemetery of Juliaca, simple wooden crosses standing straight and tall, weathered by the extreme winds and hung with wreathes of plastic flowers, yellow blooms springing freshly from the ground. And as for the cast of remaining characters, we had more space to get to know one another, now uncrowded by negativity and enlivened with gratitude.

Markus, the English doctor, had an amazing life full of adventures and hardships. He had lived in India until he was five years old, when his father, a diplomat, was assassinated. His mother moved him back to England and remarried when Markus was twelve. He and his stepfather didn't get on, and when he was seventeen, his stepfather kicked him out of the house. Since then, the only thing that had kept him going was his focus on becoming a doctor. He had just spent four months camping in Patagonia in the winter, a place where he had always wanted to go since he was a child but didn't know why. I felt a calm quietude having Markus on our expedition, knowing that if any of us fell off a cliff or broke a leg, there would be someone there to fix it, a certainty not otherwise available in rural Bolivia.

As for Muriel, the Parisian artist, I would have loved her if for no other reason than the fact that she was *sola*. Unpretentious, free-spirited, she seemed to float around leaving behind her a trail of fairydust. Although the language barrier kept us from connecting more deeply, I loved how she expressed herself through what little she portaged. She didn't pack the items that you and I would pack. I never saw an extra pair of underwear, or a sweaty sock with holes in it, or a change of shirt, but she faithfully carried a clarinet which she stored in two halves in her plastic thermos. She also toted an audio recorder and a Super-8 movie camera that she had received for first communion. A photographer and artist, happy and free, she was always singing, as fairies tend to do.

Sebastian was a Frenchman, a biological engineer serving his mandatory military service -- in Tahiti. After having lived there for nearly two years, he claimed, "I will never go back to France. There must be a better way of life, although my parents don't understand."

He was traveling with his best friend, David, who was also a Frenchman gone Tahitian, but I sensed his island fever was more temporary.

And finally, there was Fabio. Born in Rome and having lived his early adult life in Australia, Fabio had become a world traveler extraordinaire, resident of the globe-at-large. He was an expert on around-the-world airline tickets, having figured out a way to use the frequent flier air-miles he racked up on each trip to pay for his next ticket. Fabio was a fanatic. He did everything full-out with a temper as fiery as his ginger hair. Whether it was his obsession with soccer, or his reflections on his divorce after only four years of marriage, he was headstrong bordering on abrasive, although quite willing to share what he'd learned about life. Regarding his recent break-up which he was now working through, he said, "We wanted different things. It just can't work when you want different things." He had wanted to travel; she had wanted a family and home. He had tried to stop traveling -- for her -- but couldn't. It just was not who he was.

***

We emerged from between two mountains, and there it was -- The Salar... My brain struggled to make sense of it. A giant expanse of white for as far as the eye could see, it extended out to the black mountains in the distance with nothing in between. The sun glared into our nearly snow-blind eyes as Eliseo Abraham chose one small line to travel across a swatch of the 12,000 square kilometers of Salar de Uyuni.

Once a prehistoric salt lake, the flat barren landscape void of geographical relief stretched out in a sea of pure whiteness. In pictures, you'd swear it was snow. In real life, you'd swear it was the moon. By this time, Eliseo Abraham appeared exhausted, perhaps by the morning ordeal with the Australians, perhaps from lack of sleep, but as we drove and drove across the salt with no road and no obstacles, he leaned back in his seat and closed his eyes. I thought I heard a little snore and although disconcerting at first to have your reclined dozing driver rocketing through the landscape at 80 km per hour, I finally sat back, gazed out the window at the wonderness, and giggled at the impossibility of it all.

After nearly an hour of effortless whizzing across a featureless landscape that never changed, I was able to make out a small island in the distance. Difficult to distinguish against the dark mountains, it soon became clear that we were looking at a small bite of land inside this great basin of nothingness. It stood small, high, and full of three-armed saguaro cactus poking out from all sides like a pin cushion. The island seemed totally out of place, although it's hard to say what would be "in place" in a scene like that. Finally, Eliseo Abraham opened his eyes and told us that we were heading towards Isla de los Pescadores. He explained that tourists were usually permitted only a few hours on the island, but because of our patience with the mishap with the Australians, he would try to arrange for us to spend the night there with the ranger. If we stayed, we would be able to witness the most magical spectacle that the island offered -- sunset and sunrise on the salt, a time when the tints and tones in the sky are perfectly reflected on the white salt mirror providing an immersion in 360 degrees of color.

When we arrived, Eliseo Abraham went off to speak with the ranger while we excitedly climbed to the top of the island, stepping through knife-edged volcanic rocks that cut into our leather boots. As we walked along the trail, we read aloud a sign in Spanish that was hand-painted on a rock: *Do not touch cactus.*

One minute later, Markus picked up a piece of cactus from the ground.

"Ouch," he said rather calmly, his fingers full of fine-needled barbs.

Two minutes later, Sebastian did exactly the same thing. *Why do boys never learn?*

When we reached the top of the island, the six of us just sat, looking out over the white of the salt flat that extended to the mountains at the horizon. Silent, in awe of this view from above, sitting amidst one of the earth's most unique settings. Some thought of the past, some of the future, and I continued to bring myself back to the present which stared back at me squarely in the eyes.

One by one, we got up and walked off alone. I hiked on, with Sebastian trailing close behind me and stopping to photograph a *vizcacha*, which looks a bit like a green rabbit. A solitary *vicuña* wandered across the salt below, looking like it might break through the thin layer of what-seemed-like-ice. The sun was low in the sky, and as I framed up a photo of a single cactus silhouetted against the salt and mountains, I spotted through my viewfinder an eagle soaring in the distance.

What a beautiful picture it would make, I thought as I began to recompose the photo. I waited. The eagle flew closer. Then closer, and closer, AND CLOSER... I pulled the camera away from my face just as it went right for my head! I ducked down into a crouch, my knees under my chin, and as silently as a shadow it landed on my back.

I yelled in a whisper for help to Sebastian who was a few steps away. I could feel its razor-sharp talons digging into my skin, not yet drawing blood but suspended at the skin's fulcrum point of ripping. In my mind's eye, I could see the eagle reaching down and tearing a big bite out of the back of my neck. His weight was incredible, and as I covered my ears and squeezed my eyes closed, I repeated, *Get him off. Get him off.*

But Sebastian was frozen. He stared at me, at the bird. I was crouched on the ground, trying not to move, feeling the talons adjusting, settling. Sebastian slowly moved toward us, put his camera to his eye, and snapped a picture! The animal flapped its wings downward in a great windstorm, and lifted off my back, his blackened form ascending into the pink sky. We stood there, motionless, as the salt turned fiery-rose.

***

When I later told Louis that story, he said, "That's a sign. If you had lived back in the times of the Native Americans, you would be the Medicine Man."

I thought about it. *A shaman. A priestess. A chief. In a different place, in a different time? Was it possible that we gained knowledge in a previous life to which I was now being allowed to access?* I considered the visions and déjà-vu I had been experiencing recently. *What could it all mean for the life I live now? Where do those intense flashes of insight come from when you travel? What are they? And why do I sometimes feel like I've been here before?*

"Synchronicity… is ultimately what it feels like to remember the future."
<u>Nine Kinds of Naked</u>, *by Tony Vigorito*

***

That night on Isla de los Pescadores, we slept on woven floor-mats in the ranger's wooden refuge built into the side of a cave. Pink shown down through the skylight, Muriel played soft songs on her clarinet, and I drank my first Bolivian beer with these marvelous traveling companions. *I think I could do this forever.*

5:43 a.m. *Don't oversleep the alarm. You only get one chance.* I bundled up against the *altiplano* winds, sure-footedly scrambling up the sharp volcanic rocks, gracefully dodging the silhouettes of cactus.

All you hear is the sound of your heart beating in your ears, and the cold air stings your eyes as you blink away the sleep. Awkwardly gripping the pen with purple woolen gloves you scratch down thoughts of what it is like to be here in the dark, on the moon. You stand atop an island-mountain, waiting for the sun to rise over the great salt flats of Bolivia.

The western sky glowed, reflecting shades from carnation to fuchsia in its clouds and in its vast expanse of salt below. A tunnel of pink. Above, below, beyond. Pop. The sun jumped over the horizon, shrouded at first by the thick clouds that stretched in strips across the distant mountain range. But slowly it climbed, casting a golden glow on towering cacti, warming the back of my neck. I focused on that warmth, touching lightly with my fingers the space that could still feel the weight, the light scratches, the pressure of the impossible.

***

When we returned to the refuge that morning, Eliseo Abraham asked, *"Do you want to go see mummies? Very tiny people who lived in a time before the sun. One day, the sun came, and these people died because they were not accustomed to anything but the rays of the moon. Some died screaming. Mothers died with children in their arms. All are still in the cave where they lived many years ago."*

My arms were covered in goosebumps. I think we were as fascinated as much with his story as the mystery in his voice. We piled into the jeep, hurled our backpacks up onto the roof and drove 70 kilometers across the blinding whiteness of the salt flat.

White white white. Burn your eyeballs, white. Volcán Tunupa soared into the sky as we neared the small adobe town by the same name. The oranges and greens of mineral rocks painted the cliffs set starkly against wispy white clouds and blue sunny sky. Eliseo Abraham told us to wait in the jeep while he walked into town to ask for the key.

We drove the windy dirt road up the volcano, and as we reached the locked gate which barricaded the road, Eliseo Abraham explained that this gate was here to guard the *Cueva de las Momias.* He unlocked the gate, and the 4x4 glided through, but as we climbed the first precariously-inclined curve, the jeep sputtered to a stop. Out of gas. We piled out undeterred and began to climb the twisty dusty road up the volcano on foot. Half a kilometer later, Eliseo Abraham led us over the ruins of an ancient stone wall which overlooked the nearly-deserted town. There he stopped abruptly in front of a patch of dense brush growing out of the side of the mountain.

He pushed aside the vines and bent down to remove the heavy wooden planks that blocked and concealed the entrance. The *Cueva de las Momias* is in no Lonely Planet book. It exists in no South American Handbook. It exists only in the people who grew up here in the southern *altiplano* of Bolivia. The people of the town of Tunupa, who have lived respectfully at the base of this volcano since the time before the sun existed, keep this road locked and their lips sealed to all but the most trusted friends. But in that moment, we privileged six shared in their secret.

After Eliseo Abraham had removed the boards, he got down on his hands and knees and crawled into the small hole which he had exposed. One by one, we followed. Once I squeezed through the crawlspace, I blinked a few times to get accustomed to the darkness. And suddenly I saw them. Three full adult skeletons sat upright in front of me, their backs leaning against the far cave wall, their knees pulled tightly to their chests. The skeletons of two small children lay to their right, with half a dozen skulls beside them. With the emotional-detachment of a clinician, Markus moved closer to examine the skulls, noting that they were unusually small and elongated, quite unlike a modern human skull.

The skeleton on the left immediately captivated me; something from within radiated an unspoken majesty and drew my attention. Perhaps it was her proud posture, even in death. As I leaned a bit closer, I noticed that amazingly, she still had some hair, long, brown and matted, hanging from the right side of her head.

Muriel kneeled to get closer and said, "Look at the hands!"

And it was true. They were still covered with skin. The feet too, and part of the legs and arms. And a little bit near the eye sockets. Mummies. Real mummies. With real skin just like yours and mine. Perfectly preserved in the dry desert air. From the time before the sun. From the time when people lived by the light of moonbeams.

I looked down at the skin stretched tightly across the back of my hand, my bones and veins pressing gently upward, the maze of sunspots and knuckle wrinkles. The hands. The hands were the same as mine. And the realness of it all fell upon me as I leaned closer, fascinated, repelled, trying to make my brain make the links.

I knelt silently in the dusty talc, red earthen pottery shards at my side, the ancient human figures before me. Sitting on the floor of a cave that had been there before I could even conceive of time, I stared, awe-struck, trying to move myself back through the centuries, wondering about their lives, about who they had been, about what had brought them here, about what had ultimately caused their deaths.

When we finally filed out of the darkness in silence one by one, we emerged from the womb of the volcano abruptly into the sunlight, a vivid blue sky of windswept clouds. A white expanse of salt glittered as far as I could see. And I walked down the hill towards the jeep, and I began to cry.

***

By sunset, we arrived in our final destination, the town of Uyuni, to the immigration office to get our entry stamp into Bolivia. After all that our group had seen and done and been through together, we couldn't break up now. We thanked Eliseo Abraham for the amazing opportunities he had given us and tipped him with as much as our thin money pouches could spare. We invited him to dinner, but he was anxious to get back to his family.

At the hostel, we took turns taking the best showers of our lives. The indecent sounds of simple pleasure coming from the three side-by-side shower stalls would have made quiet an audio-documentary. In the decadently warm water I washed my hair four times to get the red dust out and decided that Dove soap was perhaps the world's most luxurious invention.

"La bon heure," my roommate Muriel sighed with satisfaction. *The simple pleasures in life.* Bed had never felt so good. Clean sheets and piles of blankets. The six of us walked out into the chill of the night for some cheap food, talked contentedly over beer and mate de coca, and went off to bed clean, well-fed, and happy. The next day we were all on the 10:00 a.m. bus to Tupiza, canyon country of Butch Cassidy and the Sundance Kid.

MINESHAFTS, WITCHCRAFT AND PRISON

The Uyuni-Tupiza route isn't the most frequented road on the Gringo Trail. Just 140 kilometers, the journey takes *nine hours*. As we traveled along the non-road in a bus that the driver mistook for a 4x4, the vibration achieved by bouncing over weeds and animal burrows worked at jiggling my teeth loose. The driver blasted Michael Jackson's *Thriller* (on a repeat loop), and as the pompoms and plastic flowers which trimmed the windshield leapt about in rhythm, two kids barfed. One made it into a bag.

At our first stop I followed the busload's Bolivian women past the hand-painted "rest stoop" sign to find one and all squatting together under their layers of *cholita* skirts in a dirt patch behind a brick wall. What could I do but follow? As I pulled my cargo pants down around my ankles, the ladies giggled unapologetically at my naked white moon glowing in the sunlight. I began to see the logic of a skirt here. Still, it wasn't enough to make me wear one.

Within the first twenty minutes of the bus ride, Marcus and Fabio had given up their seats to women with half a dozen kids each, and so stood for the first five hours until the crowd dwindled. I joined them standing for two hours despite the insistent protests of local valiant men, and once I got my seat back, I had nearly nodded off when I felt a tugging from behind.

I turned around to find an old woman stroking my hair, speaking to me in Quechua which her daughter translated into Spanish, "She wants to trade you hair."

The woman smiled at me from behind a mouthful of gold teeth, as she held up her long gray braids in an offering which hung from beneath her tiny Bowler hat. Her three-year-old grandson, Eric, wiggled over to my lap and gave me the lowdown on each animal that passed by the window's rolling landscape. And the sun began to set across the dry plateau.

At 7:00 a.m. the next morning, Muriel returned from the bathroom down the hall in the hostel to announce that the toilet was clogged with "the rest of another tourist." All six of us walked to the central market for breakfast, a photographer's dream filled with figures huddled in the cool shadows to fry empanadas and sell chili peppers the colors of traffic lights. Invigorated by strong coffee and five bananas each (for the price of 1 boliviano -- about 18 cents), we headed out on foot into canyon country.

It took a few hours to walk past the outskirts of town, dogs barking at us from atop corrugated tin rooftops and children playing games in the dust. At midday, we entered Quebrada de Palmira, a canyon of red rocks reminiscent of the American Southwest. By mid-afternoon we reached what the backpacker community refers to as the "Valley of the Phalluses." Thousands of rock towers reach into the sky like giant stalagmites which escaped their caves, rising from the desert floor to thirty, forty, fifty feet in the air. Amazingly, all resemble penises. Big, small, fat, thin, warped, crooked, top-heavy... Some were half eroded away. Some looked like a threatening slideshow from high school health class -- *Don't let this happen to you.* Muriel even found one that was shaped like South America.

In the narrow valley among the sheer crumbling cliffs, it wasn't hard to imagine Butch Cassidy and the Sundance Kid choosing this spot to hide out. The phallus towers offered cover for hiding from the law or dodging bullets, and although the lawless duo had had some fruitful years robbing banks in the Old American West, by the time they made it to Bolivia, they were wanted and desperate. The landscape mirrored that desperation. Blazing desert with no life in sight. Red rocks and dust, beautiful and silent. Butch and Sundance met their end in a gunfight nearby Tupiza in 1908.

We sat down for lunch in the shade of a phallus. I wrote. Fabio climbed boulders and jumped gaps until he fell into a cactus on a particularly macho attempt. Markus carved a pineapple which he'd carried in with surgeon-hand precision, gracefully dropping each piece of rind into the dirt. Muriel was crouched down, intensely filming something inside a small dark hole. We sat in the timid breeze and intense sun, enjoying a climate suitable for shorts for the first time in a long time. And suddenly I noticed that I was singing -- and had been for the last three days.

***

After a few day-hikes in Tupiza we six climbed aboard the bus once again, this time for Potosí, a town shadowed by Cerro Rico, once the largest-producing silver mine in the world. Local miners still work there in medieval conditions for tin, zinc, copper, lead and what little silver still remains, blasting with dynamite in the labyrinth of tunnels.

Eduardo Garnica was destined to be a miner, too, but after his father died in a cave-in trying to earn enough money to feed his seven children, Eduardo was determined to lead a different life despite small odds in this impoverished part of the country. In 1999 he set up his own *agencia de turismo* and invited interested travelers into the miners' worlds to see first-hand the harsh conditions which have not changed for hundreds of years.

The trip is not for the faint-of-heart, nor the claustrophobic. It was fun at first. Eduardo outfitted us with coveralls and rubber galoshes to wade through the mine's calf-deep water. He supplied us with hardhats and attached headlamps to illuminate our way. Then we took a little ride in a real mining car. But things got very dark very fast. Today in the cooperative mines, thousands of men powered on cigarettes and coca leaves work 8- to 12-hour shifts, hundreds of meters underground, in heat reaching 110 degrees, crawling on their hands and knees though tiny tunnels to use their hammers and chisels to extract minerals which bring heart-wrenchingly low market value. Some men work in the tradition of their fathers, all work for subsistence. Life expectancy after entering the mine is less than ten years after which most die from lung diseases produced by the fine dust and poisonous gases underground. Workers begin as early as ten years old, and although child labor is illegal, it is also uncontrolled.

Before we went entered, Eduardo crossed himself and said a prayer. We sloshed through a foot of water in sauna-like temperatures until we reached a small room in which sat a life-size idol, half-man half-rabbit, who represented the god of the underworld, familiarly referred to as *El Tío*. Eduardo offered him cigarettes and grain alcohol called *chicha* which he sprinkled from a tiny bottle. He prayed to *El Tío* for our safety and told us to do the same. Cave-ins are so common that the word is never spoken aloud, and the mine workers (all of whom are men) believe that women underground are bad luck. Their wives were never allowed to enter the mine. For now, exceptions were made for the tourists.

We left the chamber and moved still deeper into the tunnels of the mine. The oppressive heat increased as we ventured further, and the intense humidity made it hard to breathe. My heavy legs moved in slow motion, even as we trudged downhill. Eduardo showed us how to maneuver down a series of rickety wooden ladders that led through dark holes in the floor. When we reached the bottom of one ladder, we climbed down the next and the next as I held the rails tight in the complete darkness. My sweat never evaporated; it just poured from my forehead and dripped off my chin in small droplets. As we passed three men who were tapping with hammers on the rock walls, they stopped to greet us with a welcoming smile.

At the end of the blasted corridor, Eduardo stopped, explaining that we were ready to descend to the next level. By this time, I had no idea how deep we had gone. Time seemed to have been warped by the heat, but it felt like we were already quite close to the center of the earth. His tone had changed, become more grave. Eduardo then pointed to a small hole about 16 inches wide in the dusty ground, indicating this was where we were supposed to descend, but there was no ladder protruding from the top like there had been on the other descents.

Without pause, Eduardo took Muriel by the tiny fairly-like arms and lowered her down -- her arms stretched above her head -- into the narrow dark hole in the ground. And she was gone.

Without a word, he reached for my arms next, my feet now
frozen to the ground, petrified. I had not known until that
moment that I was terrified of small spaces. As my breath
tightened in my chest, Eduardo and Marcus held my arms tightly
as they lowered me slowly, feet-first, down into the hole. The
hole was much deeper than I had expected, and I kept waiting to
hit the bottom. Like jumping off a cliff into a pool of water
below, the anticipation of impact seemed to go on for much
longer than my mind thought it ought to. My open eyes stared
wildly at a solid wall of dirt just inches from my face as I traveled
slowly, timelessly downward. The powder-like dust caught in my
throat, and I started to cough, choking, unable to breathe. When
Eduardo and Markus could reach no further, they simply let go,
and I dropped the last 12 inches to the dirt floor where Muriel
stood, her eyes as wide as mine. The rest of our group followed,
appearing beside us one by one, except for Markus who was too
"stout" to fit. Eduardo jumped down the ten foot gap from the
top, and we continued our tour, greeting and speaking with men
whose faces were blackened with soot, streaked with sweat. We
gave them gifts of tobacco and coca leaves that we had brought,
and I thought how they looked so young, younger than me. I
wondered how many children they had, and how long those
children would have a father.

When we emerged from the mine only an hour after we had
entered, we were all deep inside ourselves. Eduardo tried to lift
our spirits by taking our photos holding sticks of dynamite. Then
he set them out in a deserted quarry, ran fuses and let us light
them. Blowing up dynamite really is quite exciting. Fingers in
our ears, we lit the fuses one after another watching the tiny lines
hiss and travel until -- BOOM! Pulverized rock flew twenty feet
in the air, and dust clouds lingered and drifted towards us in the
wind.

But in the end, it was the stories the men told with their eyes
that stayed with me through a fitfully sleepless night. The
certainty of what their lives would be, the dodging of fate that
Eduardo had pulled off, and the knowing that most of his friends
and family would not be so fortunate. And then there was me,
for whom life was nothing but opportunity. Going down inside
that mine was something I will never forget. The heavy air inside

choked me underground, but by the time I reemerged, the heaviness had moved to my heart.

***

After the mine tour and a farewell dinner, our travel group split up and went our separate ways. Some were in a hurry, some almost out of money, some would never stop, wandering to the ends of the earth and back again. As for me, I was headed north to La Paz, the world's highest capital sitting at 3600 meters above sea level. I nestled in for a long bus ride, supplied with my walkman, saltines and toilet paper. I suppose I had been expecting to drive up into the city, chugging up dramatic mountain switchbacks. Instead, as dirt turned to pavement, I was suddenly looking *down* into La Paz, sunken into a crater deep below the highway's edge. Chaotic concrete sprawl clung to the rim of the canyon, cascading down its walls like a tremendous urban waterfall.

As the bus turned off the highway and made its windy way down down down into the canyon, mountains soaring from its outer edges, the city waited to reveal its layers, new and old, rich and poor, traditional and modern. I was soon to discover that La Paz displayed its many faces throughout the many hours of a day.

I was ready for some solace after an intense few social weeks with the Uyuni crew, and I splurged on a single room, spending $4 a night instead of $3 for a dorm. I enjoyed my alone time, reading, studying Spanish, talking to myself, brooding about life's unresolved questions, and generally enjoying my own company. I stumbled upon a Krishna vegetarian restaurant while dodging indoors to avoid a student demonstration and its accompanying gunfire one day, and ever-after became a regular there for journal-writing and the daily set-menu lunch. Integral bread, salad, vegetable soup, tea, and a plate of empanadas or lentils or whatever they brought me, all without any surprise animal parts to pick through, for just 8 bolivianos ($1.20).

The people I met in La Paz were warm and welcoming, and I challenged myself to let barriers down and strangers in. I felt more inspired with my attempts at the Spanish language than I had in months, ready for leaps and bounds, hills and valleys, having learned to accept the tough spots along with the soarings. But I felt like I was climbing at warp speed. *Tranquilla* and happy.

My mind whirred at all there was still to see, to experience, and I puzzled my brain on how to minimize my "stuff," scrape money together, and extend and extend that feeling.

***

For two weeks, the rain poured down on La Paz. I loved to watch everyone get caught in a downpour and run and crowd into tiny spaces under the building awnings. Sometimes it hailed, and afterwards the merchants would use a long stick to push up on the blue tarps which served as roofing for their street stalls, sending balls of hail flying into the air and landing on unsuspecting passersby of which I was often one.

The town seemed to live and breathe as its own organism, changing from morning to night its mood, its crowd, what its street vendors sold, what welcomed me. The mornings saw stalls lining Avenida Santa Cruz selling warm doughy breads filled with creamy white cheese, and by nightfall they had been replaced with vendors selling hairbrushes from China and yelping puppies. Women sat on the ground beside giant piles of oranges glowing in the afternoon light, or offering up delicious juices of mango, papaya and fruits I'd never heard of grown in the warm wet valley of the Yungas on the other side of the Andes. Vendors pushed wheelbarrows full of popcorn up and down the plaza, loose and mounding above the sides, somehow not losing a kernel despite the wind. It all seemed so amazing, so rich.

The diversity in a single block ranged from high-rise office buildings, to great open squares, to traditional covered markets. From men in business suits hailing taxi cabs, to women in traditional dress hauling 50-pound sacks of potatoes up the steep streets on their backs. But the visual highlight of La Paz was without a doubt the *cholitas*. In their easily-recognizable Bowler caps perched atop their heads, these women also wore sweaters or aprons with a full layered skirt, their hair braided into two long strands tied together in the back. The ancestors of these Aymara women were singled out centuries ago by Spanish colonizers and required to wear this garb to differentiate them from the Spanish women. Today the *cholitas* have turned oppression into proud expression of their cultural heritage and are found in all realms of economics, politics and social class, long regarded as masters of local commerce from the marketplace to the tourist stalls.

As I passed stall after stall stacked with thick llama sweaters, scarves and gloves in every color of the rainbow (so different from their muted gray-and-brown Chilean counterparts), I finally arrived at my destination, the Witch's Market of Sagarnaga. Many merchants here are standoffish with tourists, and I started to feel a bit uncomfortable in a place where I do not belong as I tried to walk casually along the street. Surely those who are true believers in the powers of witchcraft do not appreciate tourists gawking and snapping novelty photos. I was told that the *brujos* (witches) themselves rarely make an appearance here, but a haunting vibe exists all the same.

Finally, I stopped at a stall whose merchant met my eyes. She didn't look like a witch to me. She was not old and hunched, her fingernails didn't curl into long twisty claws, she didn't have warts on her nose. So much for fairytales. (So far this journey had done a great deal to disprove fairytales.)

I smiled, she nodded in recognition, and my eyes greedily scanned her wares. Herbs and powders in plastic sacks, something with toenails in a glass jar, dried llama fetuses (used to rid malevolent spirits before a new home can be built) leaning rigidly against a table.

The woman asked me what I needed protection from. This stumped me. I explained I was simply a traveler. She paused and then handed me a small stone statue of a condor. This magnificent bird with outstretched wings was lucky for travelers, she explained, because it could see above and beyond where I was going and would help watch out for me. I nodded, and she wrapped it with strands of yellow and fushia llama wool and gave me a few coca leaves to help with the altitude.

As I trudged back down the steep cobblestone street transformed now into a downhill slalom in the slick rain, I turned the cold stone bird over and over in my hand. *Not a bad choice,* I thought. If only I had had the courage to ask her more about what life might have in store for me, medicine-woman to medicine-woman.

***

Rain whispered on the roof as I returned to the hostel. I opened my door, dodging ceiling drips and stumbling in the flat gray light, leaving wet footprints on the wooden floor of my tiny closet of a room. I dropped off my purchases and walked back into the common living room where four guys were sitting at a table with their guidebooks. One was from the States and was incredibly obnoxious, going on about politics and how important his antitrust law career was. The second was a Canadian with a familiar face (maybe it was the full beard and shabby clothes that made him look like every other long-time traveler), and the other two were Dutch. The Dutch boys were both gorgeous, both insightful, both giants, and both very cool guys who happened to be heading south, having just come from all the places I was headed towards. There was an unwritten code among travelers. Generally, Europeans didn't trust Americans, unless of course they were women which aroused an interest simply because it was unusual. Generally, solo travelers hung out with solo travelers, and if you'd been on the road longer than six months and seemed mellow, that was when you got to share in the secret stuff: what dirt roads to take, which *hospedaje* owner was the best cook, who had the best showers, and how to get to the secret caves, trails, and *pueblitos*. I had that connection with the Dutch guys, and we talked for hours before I noticed the American and Canadian had left.

When I went to bed that night, I lay awake feeling simultaneously stirred-up and reassured. Although it was an undeniable fact that my savings were dwindling, I hadn't yet been able to decide when I was *supposed* to go home. *When I completely ran out of money? Or maybe I should go home for Christmas? It was just around the corner. It would make my family happy.* But after talking to these travelers and hearing about all there still was to see and do, other ideas bounced around in my head that were far from *should-ing.*

A white Christmas? I've never had one of those, and there are so many beautiful mountain towns in Bolivia and Peru. And what about the turn of the millennium? What about Machu Picchu, the Inca center of the world?

By then my mind was racing with excitement, with possibility, and sleep was impossible. I tried to breathe myself into calmness and believe that things would work out and answers would be revealed in good time. After all, I had not planned the very best parts of my journey; they had just happened. I tried to think of what Louis might say. I tried to think of moontime. I tried to remember that the universe will gently guide you if you let it. And with that magic swimming in my head, I drifted off.

***

The next morning I met up with the four guys again in the living room, and over breakfast they asked me if I'd made any decisions about my travel plans. As if possessed, I found myself telling them I didn't know *when* I was going home, but I thought I'd spend the holidays here in South America. It surprised me even as it came out of my mouth. And then it made me smile.

Within minutes, as if to strengthen our level of commitment to travel and ourselves, the five of us decided to go together to the most secret spot in the whole country, a place to which access is passed along only by word of mouth from hush-hush traveler to hush-hush traveler, and quite possibly the strangest place I've ever been: inside San Pedro prison.

One of the Dutch guys had met a guy on a bus who told him this: *Go to the prison gate and tell them you want to see Thomas, the English guy. The guards will know what to do.* Well, we went to the gate, and we asked to see Thomas, but the prisoner who came to meet us was named Fernando, and he looked like he had stepped straight out of West Side Story, slicked-back hair, tight sparkling-white T-shirt and all. Fernando explained that it was he who had once been the prison-tour-guide king, and last month he staged a *coup* to get his business back from Thomas. None of us asked for details or verification. All we knew was that Fernando was charging twice the price that we had expected to pay at 40 bolivianos per tourist. Today he had five tourists; the day before he had had nine, and the Sunday before that, he had hit the jackpot with 40! He needed to make $US25,000 by February to buy his way out of his eight-year drug trafficking sentence. Fernando was a man with a purpose.

With much hesitation, we handed over our passports to the guards at the front gate and stepped inside as the sliding bars clanked behind us. For three hours, we toured the prison with Fernando, visiting and learning about the different sections and how one gained status. When you were sentenced to La Paz prison, nothing was handed to you. It was all about money. It was each prisoner's responsibility to buy or rent a room to live in within a section, and different sections were different prices.

Each prisoner had to pay the rent on time to the "delegate" of the section, who said he used this money for improvements but really just pocketed it, and then each prisoner had to find some way to make a living *inside* the jail in order to *pay* for rent, food, protection, privilege, etc. The less money you had, the more difficult your stay there would be. If you couldn't find work, you had to work in the kitchen where no one but the poorest prisoners ate because the food was full of tranquilizers by order of the government. But who needed to eat there when inside the jail, the prisoners, themselves, ran a dozen different restaurants, three markets, and even a shop where a Québécois man made fresh crepes every day?! Inside this prison, there were tourist businesses, alcohol businesses, drug businesses, weapons businesses. There were artists, teachers, businessmen and doctors (mostly jailed for malpractice). There were drug dealers, loan sharks, bookies and pimps. And in addition to the 1400 prisoners living in this former monastery which was designed to hold only 800, there were 200 wives and 50 children who lived *inside* the prison (and came in and out every morning to go to school and do errands out in the world) because the prisoners who were husbands and fathers couldn't afford to pay two rents (one inside and one outside).

And do you know how many guards there were on patrol inside the prison? None. NONE! There were plenty at the front gate to check tourists and visitors in and out, but the guards did not dare come inside. The community of prisoners simply did not allow it. It appeared that once prisoners went in, law enforcement stopped. Instead, the community was enforced from within, run by the guys who had the most money, who could substantiate the most threats, who held the most power and the biggest reputation. Our guide, Fernando, told us he was the number two guy. This was partly because his cousin was the number one guy (this offered him protection) but also because he had done time in a New York State penitentiary where he had learned English, thus making him the best-qualified to give tours to foreigners and make a ton of money off tourists. That gave him power and a very high spot in the food chain.

And so, there we were, in the middle of a world where we didn't belong, potentially in grave danger at any moment with no guards to save us. I had to pinch myself... *I'M IN BOLIVIAN*

JAIL. AM I FUCKING NUTS? I listened to stories of the convicted rapists and child molesters who were initiated into prison by getting chili peppers stuffed up their asses. I bought a colored pencil sketch from a very talented French artist who happened to be shooting up heroine when we entered his room to browse through his gallery. It was unreal. But it was not chaos, not at all. It was a carefully-balanced, carefully-ordered system. There were bosses and employees, sellers and buyers, haves- and have-nots. I was not in the danger that it might seem. I was an integral part of Fernando's business, his reputation, his meal ticket, his potential freedom. He had very powerful connections in the prison, and he was not going to let anything happen to me because if it did, his very profitable business would be shot straight to hell as news of any tourist harmed would spread throughout the backpacker community even faster than the word about the prison tour itself.

And so, as I walked the halls with murderers and armed robbers, none of who were in cells or behind bars but only behind the great walls of this city within a city, I was forced to look at people beyond their label, beyond the ideas of crime and criminals, to scrutinize what was legal and illegal and how much sense that made, and it brought these concepts into a new light. And just like everything else I'd experienced in my travels, once I was able to see something up close, examine it, take a bite out of it, and walk in and out of it unharmed, it stopped being so scary. It was no longer cloaked in the shrouds of unknown. Like magic, it disappeared from the realms of "what if," and then, I was not afraid.

MOON DOG, MOON BOW…

During my three-day relationship with Sergio, the sand sculptor, I walked around Montezuma with googley eyes breathing in the romance of every fallen flower, every hummingbird's wing, every bend in the meandering stream. The world radiated energy. Sergio worked every day in the one-room adventure booth, and I found myself once again on my own. I still wrote in my journal at the streetside café, still sighed at couples holding hands, but the lightness in my heart had bridged my role as observer with my yearning to be a participant in the jungle magic of this place.

I hiked to the nearby waterfall humming to myself as I slipped and slid along the mossy stones, and when I arrived, I saw her. *There's that girl again.* I had picked out a potential friend (although she did not know it) having seen her a couple times around town. Gray T-shirt, blond short haircut, low maintenance. A woman who had not only met my gaze but met it with a smile.

If I see her again, I had told myself the day before, *I'll introduce myself.*

And there she was again, this time at the waterfall. I took a deep breath and the deeply-buried feelings of the first day of school came flooding back from the recesses of emotional memory. *Be brave.*

I slid into the waterhole casually, swimming around until I finally made my way over to where she was sitting. She smiled, and I said hello.

Her name was Sophia, and not surprisingly I had intuitively sensed that we had a lot in common. She spoke in an easy way, devoid of the image-consciousness I had gratefully left behind in the States. She had been traveling in Costa Rica for a few months, had been to many of the same places I had been, and would shortly be flying back to Oregon to begin a trip to Australia.

After about thirty minutes of chatting, she turned and said, "This is my boyfriend, Ben."

Suddenly, and for the first time, I saw a person sitting right there just behind her. I suppose he had been there the whole time, listening quietly, but how strange that I had not even noticed him, having been so focused on the discovery of a feminine energy for which I had so longed.

After the day at the waterfall, Sophia and I exchanged greetings frequently as we saw each other in passing on the street and became casual travel friends. It wasn't much, but I was grateful for that openness and the vague reminder of female companionship.

In the meantime, my culturo-gender bridges were rapidly dissolving into dilapidated disrepair as Sergio began to illustrate for me that my mental map of a romantic relationship in a foreign land was far far different than his. Without being able to communicate to resolve this matter, tensions grew exponentially with every meeting. And I was not alone in this experience. It served as the topic of numerous tirades of other women travelers I met throughout South America. Sergio, after three dates, had metamorphosed into a wolf. And it was ugly.

Perhaps it offended me so deeply because I had absolutely not seen it coming. Perhaps it offended me so deeply because I had chosen him for the very reason that he had not seemed like one of *them*... The horndoggers. The other bastards you could pick up in any surf town. *Can't you see? The reason I picked him was because of his unassuming-ness. His big goofy grin, his blushing cheeks, his sweaty palms. I could have signed up for* this shit *anywhere. The man was an artist, for fuck's sake. If he wasn't all about the romance, who was?*

By date #2, our beach walk under the stars degenerated into pawing and grabbing, but with some bashful-yet-determined hand-pushing on my part, he backed off quickly and almost looked a little embarrassed about it. By date #3, he was dry-humping my leg up against a beached boat. *Ahh, Sergio... What happened to the way it used to be? The romance, the sunsets. It seems like just the day before yesterday...*

Being a young inexperienced woman who had internalized society's pressures to be polite and subdued, I decided that I would not to try to explain all of this to Sergio. The language barrier would have made for a difficult and awkward flipping of dictionary pages, and moreover, a discussion about his behavior would require that I actually *confront* him. And confrontation could upset him, which could mean he might not like me any more, at which point I'd be forced to admit that romance was all an illusion anyway. So I did what any reasonable woman would do. I skipped town. Without a word.

This was no easy task since the adventure kiosk where Sergio worked sat about twenty feet from the bus stop. On the day the bus came, I waited inside a shop off the main plaza, and when I heard the bus rumble to life, idling and spitting black exhaust as the driver climbed aboard to find his seat, I jumped on and hid behind another traveler's giant backpack.

OK, OK. I was a coward. But I was an avoider by nature. Maybe that was why I left the States in the first place -- my home, my work, my unresolved relationships -- because I knew there was something just not right, but I didn't want to hurt anyone's feelings about it. It was just how I did things. And I got on that bus. And I never saw Sergio again.

And so, as the bus pulled away, sending a cloud of dust across the middle of the square and enveloping the little adventure booth, I held my breath as I sat down on an empty bench seat, finally daring to glance towards the back of the bus at the other tourists leaving Montezuma. And the two familiar smiles of Sophia and Ben looked up from the bench right behind me.

***

The three of us shared a day's bus-ferry-bus ride back to San Jose, and Sophia and Ben told me their story. After dating for six months and spending two months together in Costa Rica, Sophia was going off to meet an ex- in Australia; the details were awkward and vague. Ben planned to stay on in Costa Rica for another few months. The future of their relationship was uncertain. *Time*. *Space*. The recurring buzz words surfaced, unspoken jolts of fear, calm and anxiety rising in turn.

As the city lights of San Jose came into view, they told me of Hotel Musoc, three-stories of cinderblock where they planned to stay the night, just upstairs from the bus station. We checked in together about 7 p.m., and I hugged them both goodbye. They walked down to the hall to room #3, I climbed the stairs to #24, and another travel relationship came to a close. I couldn't help wonder what would become of these brief friendships providing tiny glimpses into lives otherwise so distant from my own. Fleeting intersections on life paths.

The night was crisp and cold as I sat on my single bed and peeled a mango with my pocketknife, a picture window framing the cityscape against the clear still sky. I slept soundly under three wool blankets and awakened early the next morning, excited to walk down to the bus depot and buy my return ticket home -- to Playa Grande.

The receptionist buzzed the wrought-iron gate which released me from Hotel Musoc, and I wandered the blocks of the Coca-Cola bus terminal in the relative safety of daylight as buses awakened one by one, shuttering to life. I bought my ticket and paused outside a café with homemade corncakes stacked in the front window case, half a dozen people sitting inside drinking coffee at tables set for one. The Señora smiled at me, offered me a chair, and brought me a *café con leche* in a tall narrow glass, balanced carefully on a child's plastic saucer decorated with rainbows and unicorns. I sat back and sighed softly as I skimmed the congealed buttery layer off the top of the coffee and watched the faces around the room. Strangers spoke, greeting each other as they entered and pulling out chairs at their empty tables. This was a place that made you feel welcome and known and home, even if you weren't.

After coffee, I hurried back to the hotel to pack my things and catch the bus which was leaving in an hour. I entered my room and closed the door, and not one minute later, I heard two sharp knocks.

"*Pasa*," I shouted to the person who I assumed was the cleaning lady. But nothing happened. I stuffed the last of my grimy T-shirts into my backpack and walked over and opened the door. Ben stood in the doorway shaking, tears streaming from his soggy mess.

"I just -- *sniff, sniff* -- don't want to be alone right now."

God. The poor kid looked miserable. My normally-suppressed maternal instincts got the best of me, and I put my arm around him, and I told him, "Then you can come with me."

And in that moment, I had an idea. I had already told Louis that I was leaving Playa Grande for Guatemala next week, and since he still needed someone to help him for the month or two left of high season, Ben could stay on there and work. It was perfect. He was looking for a friendly place to be, Louis was looking for help, and I could teach him my job that week and leave for Guatemala for good knowing they were both in good hands, my loose ends tied up neatly in a big fat bow.

I told Ben to grab his stuff, "Our bus leaves in twenty minutes." A smile perked up on his red swollen face, and we jogged down the stairs together to catch the bus.

For the entire dusty bumpy bus trip, we talked. A poet, playwright, and odd-jobber on Oregon's coast, Ben was intense. Interesting. Passionate. He spent most of the seven-hour bus journey blathering on and on about Sophia: how much he missed her, how amazing she was, how he hoped they would end up together. And I decided that anyone who loved his girlfriend that much could be a friend of mine...

WANING GIBBOUS…

And the bastard fucking kissed me.

Not six days later.

I took him back with me, and we spent a week together in Playa Grande as I taught him my job. And on the night before I went back to San Jose, on the night before stuffing my over-accumulation of belongings into trash bags and throwing them into the back of Louis and Marianela's truck to catch a ride back with them to the capital, on the night before sitting between them for six hours as they bickered and as my stomach sweated through my money belt and soaked my ticket to Guatemala, Ben kissed me.

***

"Of course you'd fall in love with your friend's boyfriend," said Louis. "Why don't more people? You love your friend, why wouldn't you love the one they love?" There was a new Louis-ism for the books.

How dare he? He had a girlfriend who he was crazy about, right? I thought he was safe. I thought I was safe. So I had been able to be my complete self. Not my guarded self. Not my this-guy-wants-something-so-I-have-to-be-standoffish self. Just my 100% open loving human self. The kiss seemed like it came out of nowhere, but then I remembered back to a night after leaving the testosterone-seething Rancho

Diablo when I told him, "It's so nice to not have to worry about you."

"You have to worry about *every* guy," he had said as he cast his eyes toward the ground.

I remembered back to how he had followed me around all week; *he was just lonely.* How he'd look at me just a little too long over dinner; *he felt comfortable in my company.* How I'd look up from reading in the hammock and he was staring at me; *he was happy to have found a new home.* And on that last night, under the stars, he kissed me. And he told me that he'd fallen in love with me. And that I should stay, in Playa Grande, with him.

Maybe it was out of loneliness, or boredom, or just to see if he could pull it off, but it shocked the hell out of me. In his eyes I had seen a great sadness, a great longing, a compassion, a depth. A great needing to be loved, to give love. And I wondered if I had had feelings for him and just never noticed, or if I just liked the idea of being loved so suddenly and so deeply.

But the next morning, I got into Louis and Marianela's truck anyway. And I said goodbye to him anyway. And soon I was off, striding toward my plan, moving down the dirt road towards San Jose, towards Guatemala, towards the rest of my life. And after about ten minutes in the truck, Louis turned to me abruptly and said, "I think Ben really fell for you."

And then he burst into laughter. Hysterical uncontrolled laughter. Nothing pleased him more than fate's sharp stick poking at people's wobbly certainties.

It was a long six hours. Somewhere between the unsolicited commentary on the direction of my life, the Brahma cows wandering onto the road, the blaring horns racing by in Doppler Effect, it just kept echoing in my head: *You've gotta do what's happening.* And as we pulled into the neighborhood of Vargas Araya and Daisy's house came into sight, I jumped down from the truck, and Louis said, "I'll see you soon," and cackled and drove away.

I scowled and opened the door. And as I filled Daisy in on the details of my life over the last few months and the last turbulent 24 hours, it seemed that I was seeking advice, that I was struggling; that I was actually considering making a decision, and that decision was eminent and timely. And like the wise maternal archetype, it was she who offered the simple words that helped me let go and just feel -- not think, just feel. In Spanish, she advised, *"Amy, do what makes you happy."*

So the next day, I got back on the bus, and I returned to Playa Grande, and I returned to Ben. I took a sharp U-turn, and screeched around back towards the fork in the road, and changed the course of my travels and the fortitude of my emotional walls.

***

The forks in the road of life are a funny thing. One leads to the next, to the next, to the next. And if you hadn't made one bad or even one questionable decision in your past, would you have ended up in the *good* place that you now find yourself? Each bend in the road can only materialize after the previous choice -- good, bad, or ugly -- has been made.

Looking back, I can see Ben, even in the beginning, as a shade of what he eventually showed himself to be: a manic-depressive, narcissistic, insecure, two-timing, image-wielding, opportunistic shyster. In fact, for the benefit of the reader, and in the tradition of changing people's names when retelling a true story to protect the innocent and not-so-innocent, let us heretofore refer to him by a name he has righteously earned. Let us simply call him, The Asshole.

Maybe on the night before I left Playa Grande, in that moment, he really did believe he loved me. And maybe the conviction with which he spoke, his intensity, the certainty and desperation which oozed from his eyes as I-absolutely-cannot-live-without-you, was enough for me to raze everything I had planned, and maybe that was a good exercise. But even knowing what I know now about the consequences of my decision, even having watched a monster emerge and slink from its cave, more rampant and less apologetic each day, I would not take it back. I willingly opened my heart to the Asshole -- in an isolated place, for a brief time -- and maybe I did it just to see if I could. Sure, he convinced me it was safe to do so. His was the most intense, you-are-the-center-of-my-world entwining I had ever felt. He sketched me while I read in the hammock, he wrote verses for me of melancholy-inspired beauty, he stared at me while I ate, and drooled over me as I slept, and made me feel like there was no one else in the universe but him and me -- for about a week. And no one had ever done that before. And I fell for it.

Welcomed it. It was worlds apart from the flat, tame affect of the vast majority of American men who are trained to reject emotional depth, and I believed that I had finally found the world's most romantic man.

I willingly opened my heart to him. It was he who opened the door, but I chose to walk through. And in the two short months that I was hopelessly temporarily committed to the Asshole, I learned more about emotional depth and breadth, and expectations about men and relationships, and using my voice than I had in the previous 24 years. And despite how I suffered when he eventually left, I wouldn't trade it. The Asshole blew open my tidy picture of the world. And had that door not opened, I can't be sure that I would have met the others, all of whom taught me important (albeit less jarring) lessons about love and life. And if I had stayed in my tidy little world, I may have never discovered how much I had to give, how much hopeless devotion I could receive, and how to let go of all my clutching and just fall -- just leap -- into the unknown.

But I still haven't been to Guatemala...

ISLA DEL SOL

After taking a last look at my beautiful Dutchmen of La Paz (so I could transpose them at will into my threesome fantasies), I headed toward the bus station with departures for Copacabana, a quiet Bolivian town on the shores of Lake Titicaca, world's highest navigable lake at 3800 meters above sea level. All the buses were full, but my smile and my recently-adopted everything-is-negotiable approach prevailed, and eventually, I found myself on a slice of backbench squeezed between Pedro and Pedro.

Pedro, age 50, was an artist, Tai Kwan Do sensei, potter, Hare Krishna, Aymara Indian, locally-known Bolivian actor, and all-around wacky guy. During our four-hour journey, he spun tales of ancient legends of the lake passed down through generations of Titicaca dwellers while animatedly bouncing around in his bus seat like popcorn. Bolts of energy burst from his wiry little body as he gesticulated wildly, waving his arms for emphasis every time he mentioned a higher power (which was often). The other Pedro, significantly younger, sluggish and not nearly as magnetic, was once Pedro the Elder's Tai Kwan Do student. Now built a bit like a pumpkin, he worked a suit-and-tie job in Buenos Aires and mentioned every few sentences that he was single. Friends of fifteen years, they both seemed a little nuts -- and I couldn't get enough. *I must be growing.*

When we arrived in Copacabana, Pedro the Elder invited me to stay at his grandfather's home, a historic house built on the banks of the lake hundreds of years ago. After dining that evening by a blazing fireplace in an adobe restaurant, the three of us strolled along the muddy banks of Lake Titicaca, gazing up at the star-studded sky as Pedro pointed out the constellation of *Las Tres Marias* and sung Hare Krishna songs softly to La Virgin del Lago. My mind settled, my heart rested, and I felt it... *This is exactly where I want to be.*

***

The next morning, Pedro and Pedro in tow, I rubbed sleep from my eyes as a cool forceful wind struck my face and fluttered my jacket. Sitting in silence at the bow of the boat, I looked out over the wind-chopped water as we motored the two hours toward Isla del Sol. Lake Titicaca, over 9000 square kilometers in area, is shared by Bolivia on the southeast side and Peru on the northwest side and has been used as a gateway for thousands of years. The Incas believe that Isla del Sol is the birthplace of their people who are descended from the sun, and ancient history and tradition are deeply rooted in its deep waters.

As the island came into view in the distance, its steep hills reaching up toward the clear cloudless sky, this place was unmistakably a bridge between the three worlds prominent in ancient Inca beliefs: the world above, the world below, and the middle world we live in. The surface of the lake, which stretched infinitely below into a world of unknown, invisibly supported the tiny island bobbing atop it as the sky reached down to kiss the horizon. The island floated in space, surrounded by layers of blue, as the trio merged into one. It was as if I had stumbled across a gateway from which all three worlds could be unlocked in one moment. As if all one had to do to move from one to the next was take a deep breath and plunge.

Stepping onto the dock was like stepping into Oz; colors glowed from every wildflower, every trickling brook, every blade of vibrant green grass, and the warm sun beat down on my arms like an embrace from the sun god himself. Pedro the Elder, Aymara descendent of the ancients, took my hand, and we walked slowly toward the bottom of the Inca stairway. The massive stones, stacked carefully into the hillside, glowed golden in the sunlight, and I imagined these same stones supporting the footsteps of the ancient Incas thousands of years ago, climbing to the top of the sacred island with their prayers and messages. We walked slowly, looking, listening, as women in traditional dress leading their llamas on short ropes descended the narrow stairway passing closely beside us. We paused to drink from *Las Tres Aguas*, a fountain whose three sacred waters are said to originate in Cusco, the ancient capital of the Inca empire. According to legend, if you bathe in this water, you will be cleansed of lies, laziness, and thievery. Pedro stopped to splash some across his arms and mine, and the coolness somehow felt like it permeated more deeply than just my skin.

By the time we left the fountain, half a dozen children, each under three-feet tall, had gathered to ask to carry our bags and lead us to selected guesthouses where they would receive a few cents from the *dueña* for their efforts. I smiled at the thought of any of these tiny children with bright faces and diminutive frames carrying my pack (which was bigger than they were) to the top of this island which rocketed vertically into the sky. But as they scampered up and down the stairs effortlessly, and as I plodded along with gasping effort at 12,000 feet above sea level, the idea started to appeal to me. I paused to rest every fifty meters or so, and after a grueling half hour hike straight up the seemingly-unending stairway to heaven, we arrived at our Lilliputian leader's pick, a ridge-top guesthouse with a view of both sides of the lake for 8 Bolivianos/night (about $1.35 per person).

After an enormous plate of rice and fresh lake trout, we took a short *siesta* in the sunshine (Pedro the Perpetually-Single snored), and I was slowly rolled back into consciousness by the haunting melodies of the *zampoña,* a traditional Andean panpipe made of two rows of reeds of various lengths. Pedro the Amazing was blowing softly into the pipes, creating the low hollow resonance that sounds like the wind in the Andes themselves. He rose, motioned for us to follow, and before I knew it, he was skipping up and down the hilly trails, holding steadily his tune on the pipes as he played and bounded, not once missing a nuance of circular breathing. Pedro the Single and I trotted after him, jumping off boulders, bouncing through fields, stumbling and sliding down slippery slopes, panting back up again, enamored at the constancy, the beauty, the joy, the fluidity of our leader. Even without hooves, Pedro was Pan to me…

As I uncontrollably barreled down the last steep hill, my cartoon legs running wildly in a blurred wheel of speed, I managed to stop just before running right into the lake. I stood hypnotized at my first close-up look at the amazing clarity of the water from this island shore. Pedro the Pied Piper stood not too far off, talking with a little boy (who I think was even smaller than the ones who had tried to carry our bags to the guesthouse), barefoot and shirtless in his tiny wet elastic-waisted shorts. Pedro had negotiated with the boy to take us in his father's rowboat across the water to a rock a few hundred meters offshore which peeked out a few feet above the waterline. As we piled into the humble nearly-waterlogged vessel whose paint had peeled away long ago, I watched that small child row, the lean muscle of his seven years straining at every stroke, and I wanted to reach out and hug him and tell him not to worry, I'd row us there. But he was a little man, much too soon maybe, but a little man none the less, and he had a quiet confidence that I dared not disrupt as he glided along silently through the water.

When we arrived at the rock, I followed Pedro the Elder to a set of small stones which were set there as a shrine to the gods. He had brought his own stone offering to make, and after he set it next to the others, we sat quietly for an hour or so dipping our feet into the sacred waters of Lake Titicaca, soft splashes against the boulder. I looked down inside her, deep deep into her clear waters. Gleaming silver stars twinkled amongst the greens and whites and blues. Something called to me from down there, the life in it all, and I wanted to jump in and dive down until my breath burned in my chest and see what presence was looking up from deep below. Another world, a lost city, a lost people, and I remembered the legend of a beautiful woman who lives under this water. Copacati, Incan lake goddess, is said to be "destructive," responsible for ruining countless lakeside villages when angered. Powerful women are often misunderstood. But in that moment, looking down into her sparkling clear deep realm, I felt her presence, whoever she was. And I believed.

And at the end of a day of exchanging stories of the past and of journeys yet to come, we ascended again the grand hills of Isla del Sol, quietly weaving through paths alongside children tending sheep and men pushing and pulling donkeys, as song flowed from Pedro's *zampoña* in even time. And from the tallest ridge, snowy mountains rose out of the clouds of Bolivia and glowed crimson, and the sun disappeared behind the shores of Peru as the first few lights came on in far away villages. And the island went quiet with nothing but the wind.

***

The next morning, I said goodbye to Pedro and Pedro and thanked them for their inspiration, their knowledge, their energy. Time warped in these places of magic and discovery, and after spending only 48 hours together, I was not surprised to feel I'd known them much longer. Over the last year I had better learned to live in the now, to be grateful for those whom I had met and learned from, and to ask for nothing more.

Years later Pedro the Elder came to me in a dream. He told me without speaking that he was there to be my spiritual guide, the song of his *zampoña* echoing through my subconscious caverns. When he stepped back, a long narrow stone path stood before me, winding its lonely way into a lush base of green hills, meandering amongst the thick trees. He just smiled at me. And I knew I would never feel lost again.

On the lazy Sunday when Pedro and Pedro left, the island slept as I ate a pile of eggs and fried potatoes and stirred two spoons of sugar into my coffee cup set on a green woven tablecloth. The day moved from cloudy to gloriously sunny to cloudy again as I climbed out along the ridge and sat in the gravel and wrote, surprised to see how much my new journal had filled in less than a month. I reread old entries and felt inspired, stronger, moved. And I looked up to see purple-black stormclouds sweeping in overhead. The lake had turned a midnight blue as the wind drove steadily at my cheeks. I looked up at that great big sky. At that great big world, above, below. Sky and earth and water. So big. It's all so big. And as I leaned against an ancient stone wall, atop a hill, atop a lake, atop the world, the bigness of it all brought tears to my eyes which blurred in the darkness and wind and cold. *How big was it?* The earth below my feet I'd only begun to know. *The Americas. Mountains and meadows, jungles and deserts. But what about above? What about below?* The water glistened and twinkled and winked at me in reply. There was so much. So much to explore. To discover. The world seemed to go on forever, and I wondered how long I could to chase it.

For the next few days, I enjoyed my own silence in the silence of the island. The hills were silent. The lake was silent. No waves. No lapping on the shore. No voices. The resounding sound of nothingness, of reverence in the home of the sun god in the birthplace of an ancient people. I watched mothers bend backs planting yucca in the fields while babies wiggled in the shawls tied across their shoulders. I ate stale bread on hillsides with sweeping views of crystal waters and barren land. Crisp air froze fingers, nose, toes. I tried to remember what the word Monday meant. I reveled to be in a place where water was sacred, life was tranquil, values and priorities straightforward. And I resented how the self-righteous could get off calling most of South America "backwards." *How some people's priorities had gotten so fucked up?*

***

One step, then another. The iciness took my breath away. Another step into the sacred lake. *A step to purify. A step to forgive. A step for strength* -- as Incas have for thousands of years.

My breath was short now. Another step. I splashed water onto my thighs, then my stomach, then my arms. Another step, deeper and deeper. Crystal clear down to my feet. Past the hairy green plants, into the soft white sand. Another step.

I looked up into the afternoon sun descending in the sky. I looked below at the purity, the depth, the immense presence of the water. I took a breath and then lost myself inside it all, coming up gasping, the coldness squeezing breath from my lungs. And then I looked at the sun god, and I prayed.

Give me strength, give me courage. Lead me on my journey. And again disappeared into the world below. Gasping. *Give me health and health to my family and friends.* Submerse. *Omniscient goddess of the lake, powerful sun god, watch over me on my journeys and help me to find my way.* Another breath and I was gone. When I emerged, my head ached from the cold. I felt nothing of my body. *Help me to find love.* Gasp. Shooting pains in my head. *Help me to be good to all those around me.* Again. *Bless all of your earth children with your wondrous powers.* And then I held my breath, dove beneath, and I swam. I felt the air constricting inside my frozen chest. Swirls of colors danced before my open eyes, and I felt weightless in another world. I wanted to stay -- in that beauty, in that silence, in that place where everything and nothing hurts. And when I surfaced, I looked up at the sun, and I sunk down into the water so that my eyes were just above the glinting surface of the lake that flowed endlessly to the horizon, and I felt a great pressure build up inside me and I was overcome with gratitude. Something there had penetrated deep within me, a sacred presence now living, just a little bit, there inside me. The power of the water, of the sun. They have always given me strength, something I could not explain, something I just felt. Feelings are undeniable. There is no need to justify. They just are. My skin burned in its thawing as I emerged from the water, and I sat on the stone beach and slowly bundled up in warm layers against the approaching nightfall.

***

The day before I left Isla del Sol, I hiked twelve kilometers up and down the steep island through ancient archways and amidst the ruins of stone labyrinths. *Chica fuerte* takes on the world. And on that night, I had returned somewhat late to the guesthouse to realize that the other three tourists who had been staying there were gone. With only one tourist left, the *dueña* decided to save money and not turn on the generator. And as I spent the night in complete darkness with only candles to light the kitchen, I was served *trucha* for dinner -- again -- lake trout that I just had a funny feeling about. It's not that it smelled bad. It's not that it looked suspicious. And yet I was unsurprised when within twenty minutes, I was overcome with my first violent bout of projectile vomiting. The nausea gnawed at me the entire night.

Now, seeing as how this night was also the *dueña's* husband's birthday, she left the premises after dinner to give him some space, and I was left alone with the "man of the house" and a dozen of his closest drunkest friends. The party got louder and louder, and I felt worse and worse, and soon enough, there were slobbering men full of Pisco running up and down the dark hallway yelling outside my room as they stumbled to and from their card game. I mustered up the little energy I had left and pushed the dresser *and* my bed up against the door as a blockade so no one would "mistakenly" come in to my room. And I spent the rest of the night staring at the ceiling, trying to disregard the stomach cramps, trying to lay as still as possible so as not to upset my fragile little system, and every half an hour or so, I would climb out the window and run to the outhouse to barf anew into the already-ripe non-flushing toilet.

I watched as the quiet dawn light peeked through my window and rolled over with a groan. The yelling had died down in the next room, and I moved the bed to crack the door and peek out. There was a man lying in the hallway snoring, a line of drool running from his mouth to his chin to a small puddle on his red shirt. Enough was enough. The thought of getting on a boat in that moment sent the nausea rushing back, but I had to get out of there. With surrender and humility, I walked next door to find a small child to carry my backpack down the enormous hill, down the golden stones of the Inca steps, down to the boat launch, on to the ferry. I thanked and paid the child (too much -- out of guilt and embarrassment), and as the boat started up billowing clouds of diesel fumes, I focused on the horizon and tried to ignore the verbose traveler sitting next to me.

When I arrived on solid ground again, I dragged my sad little body to the favorite gringo guesthouse of La Cúpula, and was given a single room with private bathroom (I thought it best). I slept from noon until 9am the next day, woke up, took a shower, then slept all that day, too. And when I finally got out of bed, I sat down to a bowl of muesli, papaya and banana at their vegetarian restaurant and felt a little piece of paradise slide in. And I knew that to fall from the hands of food-poisoning into the lap of vegetarian luxury, from a barricaded bedroom to cozy quarters and hot shower -- all within 24 hours -- these are the contrasts of life, and of travels.

THE INCA TRAIL

As the last light drained from the sky, the bus faithfully dropped me near Cusco's main square, and I made my way to a hostel that another traveler had recommended. A little more than I'd usually spend, but I was exhausted, freezing, and ready for a room with a heater. My body ached from an oncoming cold -- my neck, shoulders, and back having tensed against every pothole as I bounced from seat to roof and back again on the springy bench of the back row. Fighting to keep my eyes open, my throat on fire, I dropped into bed with a long sigh.

The next day I began wandering the streets of the remarkable city. *How did a thousand years of indigenous history meld with Spanish tyranny and international tourist comforts in such a neat unconflicted package?* All were evident, yet none detracted from one another. The graffiti of the ages. Signature stonework of Inca walls stands unassumingly on corners and side-streets as it has for centuries through earthquakes and invasions, careful assemblies of perfectly-cut rocks without mortar. Cusco's rainbow flag flies high above the Plaza de Armas, a square of shiny emerald grass flanked by a Spanish cathedral and an Irish pub. I knew this was somewhere I wanted to stay. And so for the next three months it became home while I half-heartedly taught English and whole-heartedly enjoyed the endless layers of wonder around me.

Cusco, once the foremost city of the Inca empire, was founded by Manco Capac in his quest to find *the naval of the earth*, literally *qosq'o*, in the 12th century. The city was built to celebrate the earth and its animal symbol, the puma, and literally took its shape. Saqusayhuamán, the religious center of Cusco, was the puma's head. Its heart was the main square, and its tail was the main road of Avenida del Sol which led to Koricancha, the Temple of the Sun which was once covered in sheets of gold.

Manco Capac was the child of the Sun God, Inti, and the Goddess of the Moon and Protector of Women whose name was Mama Quilla. Inca creation myth believes that a fox fell in love with Mama Quilla, and when he rose into the sky, she squeezed him so hard against her that he made the dark spots on the moon. The moon goddess also had her own temple in Cusco, once featuring hundreds of handmaidens and a wall-sized disc made entirely of silver.

Cusco and its surrounding valleys are a kaleidoscope of Inca history, culture and architecture. When Pizarro and the Spaniards invaded the city in the 1500s, not only did they raid the Inca's gold and desecrate their temples, but they built their own churches right on top of Inca sacred places in an effort to eradicate traditional beliefs and impose Catholicism. Stones were taken directly from the temple of Saqusayhuamán to construct the cathedral in the center square. However some of the carved stone blocks were so big (15 feet high and weighing 300 tons) that the Spaniards could not figure out how to move them; surely the Incas wouldn't tell. So the biggest rocks stayed where they were, and twenty percent of the original structure of Saqusayhuamán remains in its original location just outside the city.

At nearby Chinchero, the Spaniards tried the same thing, but the earth soon sang poetic justice. When the *conquistadores* built a church atop the temple there, it stood for a hundred years until a great earthquake caused the new construction to crumble away. When the church tumbled down, it revealed the still-standing far-superior Inca structure standing resiliently beneath it. Today the temple remains in that state, modernism crumbling under the traditions of the ancient.

Symbols of Inca life mirrored the world around them, and every detail had meaning. Temples built to worship the sun were constructed in semi-circles to represent its physical shape. The dead were buried in the fetal position and tucked into holes in the sides of mountains so they could return to the sky and be reborn. I began wearing an Andean Cross around my neck, to remind me of the Inca's important principles. Four equal sides of the amulet represented north, south, east and west. Three additional cuts in each of the four sides also had meaning. For example, one side symbolized the condor (life above), the puma (life on earth), and the snake (life below), as well as the links between the worlds. Another side represented *mita* (work for self), *minka* (work for others), and *ayni* (reciprocal work). A line stretching vertically represented the line from sky to earth, a male energy. And a horizontal line stretching across it represented a line across the earth, the female energy of Pachamama, the Earth Goddess.

These were people who lived in harmony and respect with the earth. I wondered if they might offer any insight to modern "humanity." But despite my immersion in the city and its founding culture, I could not shake the nervous anticipation gnawing lightly in the background. *Amy, do what you came to do...*

Machu Picchu was the only place in South America that I had heard of before I'd left California. Even then, the two words offered only a vague impression, a magical name of mist and mystery, a lost city shimmering in a valley of secrets. And I wanted to see it.

And the only way (in my stubborn mind) for me to get there was to do as the ancients had done, follow their inlaid stone paths, climb the same hills. Four days of hiking the Inca Trail. And it was daunting...

I had made the mistake of speaking to other travelers recently returned from the excursion, and I was intimidated by how difficult they said it was. These were tough-looking travelers. They had dirty backpacks. Stubble. Muscles. Goretex. They must be experienced in these things.

And I was a very good excuse-maker; excuses are reliable failure-shields. I still resisted doing things that were hard. *But this was ridiculous. Look where I was. What I had already done.*

Finally one morning I awoke feeling surprisingly settled. Alone, quiet, confident, free. And then I knew... I was ready.

***

What do you think about when you're climbing Dead Woman's Pass? *Man, my legs are burning...* Yes, there's that. But I was surprised that more often my thoughts began with "I am grateful..." *I am grateful I've climbed trails like this before. I am grateful my shoes fit. I am grateful a porter is carrying my tent and food. I am grateful I am not in pain. I am grateful I know to choose the path of least resistance. I am grateful I know that tiny step by tiny step, my legs are still moving forward, uphill. I am grateful I feel stronger than ever. I am grateful that I am doing the one thing I was sure I wanted to do here -- to climb to Machu Picchu.*

It was hard to believe I was actually there doing it, hard to believe how the mountains seemed to rise up straight into the sky, how the lemon-colored wildflowers glowed against a brilliant blue above, how the little green leaves hung from stems so fine they looked like they were suspended in mid-air. My mind whirled back over the first two days of the hike: The roar of the creek while I slept curled up in a warm dry tent. The clouds and mist covering the valleys. Dipping my hands into the clear freezing stream to wash the black dirt from under my nails. Walking the same ancient Inca steps that had survived over five hundred years of people trekking upon them from the faithful, to the explorers, to the tourists. As I climbed, my mind rested, meditating. And my body moved quite separately, in even steady motion.

I was actually surprised when I reached the top of Dead Woman's Pass (named not because women can't climb it, but because ancient skeletons of Inca women were found there). Our guide had said that hikers normally take four hours from the morning's campsite to reach the top of this steepest and most-difficult pass on the Inca trail. It was hard at first. My legs burned but did not shake. I took the baby steps I knew worked for me and stopped to rest with everyone else. But I knew it was too much resting time. They stopped every five or ten minutes. Many had recently arrived to the Andean high altitudes via international flight, but I had the advantage of becoming acclimated gradually over land. After an hour and a half, I decided I could walk as slowly as I wanted, but I would rest less often. I knew my pace. For me it was more tiring to start over again with a slow heart rate after a rest than to just keep moving, however slowly. The porters who carried fifty kilos on their backs passed me by, sweating but not missing a step in their rubber-tire sandals. I watched them pass the two-meter-tall Norwegian hulks. I watched them pass the macho Australian guys. And I just kept on going, at *my* pace, like a little mountain goat, not looking down and only occasionally looking up. I was surprised to find that people started pacing themselves off of me -- me, the girl who almost fell off Volcán Villarica not so many months ago. I was amazed. Encouraged. My legs felt hard and strong as they flexed. I took tiny steps. No pride. No racing. Just steps. I knew all I had to do was keep going and eventually I'd get there. There's no rush; you get over one mountain pass and there's another, as in life, but you enjoy the walk. I arrived at the top with a very red face in only 2 ½ hours, surprised to already be there, surprised the journey had ended so soon, and strangely, almost disappointed that there wasn't more to climb.

The next morning's route began with a rambling ascent to a small village atop a pass where you could see both sides of the world. Green valleys plummeted, and gray clouds drifted in. A climb through the high jungle of Peru, the crumbles of Inca stonework dotted the hillsides, and vines of violets draped the path. But as we descended, rains moved in, and my mood turned. After days of pounding steep ups-and-downs upon the unyielding stones, my knee began to ache, and I cursed every step of the three thousand I now descended. Some steps were six inches high, some were three feet. And you never knew which was coming next. *Fuck. Step. Fuck. Step. I am grateful for... I am grateful for... I am grateful for these coca leaves the guide has given me.* Chew, chew, chew... *Is my mouth* supposed *to fall asleep?*

As the rain dripped off my hood onto my chilled face, I finally arrived at the bunkhouse lodge where we'd spend the night (a break from the tents we'd been camping in). The next morning we would head out at first light to Manchu Picchu hours before the trainloads of visitors from Cusco would arrive. I drank coca tea to warm up and had a glorious shower. Freshly-soaped and relaxed, I splurged on a beer and dazedly engaged in conversation with fellow travelers sitting at a long table, carbonation tickling my throat, anticipation for the morning bubbling inside me.

At 4 a.m. the fog clung firmly to the damp ground, and the low sun burned a dull yellow. Two final hours of hiking -- running -- and I had arrived. The Gate of the Sun. I stood atop the last hillside pass inside this single trapezoidal doorway, its archaic stone blocks fitted together as flawlessly as a jigsaw. There I looked down into the deep valley at the fine work of one of the world's most advanced civilizations, stretching across cushiony green meadows to rest at the base of the soaring peak of Huayna Picchu, joining this world to the one above. The Lost City of the Children of the Sun. Machu Picchu.

More marvelous, more mystical than any photos could convey, it stood silent and alone, nestled in deep jungle surrounded by sheer cliffs to guard its secrets. The reason Machu Picchu was built is still unknown. But that morning, as ghosts rose up from inside its crumbling stone walls, from the ruins of soaring towers and ancient places of sacrifice, there was not a living soul to obscure its majesty. I smiled with satisfaction and complete exhaustion.

I realized now that these last four days of hiking, the last year and a half of travel, had not been about getting here. It had been about opening my eyes. It had been about learning, and moving, and observing, and listening. About climbing, and striving, and straining, and breathing. It had been about finding out -- and believing -- that I am more powerful than I ever could have imagined.

"A cloud does not know why it moves in just such a direction and at such a speed. It feels an impulsion... this is the place to go now. But the sky knows the reasons and the patterns behind all clouds, and you will know, too, when you lift yourself high enough to see beyond horizons." Illusions: Adventures of a Reluctant Messiah, by Richard Bach

***

That evening I returned to Cusco with my hiking group, my mind replaying images of seventeen-degree angles and trapezoidal windows, of sundials and princess towers. And as I wobbled out of the minibus onto the curb, guess who was standing just inches from my dazed face but Stefanie and Caroline, the two Canadian girls with whom I had spent my birthday in Salvador, Brazil! We stared at each other, each wordless and a bit stunned. As we began to catch up, I was thrilled to discover that Stefanie and Caroline both planned to stay in Cusco until after the New Year's Millennium celebration, and they, too, were looking for a long-term place to stay. We decided to keep in touch over the next few days as we each searched for our new home.

The next day I met *Huevo*. His name was actually David, but he had been called *"Huevo de San Blas"* since his round, egg-shaped adolescence. I wandered up to San Blas square to treat myself to a restaurant that Simon had recommended, one that was popular among Brits. It was owned by an English woman named Tanya and her Peruvian boyfriend, and featured a fusion menu of creamy Indian curries, English roasts and local specialties. When I arrived at the address, there was no sign on the door. It looked closed, but I knocked anyway.

"Are they open?" I asked aloud, but mostly to myself.

A worker came to the door and called into the living room, "Are we open?"

A mischievous face shot around the corner, looked me up and down lasciviously, smiled and said, "Oh yes, we're open. Come in."

Quirky and fascinating with an overstated air of flirtation, Huevo made me feel right at home. I sat down and chatted as he channel-surfed in the restaurant's living room and nursed his hangover with *papaya con leche*. Huevo was thin (having left his egg-shape behind), and he barely scraped five-feet tall, including his wild head of curly hair. He was magnetic.

Huevo was one of the first Peruvians I had met who had traveled the world. Most recently: Ecuador. His favorite: Columbia. He was a chef and had lived in London for a few years where he had met Tanya. They had come back together to Cusco, his hometown, and opened the restaurant. On that particular afternoon, Huevo made me a plate of tropical curry. It was the first of many amazing dishes to come.

HUEVO'S RECIPE FOR TROPICAL CHICKEN CURRY

At high heat, melt lots of butter in a pan. Add chopped onions. Brown white-meat chicken pieces (cut to medium size) and cook.

When fully cooked, add fruits such as banana, peaches, strawberries (all cut bigger than bite size).

Stir and add a few tablespoons of curry powder. Cook, then reduce heat and add evaporated milk. Cook until it thickens.

Lay out on a plate with rice, molded into the shape of a little mountain. Garnish sides of the plate with freshly chopped basil or parsley.

***

A few days later I was walking with Stephanie and Caroline when I saw Huevo again. He was making general mischief in the main square, accompanied by Tanya and her new two-month old sheepdog puppy. When Huevo spotted me, he reached for me in an exaggerated embrace, looked me up and down again, and said, *"Me gusta, pero un poco grande." I like, but a little big... Wink, wink, smile,* as he buried his head in my chest, standing nearly a head shorter than me.

As I squirmed away, he reached down to pet the dog and asked me what I was up to. When I told him we were looking for an apartment, he jumped up and hugged me again. He and Tanya rented a duplex, but their downstairs subleters had recently moved out. They were looking to sublet the three-bedroom bottom-floor for just two months, the remainder of the lease, and exactly the amount of time we were looking to stay. Stef, Caroline and I mentally divided the rent by three, and my share came out to $40 a month.

And that is how I came to live at 369 Tanda Pata Street.

CHRISTMAS IN CUSCO

Welcome to our humble abode on 369 Tanda Pata Street. There is no kitchen, there is no furniture. There is no water -- most of the time. I sleep on an exercise mat on loan from Tanya. We acquired our unique home furnishings at the central market: sugar sacks for wall decorations, empty apple crates to hold our clothes, assorted medication boxes for our assorted illnesses. Our walls are painted a rainbow of blaring colors: grape, orange and peach.

Caroline laid down on the floor and asked, "Is that wall crooked or am I high?"

Actually Caroline, that wall is crooked... But I'm going to go with "Both."

The water turns off at 6 or 9 or 12 or 3. Then we can't flush, and the monster awakens in the pipes. When there *is* toilet paper, please place the used squares in the overflowing bag to your right. Stefanie reaches to flush. *Dink. Dink. Damn. It's after 11 p.m. But wait! Sometimes there's a little water hiding in the hot water tank to aid in an emergency flush.* She crawls onto the shower ledge, trying to avoid being molested by the moldy shower curtain that never dries, and dips a cup into the tank. A good-enough flush. She then reaches for the soap, having quickly forgotten there's no water.

At 7 a.m. we are blessed with the return of our water. We wake up early because it takes the tank about an hour to heat its five-gallon capacity. Turn on the tap. *Boom! Boom! Boom! Are those fireworks or is it the toilet?* The pipes grumble and roar. I get into the shower which spits at me like a llama. *Hot. Hot. Hot. Scalding. Cold. Hot. Cold. Cold. Hot.* It's been two minutes. I get out before it turns cold again.

Dinnertime at Tanda Pata is cooked over Stefanie's single-burner trekking stove which we set up on our hardwood floors. Put in your fuel. Balance the cooking pot on rocks. And you've got a nearly-boiling cup of water in under two hours. Making soup takes commitment. But eating out was too risky…

***

Strange things happened to my body in Cusco. Pain, cramps, bloating the size of an 8 ½ month babybelly, and deadly gas. It would build up inside and beg you to release it but just wouldn't let you. *Pop me with a pin… Anything!* Since these intestinal issues were shared by all members of the household, there was a don't-hold-back rule. Had Tanya and Huevo sublet to a whoopee cushion factory?

But far worse than the gas was the Fear. The Fear of Farting. If you were lucky enough to release your aching bellybloat, sometimes what came out was massive volumes of air and some relief, but sometimes what came out was explosive diarrhea. And you never knew which it was going to be. How unfortunate. It made it difficult to enjoy yourself around town.

We tried eating less. It didn't help. We tried eating more. Our pants got too small, and we had to buy new ones at the market. At first we just figured the food wasn't agreeing with us and started cooking at home on the camp stove, but eventually I got so nauseous I couldn't even sleep. And one day, something very strange happened (yes, even stranger). The egg burps arrived. I started burping sulfur.

And then a tiny light went on in the back of my mind. I'd once met a traveler on the road who was talking about the "telltale sign of the sulfur burps." *What illness had he been talking about? There were so many, after all.*

When Tanya got home from work, I rushed up to talk to her. She didn't even let me finish. "It's giardia!" she proclaimed.

I then realized that the tiny pills sold locally claiming to "purify" water on tourist treks did not kill giardia, a fecal bacteria that infects water or raw food and can be passed on by people and animals. I had used those magic pills on the Inca Trail, and my mind rewound to the stagnant green scummy pond where I had gathered my drinking water and dropped in those magic pills on day three.

All of 369 Tanda Pata piled into a taxi, went to a 24-hour pharmacy, and each bought the one-dose cure (with which I became very familiar; I got giardia twice more before the year was over). And when I woke up the next morning, I felt like a new woman. And the only thing left groaning in the bathroom was the pipes.

***

The next day was the winter solstice and the last full moon of the millennium. The moon was closer to the earth than it had been in 133 years and closer than it would be for another hundred. I walked through the plaza and was bombarded by the usual scene of little boys selling postcards. *Buy my postcards. Give me money.* Somehow the impact of heart-wrenching scenes had dissipated with months of repetition. But on that day, two little boys came up and asked me for food, not money. I invited them to a nearby restaurant with a set lunch for three sols, and as they shared one gigantic meal, they laughed and jabbered and goofed as little boys universally do. I talked to them about their families, about why they weren't in school (their families couldn't pay for it), and my heart felt heavy even though I chattered and laughed along with them.

Then I walked down the block and got the worst haircut of my life. The funny part was (yeah, *real* funny) that I went to get a haircut because I was trying to get it "fixed" from the last haircut I'd gotten a few days before, the one which had *previously* held the title of the-worst-haircut-of-my-life. But the new one took the cake. The result was a puffmop perched atop my head like a blond Afro of disco days gone by.

It had all started a few days before when I had walked in for a trim and had had a bad feeling from the start. I had tried to peek into the salon without being seen to scope the place out, but the hairdresser had spotted me immediately, and she was so nice that I had to go in. *Just a trim. What could go wrong?* The hairdresser sported big bangs that were sprayed up to eight inches tall that reminded me of my 10th grade class picture. She took me to the back of the shop and washed my head in a bucket with a cup. The haircut wasn't horrible, but it was uneven, the right side being higher than the left by about two inches. And after a few days of walking around with my head cocked, I asked Tanya for a recommendation and went to go get it fixed.

This time the salon was beautiful with white-and-black checked floors and the smell of professional products. Behind the receptionist's desk, stylists flitted about and an over-animated effeminate man with a lisp asked if he could help me. *Good sign.*

My hairdresser was a beautiful young woman with caramel skin and gorgeous shiny hair that cascaded down her back, not a split-end in sight. I explained what I wanted in my quite-good Spanish.

Just even it up. Don't cut the front because it's already too short.

She said, *"No problema,"* a response that has forever since struck fear into my heart.

She began cutting, scissors twirling skillfully in the air, and I watched her carefully, very carefully, as she cut the back. She flipped and snipped and combed with flair, and with her contagious confidence, I began to relax.

She showed me the back in a hand mirror, and I was impressed. Sassy. She mentioned that the front was now too long (it sat about half an inch below the rest of the hair, which fell just below my jawline), and so she asked me if she could cut it. Lulled into a false sense of security by her performance thus far, I said OK. And I will never forget the next moment. She combed up into the air the front left quadrant of my hair and *Snip!* Just above the eyebrow. She held up a clump six-inches long in her left hand.

"Ahhhhhhhh! WHAT are you doing?!!" I gasped.

She looked surprised. "Now it's just like the picture," she fumbled.

"WHAT picture?!"

"This one," she said. And she showed me a glossy photo ripped out of a magazine of a girl with thin beautiful sleek straight hair in a fashionably-short shaggy do.

"I didn't choose that picture," I breathed heavily, but the damage was done.

Most Andean Peruvians have gorgeous slick bone-straight hair, grandfathered down from their indigenous roots, but I, my friend, do not. I have kinky, fuzzy, curly underneath, wavy on the top, the-shorter-you-cut-it-the-bigger-it-gets hair. And this was *not* the haircut for me. After securing my permission, she cautiously cut the right side to match, and thus I learned two very important lessons that I was reminded of every time I looked in the mirror for the next six months. 1) Never let your guard down, and 2) A $1.30 haircut is not a deal.

But I didn't cry. I didn't really want to. I swore a lot. But I didn't cry. And when I got home, Stef's mouth dropped, then she laughed 'til the tears came, then she said, "Let's go to the market. They have scarves there. And barrettes. We'll need lots of barrettes." And then she took me for chocolate fudge cake.

***

On Christmas Eve day, I wandered around the seasonal market in the main square, listening to vendors announcing last-minute deals from slippers to jewelry to plastic baby Jesuses *"Dos por uno!"* Children pled their cases to their parents why they NEEDED the blonde doll that moves her arms, why they just couldn't live without a stuffed Garfield. Along Avenida del Sol teenage girls listened to walkmans, women sat on the curb knitting *gorros*, and restaurant window-fronts featured furry guinea pigs turning on a fiery rotisserie, a local delicacy.

And then it was Christmas. I woke up early and lay on my exercise mat thinking about last Christmas at Daisy's house, how we'd lounged around in our pajamas eating warm tamales and laughing. I could see my breath inside the house on Tanda Pata Street. I thought about my family and the present-opening pancaking traditions we'd ritualized since we were children.

I dressed in my warmest llama llana sweater and made my way alone down the deserted winding streets to Plaza de Armas to stake out my place. Christmas Mass in Cusco on the steps of a five-hundred-year-old cathedral just days before the turn of the millennium. When I reached the bottom of the hill and turned the corner, I drew in my breath at the startling transformation of the main square.

Campesinos from hundreds of villages in the surrounding valleys filled Plaza de Armas like one giant organism made of thousands of woven-wool rainbows. Each man, woman and child dressed in traditional Christmas shawls and ponchos, each unique in color, pattern and image designating the person's village. They had poured into town on Christmas Eve Day to sell and buy goods, and then spent the night sleeping in the streets, families huddled together under layers of blankets.

I entered the sea of color, swimming through the masses of anticipatory participants, finding a place near the back, towards the center, gazing easily above the thousands of heads of slick black hair. All eyes focused on the cathedral steps, and finally the Archbishop rose slowly from his seat and swished across the red-carpeted stage. Draped in white robes, the tiny man moved slowly, deliberately, toward the microphone. His small chest supported a massive golden cross, and a three-foot-tall pointed gold hat perched atop his head despite the constant chill of the wind. He began to speak in the long drawn-out tones which sounded like so many other Catholic priests, universally cut from the same good cloth, transcending language. His audience absorbed his every word, his every gesture, heads nodding solemnly, an occasional "amen" reverberating through the crowd. The Archbishop droned on for nearly two hours when at last the doors of the cathedral behind him flew open. And out came, seemingly on its own, a 15-foot tall ivory statue of Jesus Christ, draped in gold and standing atop a solid silver pedestal. El Señor de Los Temblores, the Lord of Earthquakes. In 1650, the people of Cusco held a vigil during one of the biggest earthquakes in history until he made the earth stop shaking. And because centuries of faithful parishioners have lit prayer candles beneath this powerful icon, El Señor de Los Temblores is now stained black from their smoke.

Atop his grand pedestal, atop the cathedral stairs, high above the thousands of tiny humans gathered in the masses below, the giant statue really did look like he was descending from heaven. He paused for a moment, and then he began to "dance." Aided by the twenty men who carried him, the statue of Christ "danced" down the steps of the cathedral. "Danced" out into the square. "Danced" through the parting sea of rainbows as the procession ended just as the first raindrops of the daily downpour started to fall.

***

Weeks later, I stood looking out from the picture window in Stephanie's room down into the sparkling city lights of the ancient valley below. The moon was beginning its long arc across the night sky, waning into its last quarter, and I thought of Mama Quilla, beautiful moon goddess who cried silver tears. Incas feared lunar eclipses because they believed that Mama Quilla was in danger, being attacked by an animal. They would throw weapons into the air and gesture fiercely to defend her since if the animal achieved its aim, the world would be left in darkness forever.

I watched her now, Mama Quilla, as she cycled toward empty black, and I got that tight feeling inside my chest. I had been stagnant too long. Life felt far away. I wanted to touch it again. The magic, the mystery, the road to the silvery mother moon.

And I knew it was time to go.

And the next morning, I was on the first bus leaving for it-didn't-matter-where.

LAST QUARTER...

"I believe that we are always attracted to what we need most, an instinct leading us toward the persons who open new vistas in our lives and fill them with new knowledge." Helene Iswalski

The Asshole had a way of attracting drama. Death and destruction followed him like his muse. And Playa Grande, which until his arrival had percolated with Eden, suddenly found itself in the throes of one disaster after another.

One Sunday morning, the Asshole and I were dozing dreamily in the Rancho wrapped in salty circles of each other's sweat when Carmen's desperate cries from downstairs abruptly awakened us.

"Ben, Ben, Get up!" she shrieked in Spanish. "Louis needs you. There's a robbery. Hurry!"

And then her footsteps scuttled away, dress shoes shuffling quickly across the polished cement floor below.

The Asshole looked up at me groggily, eyes still swollen with last night's tequila.

"What time is it? What did she say?"

Against all odds, he still managed to have learned no Spanish. As I explained, his expectant face widened in anticipation, his internal vacuum for thrill-seeking sensing an upcoming fix. He grabbed his pants, tripped over them twice on his way to the door, and ran down the rickety stairs.

I got up and walked toward the dirt parking lot to find Louis whispering to Ben in hushed conspiratorial tones.

"Don't go out there. They might have guns."

Louis always defaulted to the theatrical. I guess that's why the Asshole worshiped him. Louis told me to go up to the reception desk and call the police.

"And tell them to set up a roadblock!"

In Playa Grande, we had to get a head-start on crime since there were no police in town and since response time from the nearest station was approximately two hours. Out here, it was the Ole' West as best it could be found in the turn of the twenty-first century. The citizens were the vigilantes. Tie-'em-up and string-'em-up as you see fit. In the meantime, Louis grabbed the Asshole and told him to follow close behind him as they snuck out of sight around the back of the hotel.

Costa Rica is a great country, a phenomenal country. I had always felt safe there. I didn't worry about being held up in the street or having my money snatched at knifepoint. But Costa Rica had an endemic problem: Car burglary. Not robbery. Burglary. And they didn't even take the car. They just took what was in it. *Everything* that was in it. *Every* time.

Tourists liked the beaches so thieves liked the beaches. Some dim-witted gringo would inevitably leave his camera on the passenger's seat and jump out of his rented 4x4 to check the surf, and in forty seconds flat all his stuff would be gone. These thieves were amazing. They'd get what was in the car. They'd get what was in the trunk. It didn't matter if the car was locked. Sometimes they'd break the window. Sometimes they wouldn't. Their schemes were flawless, and *everyone* was involved... Even the rental car companies supplied keys to the thieves who paid well enough. A gas station attendant at a busy crossroads might casually ask a tourist, "So where are you headed?" And the happy honeymooners would tell him, and he would call ahead to his buddy, and by the time the tourists rolled up to their destination and got out of the car to check into their hotel, FLASH -- everything was gone.

Earlier in the season, I made a hand-painted sign from a piece of driftwood warning everyone about the problem and not to leave anything in their cars. I nailed it to the front fence post at the entrance to the beach, and the damn robbers stole my sign.

So weekend after weekend, people would climb the stairs to the lone beach hotel where I worked, and vent and cry and scream about their lost passports and their lost video-cameras and their lost suitcases and their lost I-love-Costa-Rica T-shirt for Grandma. And Louis was getting tired of it. Especially when the thieves were stealing out of *his* client's cars.

Louis was always watching. As a veteran insomniac, he used to say things to me like, "If you ever feel like something's wrong, just call me. Even in the middle of the night. You won't wake me up."

And in this particular year when the thieving was raging out of control, you could find him in the pre-dawn hours, sitting in dining room in the dark like a ghost with a cup of coffee, looking out onto the beach, or into the parking lot, or into people's uncurtained windows... He was *always* watching.

And on this particular morning, he had spotted two rough-looking guys in their late-twenties, complete with shifty eyes and menacing looks, breaking into a car parked outside the hotel's walled lot. And Louis had gotten it in his head that enough was enough. But what happened next shocked us all.

The usual car thieves were from towns just outside of Playa Grande. They were generally harmless and often dumped the stuff they didn't want along their escape route. Considerate, really. It wouldn't be unusual to find some poor soul's passport or discarded backpack lying a few miles up the road only an hour after a burglary. And although these thieves were virtually invisible in eluding the authorities, they certainly had not posed a threat to anyone's personal safety.

But on this particular morning, the thieves were different. On this particular morning, the thieves were the *chapolinos*. The mob from San Jose. The real bad asses. The gangsters. Professionals. And unlike most of the petty thieves in Costa Rica, they were unafraid and undeterred. And they carried guns. I had never seen them before, but looking back, it doesn't surprise me that they materialized shortly after the Asshole did. Neither he nor Louis knew who they were up against when they began the sneak-attack that morning, but Louis is a very intuitive man, and he is nearly always cautious -- unless, that is, he's in a reckless mood...

And so from my bird's eye view at the second story reception desk, I watched Louis and the Asshole slowly creep up on the *chapolinos*. One guy was sitting in the get-away car with it idling, waiting for his friend to snatch up the goods and make an easy early-morning exit. But the driver spotted Louis and the Asshole as they came sneaking in a low crouch around the corner. The robber shouted to his buddy, turned the wheel of the getaway car, and threw it into reverse. Gears grinding, tires spinning, gravel spraying, he barreled, backwards, aiming straight at them -- and smiling.

Louis dodged to his right out of the way while managing to push the Asshole to safety behind a cement pillar. Skidding to a stop, the driver jumped out of his vehicle, and I watched as he and Louis met eyes. And from there, it all happened in slow motion. The *chapolino* lowered his gun and pointed it at Louis who stood not thirty meters away. They looked at each other, eyes locked in eternity, and then the *chapolino* made one deliberate motion. He squeezed the trigger. POP! The sound echoed off the perimeter wall. POP, POP! Louis, then in his mid-fifties, moved like a warrior. Without effort and with complete disregard for the known space-time continuum, he seemed to levitate into the air, dodging and moving and making his way behind the shelter of a nearby parked car. And somehow, he dodged three bullets.

The *chapolino* did not hesitate. He jumped back into the car, his buddy anxiously yelling from the passenger's seat, and they tore down the dirt road. My hands shaking and heart pumping, I scrambled to make a second phone call to the police to hurry and block the only road that headed out of town.

As the robbers' car disappeared in a cloud of dust, Louis sprinted up the stairs, still screaming venomous threats at the subject speeding into the distance. And when he got to the top of the staircase, out of breath, his face flushed to a bougainvillea-fushia with minuscule beads of sweat glistening from every pore, he looked at me square in the face, dead-pan, and said, "I swear that gave me a hard-on."

***

A few weeks later, on a Wednesday afternoon in the late dry season, we pulled a drowned woman from the ocean. From the same ocean I surfed in every day, from the same ocean I gazed across every sunset. Right in front of the hotel, in my refuge of Playa Grande.

The many faces of the ocean continued to frighten me -- power, mystery, breadth. One moment giving energy and beauty, the next annihilating mere humans. Shiva Creator, giver of life. Shiva Destroyer, taker of life. Mama's warm womb, Mama's strong hand.

I had been upstairs in the restaurant working on email reservations when I noticed clients starting to move toward the windows and look out toward the thundering sea. A low murmur began and soon someone walked calmly up the stairs and announced, *"There's a dead body in the break."* The Asshole and some hotel guests went down to the beach, and the *guilas* came out from the kitchen and gathered around upstairs. I finished the work I was doing on the computer, content not to see a dead body, but when the buzz in the dining room didn't quiet, I eventually walked downstairs to see what was going on.

A crowd had gathered on the beach. I couldn't see her at first, and then I spotted her body floating over the top of a huge wave. Shock. I didn't feel panic, but a deep fear. Fear of the ocean. A man next to me said they were trying to bring her back to shore, but it seemed like no one was hurrying. These were not the actions of a crowd trying to save the life of a drowning woman. These were the actions of people standing by to see a dead body dragged out of the sea. No one ran. No one screamed. Everyone moved very very slowly.

Suddenly someone shouted loudly, "We need a surfboard!" The words had such sudden urgency that for the first time it hit me that this woman may be able to be saved. The Asshole, in full dramatic hero form, took off running back toward the hotel for a board. It had been over five minutes since I had first heard about the incident. Most people acted like it was too late, and I just stood there, paralyzed, feeling sick, watching her pass over the top of another wave. Everything happened so slowly.

The waves had been enormous for days, a huge swell in from Japan had made the waves so big they were unrideable; the Playa Grande break just could not hold the size. The ocean snarled and gnashed its teeth and bit at your legs if you entered so much as up to your calves. It was hungry, and it pulled in anyone willing to approach it. I had nearly drowned myself, right there, a few days before. When Louis had seen my carrying my board toward the break, he had said simply "It's big. Don't get hurt." I should have noticed that he wasn't getting in the water. It was only a few minutes before a monster set came in from the outside, sucking up on the outside rock pile. I paddled madly for the outside, scratching for the horizon, but there was no way I would beat it. It exploded ten meters in front of me and I dove for the bottom, hoping it would wash over me. But it grabbed me, tossed me and pounded me with its fists and held me down. I scrambled wildly for the surface as my lungs began to burn with the need for breath and instead -- BAM! -- I hit the bottom. I was completely disoriented and had no idea which way was up. After what seemed like forever the wave let go, and I popped up, only to see another giant wall of water headed straight for me. I took another breath and dove down.

Wave after wave after wave broke on top of me, and I felt trapped. I couldn't swim out past it. I couldn't swim in to shore. It just sucked and pulled and sucked and pulled me back into the impact zone as I dove deeply under each successive blast. Each wave held me down like a weight pressing on my body, only to toss me up to the surface just in time to gasp and be buried once again. As the sixth enormous wave of the set held me firmly in an eternity of sand-swirled darkness, I wondered how many more waves I could take. And I actually asked myself, "Am I going to die?"

Strangely, my acceptance of this possibility relaxed me. I felt a relief that I didn't have keep fighting, that at some point, I might just have to let go. As I popped up again, my lungs burning from the salt water, the waves slowed for a brief moment, and I paddled furiously toward shore and dragged my body up the sand, breathless, every muscle trembling.

I had almost died, twenty meters from shore, on a crowded beach, at my new home, at sunset. *How could such a familiar place transform into such a merciless carnivore?* Since then, I had not been in the water. I had been too scared. Wary. Aware -- of the ocean's power.

And not more than a few days later, as the dry season rolled toward rains, in the ocean I knew so well, two 14-year old boys on boogie boards pulled a woman's body from the sea. Her eyes were rolled back in her head and her nose and mouth oozed white foam. It was the first dead body I'd ever seen. There was a long pause. Then two people started CPR. It went on for about two minutes, and when it stopped, a man burst out into screams of anguish. Two tiny children looked up expectantly at their father, then in horror they began to wail. I stood back from the crowd, feeling guilty for not helping, feeling as if I shouldn't even be there in that intimate moment of goodbyes. The crowd had accepted long ago that this woman was dead, and no one, including me, had done anything to help. I had been afraid. Afraid to jump into the waters that had just killed someone. Afraid to take charge. Afraid to do something wrong. So I had just watched. And accepted. *Did this woman have to die?* If only people -- we -- I -- had reacted faster. Reacted at all...

The Asshole walked away from the crowd and wandered back a few minutes later with a cigarette in his trembling hand. I wiped away something on his forehead, white and slimy. When I touched it, I realized it was the foam that had come out of this woman's mouth when he had helped to turn her over.

It is hard for me to understand the mystery of death. Who it takes. Why. Our universal vulnerability. Every day. You could be with your family having a picnic at the beach, and a few hours later, you could be going home without your wife, without your mother. Sudden. Unreal. And you spend the rest of your life thinking about her. Missing her. Wondering why. We all have a *time*, a magic invisible clock that ticks down inside our bodies. And with all the technology we have, we can heal diseases, send people to the moon, travel anywhere in the world at unimaginable speed, but we just can't know how long we get here. And all of a sudden, one day, your clock stops ticking and it's all over.

And on the day that woman drowned, she engraved a message on my heart. *Live every moment.* And after two hours of baking in the midday sun, the police arrived and dragged her body to higher ground, above the tide line where the fine white sand meets the coiling vines of the dry jungle, and put a sheet over her, and then they took her away...

***

The watercolor days ran on, dripping down the pages of my imagination as sunrises and sunsets melted together, growing and gaining speed as they rolled downhill. I practiced intensely the discipline of living in the moment and began to accept that love doesn't necessarily have to be forever, and that opening yourself up to new experiences is almost always painful and almost always necessary if one is to shed the layers of skin that have grown too tight.

I began to read words that reassured me of the importance of life's process, of living life as a journey. That one must do their best to love it *all*, the happy *and* the sad. And to live it all, each piece fully, each day. I'd scribe the judicious advice I found amongst Louis's bookshelves into my journal, needing to believe each letter as I wrote it, like a Benedictine monk cementing his faith by carefully recopying the Bible, word by word, in his most careful calligraphy.

"You are so young, so before all beginning, and I want to beg you, as much as I can, dear sir, to be patient toward all that is unsolved in your heart and try to love the questions themselves like locked rooms, and the books that are written in a very foreign tongue. Do not now seek the answers, which cannot be given you because you would not be able to live them. And the point is, to live everything. Live the questions now. Perhaps you will then gradually, without noticing it, live along some distant day into the answer." Letters to a Young Poet, *by Rainier Maria Rilke*

Rilke's words brought me peace as the days of the Asshole's gushing attentions decayed into nights of bluesy melancholic spells and drunken tirades. For the first few weeks after I returned, I had felt as if he and I were the only people in the whole world. He had said, "I hope that every man that has ever been with you lets you know how truly amazing you are." And he did. For a while…

But soon we began to slip out. Slip away. The world came in and interrupted us. Work. Errands. Troubled phone calls from Sophia. Thoughts of home. I wasn't sure why the Asshole couldn't be completely present with me anymore. We had such a short time to be together until he was "scheduled" to go home.

Was he giving up, regretting his decision, preoccupied? Naturally I assumed the worst. And my moods, my happiness, my sadness, my general state of being became completely tied up in his. As a sensitive person I had always been aware that I mirrored the emotions of others, but in a relationship my empathy magnified parasitically. I felt crazy, emotional, all the time, and I didn't know why. I guess that's because they weren't *my* emotions at all; I was just siphoning off the Asshole's natural temperament.

When I first returned to Playa Grande, the Asshole and I had celebrated. We drank excessively, partied, stayed up all night, but after a week of hangovers, my desire to get back to a healthy lifestyle outweighed my need to float away into an alcoholic stupor. I began to bring myself back to center, but the Asshole did not join me. Instead, he went missing more and more frequently as the weeks wore on, and I felt the distance between us growing greater. It wasn't long before I questioned my decision about Guatemala. *If he wasn't even emotionally present, why was I still here?*

When I retrieved him one evening at closing time from a Guaro-enhanced pool game at Rancho Diablo, I was nearly in tears as we walked out the gate and back into the darkness of the path leading home to the Rancho. Using a sense beyond sight and sound (I had not yet said a word), he said softly, "I'm sorry I'm not who I was when you first met me."

And I began to cry.

I felt so alone. Duped. I was angry with him for not being enchanted with me anymore. I was angry he'd convinced me to stay, *let* me stay, encouraged me to start falling and then pulled away in mid-air. And much to my surprise, I was able to tell him all of this.

And as I did, the Asshole started crying, too. He really was a drama queen. Maybe all poets are. But he was the first man I had ever seen cry. Tears weren't the end of the performance, and soon he began shouting and pounding his chest and egging me on, "Go ahead, you're angry. Tell me. Show me. Hit me. Yeah, hit me. Clock me, right here in the jaw," he pointed.

And I stopped and looked at him, brow wrinkling at the maniac's behavior, but he only had to ask me once. I wound up and knocked him, clinched fist in the face. And it felt great. The white cotillion gloves of childhood innocence fell to the ground behind me, and I stepped back to grind my foot into their shadow. Suddenly I found that I was no longer quiet. No longer obedient. No longer the wallflower at the back of the classroom.

I was a woman. And I had begun to speak. There was no choice.

The Asshole looked at me a bit shocked; then he smiled. I'm not sure if he didn't think I'd do it, or if he was just impressed that I could hit so hard. But I was on a roll. I raised the strength of my powerful new voice and spoke in strong full words from the diaphragm, no whimpering cries, no self-doubts. And for the first time in any relationship, I told him that he wasn't living up to his end of the deal, and I said, "This is what I expect. And this is why you have wronged me."

And it worked.

And things got better.

And then they got worse again... The Asshole just wasn't a good match for me.

But I learned that it's *all* part of it. The good, the bad, the highs, the lows, the uncertainty, the feelings of closeness and the feelings of distance -- they are all part of every relationship. And the talks that surface to address these issues are part of it, too. They're not the ugly stepsister in the relationship, the part where the guy acts like "Oh great, not 'the talk' again" (contrary to what former boyfriends had made me believe as they shut down even further the more I cried about them being emotionally unavailable.) Issues are always there, and these talks are the answer, not the problem -- an ongoing dialogue to update, clarify and vent. A way of getting closer. And instead of dreading bringing things up, instead of bottling it all away, or avoiding, or bolting, I began to embrace these talks when they surfaced because finally I was able to make them bring resolution. I was able to say what I needed. Clearly.

And as for my relationship with the Asshole, I learned to take it for what it was. *Amy, you got to fall in love. You got to fall fast and hard without looking back, without having to explain it to anyone, in a world with no boundaries, with a man who altered your view. Who helped teach you how to let go, and how to be honest with yourself.*

In the beginning that relationship helped bring me alive even further, and as he started to drift away, I realized that feeling so electric, so powerful wasn't just about the love he gave me. It was about the love I felt, the love I expressed, the love I made. Maybe he was the catalyst. Maybe he was the body who happened to be there at a time when I was ready. With the Asshole I felt passionate, yes, but passionate about *life*. And *that* feeling wasn't contingent on him. And that was the euphoria that I yearned to capture, to seize, to draw a roadmap to so I could get back there, without him, without anyone -- all on my own -- and carry it with me as I moved forward on my journey, south and beyond.

WANING CRESCENT...

"The poet would have stayed..., but he had come to realize with increasing clarity that relaxation, sunshine and contentment were doing irreparable damage to his muse." Corelli's Mandolin, by Louis DeBernieres

The first rain of the season lit up the world as it fell softly on the dry golden hills. Soft white mist hung just above the forest floor now carpeted with orange-and-purple Halloween crabs emerging from their holes in the thousands, clacking their claws at your toes as you passed, dancing, dancing. Giant double rainbows arced over the once-barren landscape evolving into 360 degree rainbow circles as they reflected in the mirrors of wet sand at low tide.

Onshore winds arrived, and the surfable hours in the day grew fewer. The shifting of seasons, the changing of times. The Asshole was scheduled to leave in a few days, and despite a part of me that felt incredible relief at the thought of being rid of his daily melodrama, another piece of me secretly wished he would know to cancel his flight home. Rainy season had finally arrived, and with it I knew -- finally, I just knew -- it was time to go. I had done my best to live *what's happening*, and now I supposed that meant leaving. And finally, finally, that possibility made me excited. I was ready. To start anew. Again.

In the end, the Asshole left me, on time, on the date his plane was scheduled to fly home. He left promises unfulfilled. Promises of a perfect relationship. Promises to return. With an I-love-you on his lips, I watched him disappear, blowing kisses from the back window of Francisco's minivan as it shuttered down the washboard road. I stayed strong. I didn't shed a tear. I went upstairs channeling thoughts of *distraction, back to work, make some breakfast...* Sometimes I could think myself out of feeling.

I walked into the kitchen past Carmen and Shirley and Juanita who were watching me expectantly. As I slid open the refrigerator door, I laid my hand on breakfast, and with my head still safely inside, burst into tears. When I turned around, Juanita was standing beside me, mother of five with one more on the way. She opened her strong arms and wide warm body, and I fell into her and I sobbed until I couldn't breathe. She held me and rocked me and warmed me like Mother Earth herself, and finally she said softly, *"Cinco días." Five days. It will all be over in 5 days.*

There were tears in her eyes, and Shirley's, and Carmen's. They'd all seen it before, lived it before. The heartbreak, the ripping, the uncontrollable sobs. They had all been there. A lover's promises vanished. And we sat together on wooden kitchen stools and laughed and cried and remembered.

"Aquí es su familia," Juanita said as she dried my tears. And my heart broke open with her love.

***

And she was right. The first two days were terrible. Marianela and Louis fed me chocolate chip cookies, and Sandra blended sugary banana and ice-cream shakes. I went back to the Rancho to sulk, but he was still there. His smell in my sheets, his shadow beneath my mosquito net. I went back outside. *How could this have happened? I had opened myself up to love him, changed my plans for him, and he had left me anyway.*

He'd said he'd call. He did. Twice. He said he'd write. He did. Often. If only to tell me how much he loved and missed me. If only to prolong the drama, the romance of distance. If only to make more promises. To say that he'd meet me. Meet me in Brazil, meet me in Peru, meet me in Playa Grande, meet me, meet me, empty. And the hope of "next time," of "soon" was borne forward. But he never came. Even though he promised. Over and over and drag-it-out over. And that was how I learned that most people don't do what they say they're going to do.

Louis said some people just can't. They're weak. They're distracted. They don't have the courage, or the heart to change their lives for the better. But *I* knew it wasn't that hard. I had done it. You just got on a plane. You just follow your heart or you run from your sadness, and somewhere along the line, if you sit quietly for a long enough time, you find peace within yourself. And if I could do it, he should be able to, right?

And although I slowly began the process of opening myself up again to people once I got back on the road, I lived in the moment. To experience. Maybe even to love. But just for the present. I never again trusted that they would come back. I never asked them to. And I never let the future slip into the equation.

***

On the day before I left Playa Grande, Louis asked me if I wanted to go on an errand with him to Huacas to pick up some bags of cement. I jumped into the truck, and we bumped down the dirt road in the big red truck, heads jerking from side to side like cartoon bobbles. Water exploded from muddy potholes beneath the tires as we traveled under a fresh canopy of newly-budding leaves, the jungle trees and vines seeming to have grown a foot each day since the rain began. And with the rains, a melancholy beauty had spread over the land.

After we finished at the *ferretería*, Louis pulled off to the side of the road, hopped out of the truck, and climbed up onto the hood. By the time I got out, he was reaching tall up into the treetops picking sweet red ripe *jacotes*. We giggled as we ate, and then drove on to a place he called *Mango Paradise* where we picked mangoes and ate the fruit of wild cashews (*marinoñes*). Sitting on the tailgate, neither of us spoke. We just sat and watched the flocks of parakeets and listened to swarming bees.

When we got home, we went out for my last surf. Sunset surf. We paddled out late, and outgoing tide was just about over. But we went out alone. And for two hours, I surfed some of the cleanest, most perfect, shoulder-high A-frames of my life. I watched the water turn gold, then a deep blue. The sky glowed cotton-candy pink, then bled red, then the curtain of twilight descended. Venus and Jupiter appeared, burning brightly. The silvery slivery moon would not rise until late.

Out to sea, a watercolor painting of pastels. On the shore, the most shades of blue I'd ever seen. As we jogged back toward the hotel, soft white wet sand under our toes, he said, "This is what most people dream of. Others can't even imagine it." I had lived it. Day after day.

The next evening, with the sweet scent of Playa Grande still fresh in my nose, I sat on Daisy's balcony at sunset snuggled in a fleece jacket against the San Jose chill. Coming back always felt like coming home. Daisy, Pascual, Marco and I sat down together at the dining table for *arroz con pollo* and to catch up, and by the next morning, I had bought a ticket. Without thinking too hard, I just walked into the student travel agency as I had done so many months before in California, and asked for the cheapest ticket to South America. Within a few moments the dot-matrix printer began to buzz and the die was cast. By the next afternoon, I'd be in Santiago, Chile.

***

STOLEN VERSES

in such a way as i have never
seen myself see another
i could
identify
with a man who once said
beauty in its purest form
exists

and being of simple mind
i fell through life yet toward her
blind, bound and surreal
i could not feel anything
i did not know her
could not show her how
much i needed love
i was twisting

wanting waiting writhing alone -- haunting that
i might have missed her
might never have kissed her touched her held her
loved her

                    -- The Asshole's Last Poem before leaving Playa Grande

RAINBOW RICE SACKS

Sometimes something tells me to stay, and sometimes
something tells me to move. And when I left Cusco after
two-and-a-half months, I just could not stop. I was a bus
junkie. Bumpety, rickety, broken-down, change-the-tire-again,
chocked-full, radio-blaring buses carried me through southern
Peru, from the freezing fog of Colca Canyon to the unbroken
lines of Nazca, from the sand-boarding dunes of Ica to the
barking sea-lions of Paracas.

During those travel-insatiable weeks, I had plenty of time to
think, time to daydream, time to gaze out the window at the
fleeting landscape. My mind swirled and rattled in tempo with
the wind and the bus. One day I was jolted awake in my seat
after the driver had laid on the horn, screeched on the brakes and
hit something. Nothing out of the ordinary, but something made
me open my eyes. The ocean. A big blue long-forgotten friend
staring right back at me. It reached out its long cerulean arms
and massaged the worry lines from my forehead.

I smiled and stared at myself in the reflection of the window.
A baby behind me was crying. The little girl to my left had chicks
in her lap that peep-peeped as they rustled around in a paper bag.
And there I was, with my black headband holding down my
hairpuff which had finally grown back to the bottom of my ears.
A woven bracelet, an Andean Cross necklace on a black leather

strap, fingers full of gaudy rings, dirty cargo pants, mud-encrusted boots, the whole thing. Not only had I become a backpacker -- I'd become a backpacker who'd been gone over a year.

Those were the ones who had always scared me, the backpackers who had the *look*. I remembered the first time I'd seen it, meeting a girl coming back from Puerto Viejo in Costa Rica on one of my first bus trips -- guitar slung over her shoulder, holes in the armpits of her ratty orange T-shirt, tattered hemp jewelry strung about every appendage. What had unsettled me about those travelers was not what they wore, but the look in their eyes. They looked somehow past you into a splendor that existed far-off. That *look* indicated a permanence, visual evidence to an outsider that that person's journey had changed their life in the deepest reaches of their brain, and that, well, you could never go home again. I wondered if others saw it in *my* eyes.

The *look* indicated clarity. Realization. An acceptance through experience that the world moves along at its own pace whether you're in a hurry or not. A perspective that you gain when eventually you relax into your surroundings, start *really* observing, taking it all in, absorbing the beauties and the smudges in the world and thinking about where you fit into it all. Maybe it was a giving-up of illusions of a certain future, anticipations that would inevitably lead to disappointment because your mind can always come up with a smoother transition back into your old world than the universe might have in store. And I got that. And if that meant that my journey had changed me, had molded me permanently into a different unrecognizable form -- if that meant that I had the *look* -- than I was ready to scare the ba-jeebies out of any new backpacker who boarded that bus.

***

Eventually, I found myself in the urban sprawl of Lima, stopping only to change buses in the station for destinations farther north. I bought a ticket to Huaraz, a winter wonderland of snow-capped views and quaint village charm, and settled into a hard, sticky, plastic seat in the terminal to wait for the bus' imminent departure. I spotted a girl sitting alone a few rows away, bobbed blond hair, blue eyes, big backpack. We made eye contact, and she smiled. I returned her smile shyly and went back to scrutinizing my guidebook. Out of the corner of my eye, I saw her get up and return two minutes later with a drippy lopsided soft-serve ice-cream cone. That was my kind of girl.

Her name was Ali. She was from Canada. And in all my time traveling through South America, she was one of only three women I had met along the way who was traveling alone. Not on a break from the Peace Corps, not on vacation with friends, not hanging on a boyfriend for illusory support. Truly traveling, for the sake of traveling, for as long as the money would hold out, alone.

We connected straight off. Finishing each others sentences, relaying stories with the same type of wonder and enthusiasm, it felt like we'd fallen out of an old forgotten friendship. Synchronicity has a way of never letting you down, and Ali, of course, was also on her way to Huaraz. We talked the whole way there. She was a geographer who had just come from the Atacama Desert in Chile looking for work that hadn't panned out. Just a few years older than me, she had already traveled through Australia, New Zealand and Southeast Asia (I took mental notes). When we arrived in Huaraz at 10pm, we found a hostel and agreed to meet for breakfast the next morning.

We both intended to use Huaraz as a base for hiking into the Cordillera Blanca, the highest and most famous mountain range in the northern Peruvian Andes, and decided to go together to look for a guide. But when we arrived at the tourist office to inquire, the man who worked there was so convincing that trekking the four-day Santa Cruz loop was *"no problema"* (watch out, there's that phrase again), we gained enough confidence to shop for fifteen kilos of food at the central market, rent camping equipment, and make plans to set off early the next morning on our own.

And so, with little time to think ourselves out of our independent adventure, the two *solas* joined forces and headed out into the great beyond. Loaded down with everything from powdered soup to alpaca socks, being self-contained gave us ultimate freedom to camp when and where we wanted. Damp xeroxed trail map in hand, we took a taxi to the trailhead and made our first bootprint in the Santa Cruz loop. In the following four days, we saw no other hikers.

The vast sweeping plains and towering mountains of the Cordillera beckoned before us as we started down the trail with strong steps. I felt like was floating through a dream as the scenery changed from low valleys, to rolling hills, to pampas, to snowcapped peaks. Focused on the beauty and open space that surrounded me and energized by a positive inspiring companion, I smiled and walked as the weight of my pack and the burning in my legs rarely entered into my consciousness.

Ali was really quite amazing. She made plans easily and took care of business with no stress. She gazed in wonder at the beauty of life all around her. She accepted my cranky non-talking mornings and always got up first to go to the stream for water (which gave me giardia -- again) to make the hot chocolate. She never complained. She took my picture for mom wherever I asked. She carried the heavy half of the tent. She appreciated how good food tasted outside. She made me laugh. We talked about feminism and politics and religion and capitalism. And in the toughest times, she smiled. Being with her reminded me of an encounter another *sola*, Laurie Gough, describes in her book, <u>Kite Strings of the Southern Cross</u>:

"*Into blackness we talk while setting up her tent. We talk deep into the night of our travels, adventures and loves. Travelers sometimes pour their hearts out to each other, as if we're each others angels. We say, Of course you're crazy to be roaming the world alone; I'm doing the same thing.*

'Do you ever think we should be settling down? Should we try to stay in one place for a while? Get married, acquire furniture?'

'No.'

'Me neither.'

'Silly thought.'

'I own a bookshelf, two bikes, a bunch of clothes and a bunch of books.'

'Me too, and a coffeemaker.'

'What about a man? Shouldn't we find one of those?'

'I've had plenty of those.'

'Me too. Always fun.'

'Always fun, fascinating.'

'I like the ones I know I can't stay with.'

'Of course, the ones entirely unsuitable.'

'Safer that way.'

'Then we can leave, go exploring again, see more of the world. We have

to. This is our natural state, to be wandering explorers, seekers.'
'We're born alone, we die alone.'
'We're explorers.'
'This is our destiny.'
'Our hearts are pure and free.'
'And wild.'
'We're weird.'
'Probably.'"

***

When I first began to travel alone, I became intuitively aware of a recurring feeling of acceptance when I interacted with local women. When I walked into a restaurant, a hostel, a market, my bright inquisitive eyes and respectful pause was rewarded with an almost-undetectable wink and knowing smile. I had begun to discover the sisterhood.

The sisterhood was everywhere. Its pervasiveness told me, *You are me. I am you. We know each other* -- all without words. When I traveled, I felt welcomed, comforted, excited to be in the company of women... And then I felt angry.

Why was now the first time in my life that I was experiencing this bounty? Why did I have to go abroad to find it? This unconditional boundless beauty? My culture robs women of this bond by labeling any love between women as deviant. If we become too close, we are called lesbians. If we become too powerful, we are called witches. Our bonds, magic and sisterhood are crushed before women themselves have an opportunity to discover how powerful we are as a collective group. In my culture, women have been pegged against one another for so long that we now do it to ourselves. Feminists vs. housewives, career women vs. mothers. *Which kind of woman are you? Take a stand. Pick a side.* Labels, narrowing of categories and negative connotations toward all the categories that are created keep women from joining in their powerful mystical energy that has been present (often on the periphery) throughout the ages.

But for now, I was here, on the road, where despite cultural differences, the walls between us were not as strong as the bonds among us. And on the road, I gathered energy from the sisterhood, from local women to other women travelers. All I needed to do was ask -- when I got in trouble, lost, emotionally disoriented -- and a sister would hold my hand and point me, without judgment, in the right direction.

***

Day after day Ali and I followed the not-so-definitive trail, sliding down rocky paths, jumping mud bogs which too often ended in goo up to our knees. We got chased by a bull (guys can be so territorial) and ate snowflake-and-avocado sandwiches on the spongy bank of an icy blue lake. The bright sky whisked with clouds bent down to kiss sheer mountains springing up from the ground like fresh sprouts. Two black-and-white cows inquisitively lifted their heads from a pond frosted with floating red flowers. *Campesinos* drove herds of donkeys along the path and greeted us with a *Bienvenidos* or *Buenos Dias*. As I climbed up the sandy path through the valley, wound along the switchbacks, and scaled the granite boulders along a rushing river of Crayola-forgotten blue, the sun warmed my skin, and I took in a deep breath. The chill of the wind made my nose drip and cleaned out the cobwebs in my head. I could feel my smile beaming although Ali was far ahead and there was no one to see it. Total tranquility.

For four days, we trekked the Santa Cruz hiking loop and ascended and descended thousands of meters among towering snowy passes. And despite cold nights of undercooked spaghetti and freezing mornings when the sun didn't flow into the valley until 10 a.m., I realized that I loved trekking. Volcán Villarica. Patagonia. The Inca Trail. The Cordillera Blanca. The external beauty was machine-gun-fire to the senses, but perhaps even more important was the internal journey of body and mind. A mandatory quietude for the brain to unravel insecurities, for the legs to walk off worries. And then silence. Of the mind, of the world. Out. Away. Alone. A walking meditation. The landlubber's version of surfing.

***

We continued on our journey, treading down the narrow dirt path with no one ahead and no one behind. Every once and a while, we would come upon a small house made of branches and mud, sometimes covered by a plastic tarp flapping in the wind.

Children and adults alike would look up from their work and play and wave. "Hello!" echoed the music of their voices.

The poverty here was astounding. Initially, I had been hesitant to come to South America because I worried that I would be confronted with poverty, feel sad and helpless, feel like an oppressor, a rich foreigner, and be racked with guilt. When I thought of poverty, I thought of urban poverty, neighborhoods in big U.S. cities, Los Angeles, D.C., Chicago. Crime, homelessness, hopelessness in a barren concrete landscape. But this was rural poverty and seeing it firsthand was seeing poverty differently.

The people we met in Peru's northern Andes were undeniably poor. They didn't usually use money; they didn't have much of it anyway. The only food they had to eat were the purple potatoes they had planted in the ground. The spearmint leaves growing in the sun. The water from the quick-moving stream. Their homes stood solitary, miles from their nearest neighbor, where fruit trees swayed in the breeze and berry bushes grew wild at the foot of one of the world's most beautiful landscapes.

Most of the people we met here had never been to Huaraz just thirty kilometers away. They owned very little of financial value. They had no access to healthcare or schools. But they were not hopeless. They smiled a lot, more than most people one might pass on a city street. They had so little on which to subsist, and yet they were heart-breakingly generous. Ali and I were frequently invited in for mint tea. No one ever asked me for money. A little girl once asked me for a pen, and a woman asked me if I had something to help an itchy rash which she exuberantly rolled up her sleeve to show me.

People worked hard, their cheeks wind-whipped into rosy-red circles from harsh years out on the land. They were poor, but they were not down-and-out. They were not surrounded by cement and unemployment and abandonment, but beauty, and family, and love. Their lives were not easy. And certainly not romantic. But they existed amidst a tradition of a simplicity that many modern people had forgotten. A simplicity which had not always been regarded with pity, but rather with acceptance and gratitude in greeting every day.

***

On the fourth and final day of the trek, Ali and I arrived at the tiny town of Vaqueria just in time to catch a ride with the weekly delivery truck. It would give us a ride to Yungay where we could catch the bus back to Huaraz. When the driver opened the back of the truck for us, I never would have guessed that it would be one of the most memorable days of my journey.

The sides of the pickup were built high with horizontal wooden slats, a configuration I had previously associated with the transport of cattle. I climbed up onto the tailgate, stepped over the rainbow-colored rice sacks, past the piles of particle-board furniture, and stood next to a group of women who sat in the back corner of the truck. Their long black braids streaked with gray were tied neatly together mid-way down their backs, and their dark bowler hats sat perched atop their heads ready to take flight like crows in the wind. One woman patted the rice sack next to her inviting Ali and I to sit down.

When we had negotiated the price for the ride with the driver, he had told Ali and me that we would have to hide when we drove past a nearby inspection station because he was not supposed to be transporting foreigners. My visit to San Pedro prison briefly popped into my head, and I wondered what the consequences were if the guard did find us. But we were committed now. The diesel engine shuddered and grumbled, and the truck pulled away from town. The woman sitting next to me smiled a gap-tooth smile, reassuring me with a tap on my thigh as she chewed coca leaves and spoke in the rising and falling tones of Quechua.

After about fifteen minutes the truck slowed and pulled up to the inspection point. I held my breath, completely motionless, and one of the men in the back of the truck gently pushed my head down so that I could not be seen as the guard peeked between the cracks in the boards. I could hear men talking inches from my face and the clunk-clunk-tap of the guards checking for false panels in the body of the truck. They did not open the tailgate. And then we rolled away. The other passengers smiled at me.

A kilometer or so down the road, the truck pulled over, and the driver yelled out the window, "OK. Now you can look out."

I stood up on the stacked rice sacks like the others were doing, but barely managed to peek my head above the tall wooden panels. The man who had pushed my head down now climbed up onto a desk being transported in the back of the truck and pulled his wife up with him to get a better view of the dramatic passing landscape, her layers of just-below-the-knee skirts flirting playfully with the wind. Tiny tornadoes twisted my hair into tangles as I looked up into the bright blue sky, the smell of the dusty road sneaking between the slats. Still, stretching at the tiptoes of my hiking boots, I just couldn't see enough. Just a few more inches...

Passengers moved and shuffled, trying to get a better view. One man crawled out of the truck's bed, up on top of the cab of the moving vehicle, and positioned himself in a wooden luggage box which balanced atop the cab. Triumphantly perched like a cross-legged raptor in his nest, his head rotated rapidly up, down, around, taking in the new astonishing views. Now beaming, he motioned for Ali and me to climb up and join him.

Now that looks dangerous, said my inner voice.

I hesitated, but the woman who had reassuringly tapped my thigh earlier gave me a little push, so I climbed up on top of an unfinished dresser and stepped up to the cab's roof as the truck continued its unapologetic pursual of pothole collisions. I wiggled into the wooden box whose width ran the width of the cab and whose depth was no more than four inches (I have no idea how it was attached to the truck). There was nothing to hold on to but the tiny piece of 2x4 in front of me, and I envisioned my body being flung into the grassy meadows far below the first time the driver braked too hard. But before I had a chance to look up from positioning myself, the truck arrived at the top of the final mountain pass it had been climbing, and I stopped and just looked around me. We were so high that the mountain peaks which had towered up from the valley during our trek were now so close that I could taste the snow blowing off their misty peaks.

As the truck inched ahead, it hesitated briefly as it straightened out at the top of the pass. Tip, tip on the fulcrum. And then, like a rollercoaster, it abruptly bucked forward to meet the sharp grade below and tilted to reveal a dirt road steeper than I'd ever seen. A skeletal graveyard of rusted-out buses which had catapulted off the side of the sheer cliff provided a visual history of past travels. I heard the cosmic amusement park fans begin to cheer as the truck pitched forward and ran down the hill, the Quechua passengers screaming with wild abandon, wind rushing against their faces, bowler hats flying, hands high in the air.

Thirty tenuous hairpin turns wound down into the valley below. And as we turned down each one, I felt something inside of me release. The truck crawled inch by careful inch as I sat atop it all, clutching the creaky board near my folded knees for dear life, the truck twisting and turning down the narrow switchbacks into the valley from which the snowy peaks grew.

Atop our magic carpet, I looked down from the heavens onto a world filled with sunbeams. I glanced back into the bed of the truck, and rainbow rice sacks shone brilliant colors while *campesinas* of all ages giggled, as we bobbed from side to side through muddy potholes and miles of road.

"I have never felt so alive," Ali said in a whisper.

I felt sure I could jump up from my perch and dive into the bright blue sky where the white clouds had parted. The lagoon below sparkled aquamarine and translucent, so small, so distant. Mammoth ice crystals of luminous sapphires glowed from glacial elbows, joining magnificent peak with magnificent peak. Delicate golden wildflowers bent from tiny stems, flowing into the road like streams of sunshine. The colors. The colors glowed beyond an earthly atmosphere. So high. We were so so high. And as we approached town, children ran to the road waving and calling hello, dogs biting at the tires. And still I floated above the world.

I have never felt so alive.

I have never felt so alive...

PART V:
THE RETURN TO MOONTIME

NEW MOON, OLD MOON

Online banking is great. You can access your account anytime from anywhere in the world. Now I use it all the time. But back when I was traveling in South America, I did it old school. A pencil, a few pages at the back of my journal, and lines and lines of scratched-off traveler's check numbers, bank withdrawal amounts, and paper-clipped credit card receipts.

And as I sat in a dimly-lit internet café in Quito, Ecuador, I stared at the dog-eared page at the back of my journal, and I realized that the inevitable had finally caught up with me. I had $126 in my bank account. $126 and a return paper ticket to Los Angles, California.

It hadn't taken me by surprise; I had always been quite diligent in keeping up with my accounts. In fact, in the last few weeks as the impending financial doom drew closer, I had pinched every penny. But just because I knew it was coming, it didn't mean it was any easier to look at $126.

Part of me knew it would be fun to go home, see everyone, show photos, but the other part of me knew that the high would wear off after a few short weeks, and then I would find myself in a city that no longer felt like mine, with no job, and no place to live except for the home of my understanding parents and the couches of my tolerant friends. And soon, all that would remain for me in Los Angeles would be the financial necessity of getting back to the life I had left behind almost two years before. And it just didn't feel right anymore.

I knew friends would have moved on, made other friends -- friends that didn't take off and move to foreign countries. I knew my favorite little neighborhood would have changed, and the cute guy with the dark wavy hair probably didn't even work at the coffeehouse on Los Feliz Boulevard anymore. I did not hold illusions about what it would mean to go home. I knew it would be OK, but I also knew I would probably have a really hard time at first, maybe for longer, because the *me* that had left home, wasn't the *me* that was coming back. And I didn't know where I would fit -- or even if I wanted to.

I set down my empty coffee cup, turned toward the keyboard and signed onto my email account. And what I saw there sent electricity jumping through my fingertips, a warmth radiating up into my chest. A message glowed with a strobe-like heavenly light. Slowly, deliberately, I clicked the indigo blue address: Hotel Las Tortugas.

Dear Amita,

How are you? I know it has been a long time since we've written, but things have been pretty bad here. Louis and I are fighting all the time, and I think we're going to split up. It's really pretty sad, and I've been crying a lot, and no one can concentrate on work here.

How much longer will you be in South America? I was just writing to see if you might want to come back and help us at the hotel. I want to go to San José for a while to get away, and Louis's mom has cancer, and he will have to go back to Florida. We really need someone to come manage the place, and since the girls already know and love you, I thought I would ask. I know you wanted to learn how to run a small business some day. Louis can teach you the accounting, the payroll, the worker's benefits, and you already know the email and what to do with the guests. I'm not sure how long this will go on, but we'll pay all your expenses and give you a monthly stipend you can save. If you stay here a year, you could probably save enough for another year of travel.

I just don't know what's going to happen here, and it would be good to have someone to help out who knows how the place works. Let me know what you think.

Love, Marianela

I felt it all at once, as if she had been there holding me, her arms wrapped tightly in a sorrowful embrace, tears running down her face. Her sadness, her split, her call for help. Louis's mother's impending death. I didn't quite know how to feel. At first, I just felt sad. And then slowly, it dawned on me selfishly that this was my way out. Out of going home too soon, out of the urban sprawl of Los Angeles, out of $126...

But was returning to Playa Grande a step forward or a step back? I was wary of going back to what appeared to seem familiar. Clearly things had changed in Playa Grande. But I had learned that if I expected nothing and arrived with a clean slate, then I could not be disappointed. I must remain open to all that could be. And it appeared from Marianela's letter that all that could be was quite infinite with possibilities.

As much of a gift as that letter was, as much of an opportunity, I still felt mixed about *going back*. I had left a lot of happiness there. And a lot of sorrow. I had grown, and been pulled, and been tested. But I was stronger now. And maybe things would be easier. I knew that at least things would be different.

So I signed off of the computer and pivoted in my hard wooden chair to an empty section of table. I flipped open my journal until I found a nice blank page, and I made two columns, as I always had. Pros on the left. Cons on the right. I sat there for a few minutes, scribbled some things down, but it seemed so superficial, so sterile, so void. *Where was the spot to write what I was feeling, what I really* wanted? It was just a list, staring coldly back at me, divided into stark columns of black and white. And I didn't feel so black and white anymore. So I closed my journal, and I walked out the door.

I walked up the narrow cobbled streets of Quito past towering Spanish cathedrals dwarfed by a backdrop of 5000-meter volcanoes. I took a bus out of town and stood on the centerline of the earth and watched a display of water swirling naturally in opposite directions at each side the equatorial monument. I shared a taxi up to Otavalo market where I walked among the bright reds and oranges and blues of the llama-wool rugs that hung unfurled from merchant's stalls and flapped in the strong wet wind of an oncoming storm.   I didn't speak to anyone. Or to myself. I just walked.

And soon, I knew what to do.

I just knew.

***

If you follow your heart, the one that exists deep inside your *sola* self apart from the desires of others, and you trust the universe to show the way, it can bring you to places far beyond your imagination, to happiness, peace and joy that you never knew existed. And if your faith in your self is strong enough, it can take you to a place where time does not exist --
Where days melt into one another,
And every sunset is a work of art on a canvas
        as big as the sky…
Where the tides tell us the time,
And the moon's cycles show us the way,
Waxing and waning,
Moving and flowing
Month after month, year after year.
And if you let them,
The layers will fall away --
And all that is left
Is what is real,
What is essential,
What matters…

AUTHOR'S NOTE

The events in this story took place over the two-and-a-half years I spent living alone in Central and South America. Everything I've written about actually happened, but occasionally characters, conversations, and events have been combined or streamlined for more effective flow of story. Names and identifying details of some people have been changed to protect the identities of the innocent -- and the not-so-innocent. Conversations are written as accurately as remembered and are drawn from the many journals I kept during that time, but are not intended to be exact quotations. At its core, this is a story of a journey and is not intended to be a journalistic endeavor. I hope that the reader enjoys it as such.

KEEPING IN TOUCH: AN AFTERWARD

My best friend, Kree, married a teacher she met in Paraguay and has since taught in the United Arab Emirates, Bolivia, Vietnam and Malaysia. She has two daughters, both of whom were born in La Paz, Bolivia, bilingual bicultural citizens of the world.

The Asshole and I thankfully lost touch over time after a series of drawn-out promises and after I blocked his email address. Last I heard, there was a warrant out for his arrest.

Simon and I kept in touch for many years. He completed his degree in garden design in London. After his last letter when he mentioned a new girlfriend, he no longer responded to my correspondence.

Louis. Ahh, Louis, what can I say? He's changed a thousand times since I moved away, but at his inner core, he is always welcoming, challenging, and wise. He continues to run Hotel Las Tortugas, and all the guilas still work for him. He still plays a pivotal role in fighting for the preservation of the natural environment in Playa Grande and the survival of the leatherback sea turtles whose existence is as fragile as ever. His recent opponents include Century 21 who has cut up the dry forest into tiny parcels and continued to develop the once-pristine beachfront, a new wave of expat surfers who've thrown up a cluster of small hotels, and even the "turtle scientists" themselves whose experiments and research have coincided with the recent dramatic decline in turtle populations. Louis is edging toward 70, surfs almost every day, and even dropped a few new *Louisisms* on me last time I visited. He is on wife #3.

As for the guilas, their spirits continue to flourish, and most everyone is still working at the hotel. Juanita has had two more children. Johanna mastered the English language and moved from the kitchen to reception, a job which she now shares with Carmen. Shirley had a little girl who sways on tiny legs and loves to dance. And all is well in the hearts of the strongest women I know...

Marianela married a boogie-border named Big Wave Dave, whom she divorced a few years later. They had a daughter together, and Marianela lives in Matapalo and manages beachfront property in Playa Grande.

My heart breaks to report that Alex was murdered in 2007 in a tragic assault and robbery. He taught English in southeastern Costa Rica after he'd finished college, a venture through which Marianela and Louis supported him financially and emotionally. He was well-loved by his students and colleagues alike, and he had just been voted Teacher of the Year. We have lost great beauty, humor and gentle-heartedness with Alex' passing. We are all deeply-saddened.

Paulina fell in love with a Frenchman and left Chile; she moved to Paris and had a baby girl.

Eveline moved back to Switzerland where she ate all the braided honey wheat bread she could. She left culinary school, got married, had a baby and now teaches English in elementary school.

Jan married his beautiful secretary, Carmen, and left his high-rise job to start his own eco-tourism business offering trips for Europeans around Brazil. They have two children.

Stefanie graduated with her Masters in Geology and works for the Canadian government. Caroline got married and teaches snowboarding in Squamish, British Columbia.

Pascual passed away a few years ago. Daisy and Marco were still living in San Jose a few years ago. Sadly, my last few letters have been returned, and we have lost touch.

As for me, the journey is still evolving. I met the love of my life during that second season in Playa Grande to whom I've been blissfully unmarried for fifteen years. We continue our travels, both separately and together, and have worked in various capacities, from teaching scuba diving, to going on environmental conservation grants, to becoming nuclear mechanics at a power plant. Life holds many surprises. For now, I will enjoy every moment of my happy not-so-ending...

ACKNOWLEDGEMENTS

To Arik, for his unwavering belief that I can do anything... For his countless re-reads, mugs of strong coffee with honey, encouragement, and for acknowledging and embracing the me that existed before the me-and-you.

To Kree Bjorn, who I am most proud to call my best friend, for embracing me when I needed it most, and making me always feel like a WonderWomyn.

To my parents, sisters, grandparents, for their love and support in my journey.

To Laurie and Steve, for providing me with the world's most perfect writing environment.

To Mari and the Flamingo Express, for giving me a place to be, and to Ron for his reads.

To Allan, for keeping the wine flowing.

To MM and all my friends DCPP, who make my adventures a continuing financial possibility.

To AG & CBT, for growing the seed, for inspiring in me the courage to explore a bigger world, and for lovingly nudging me out of the nest.

To Louis, for helping me grow up, and for opening me up to a world that I would have otherwise not known.

To the *guilas*, for their undying friendship, no matter how many years or how many miles come between us.

To Daisy, for being my family when my family was not there.

To Mama Ocean, for her beauty, inspiration, solitude and powers of recalibration.

GLOSSARY

abierto open

acaraje fried cakes stuffed with shrimp and peppers sold in
    Northeast Brazil

agencia de turismo tourist agency

altiplano high plateau

aquí here

arco iris rainbow

Aymara native ethnic group who has lived for over 2000 years in
    the Andes and Antiplano regions of South America,
    primarily in what is now Bolivia and Peru

baile a dance; in Guanacaste the dance pavilion is set up after the
    bullfights

barrio neighborhood

berimbau a single-string percussion instrument, a musical bow,
    now associated with the Afro-Brazilian martial art of
    capoeira

bienvenidos welcome

bolinho small balls made of flour, sugar and water, deep-fried in
    oil, which taste like donuts

bolo de trigo griddle cake of Brazil

brujos, brujas witches

buenos dias good afternoon

cachaça local hard alcohol of Brazil

café con leche coffee with milk

caipirinha characteristic alcoholic drink of Brazil made from
cachaça, limes, sugar, and ice

campesinos, campesinas people who live in the countryside

candomblé religion which came to Brazil between the mid-
    sixteenth and mid-nineteenth centuries carried by African
    priests who were brought as slaves; characterized by
    believers going into trances or becoming temporarily
    possessed by spirits

capoeira martial art with a strong acrobatic component developed
    in Brazil around 1520 as a way for slaves to defeat their
    oppressors and disguised as a form of dance played with
    music

casa house

capybara largest rodent in the world; found in South America

casado literally "marriage"; also refers to the set meal of the day

carnecería butcher shop

cascada waterfall

Centenario fine Costa Rican rum

cerros hills

chantilly whipped cream

chapolinos Guanacastecan slang for thieves, robbers

chica fuerte strong woman

chicha sweet corn alcoholic brew or hard grain alcohol similar to
   moonshine

chisme gossip

cholita Bolivian women in traditional dress, including bowler hat,
   shawls, layers of knee-high pettycoat skirts and two long
   braids tied together at the ends behind the back

cielo sky

cintura waist

como esta usted? how are you?

como se llama? what is your name?

cortado type of strong coffee made with espresso

crampons metal spikes used on shoes to prevent slipping on ice

Cristo Redentor Christ the Redeemer, a landmark statue atop one
   of Rio's hills

Cuatro Plumas one of the most popular brands of guaro liquor

cueva cave

cumbia popular campesino-style folkdance involving drums,
   claves, woodwinds and flutes where the basic rhythm
   structure is 4/4

Dios mió! Oh my God!

djembe medium-sized hand drum of African origin

doce twelve

donde esta? where is?

donde vive? where do you live?

dos por uno two for one

dueña woman owner of a hotel, house, business, etc., or a woman
   head of household

El Fin del Mundo the End of the World is the nickname for
Ushuaia, Argentina, the farthest southern city in the world
emocionante exciting; emotional
empanada deep-fried pastry filled with cheese or meat
esta there is; it is

familia family
ferretería hardware store
fiestas parties, festival
focas seals

giardia a flagellated protozoan parasite often found in unclean
water that infects the gastrointestinal tract and manifests
with symptoms of severe diarrhea, abdominal cramps,
bloating, flatulence, fatigue and nausea
glaciar glacier
Gracias a Dios Thank God!
gringo, gringa a white person or foreigner
gorro wool cap
Guanacaste northwestern province in Costa Rica
Guanacastecan the people of northwestern province in Costa Rica
Guaro Costa Rican potent alcoholic drink made from sugar cane
liquor
guilas slang for "the girls"; nickname for the female staff at Hotel
Las Tortugas

hacienda house on a farmstead, often cattleland
Hare Krishna believers of the theology that the Hare Krishna
sixteen-word Vaishnava mantra, when said aloud, brings
about a higher state of consciousness that ultimately takes
the form of the pure love of God (Krishna)
hielo ice
hierba grass
hola, como esta usted? hello, how are you?
hospedaje a hostel, usually informal, often a room in someone's
home
huevo egg

igarapé a stream wide enough for a canoe to pass through
iglesia church

Imperial a popular brand of Costa Rican beer
invierno winter

jacotes small, red, sweet-and-sour fruit with a seed in the middle

knickers panties, women's underwear

la casa de la familia the family's house
langostino small lobster without claws
Las Tres Marias the constellation of Orion; often known in South
    America as "The Three Marys," representing Mary of
    Nazareth, Mary Magdalene and Mary of Bethany
lavandería a laundry facility
leche milk
linda beautiful, pretty
llana llama llama wool
loro parrot

manjar Chilean caramel, usually spread on toast
marinoñes fruit of a cashew; yellow, orange or red when ripe;
    juices are clear but stain
mariposas butterflies
mate see yerba mate
mate de coca coca tea, made with leaves from the coca plant—the
    same plant from which cocaine is made; the tea it is only a
    mild narcotic and widely drunk in the Andean region to
    combat fatigue and altitude sickness
matrimonio double bed
me llamo my name is
media luna croissant, literally "half moon"
merengue type of lively, joyful, frantic-tempo music and dance
    where partners hold each other in closed position, dancing
    with small steps and slow turns, typically with four beats per
    complete turn
mola traditional hand-stitched cloth embroidery with intricate
    designs of animals to tell stories of the San Blas islands of
    Panama
momias mummies
mucha suerte good luck
muchas a lot; many

mucho gusto literally, "with much pleasure"; often used for "your welcome"

Navidad Christmas
no problema no problem

Olodum cultural activist group that fights racial discrimination and socioeconomic inequality through music, primarily drumming

Pachamama the benevolent fertility goddess of the harvest in Incan mythology who is frequently honored with food, water and even llama sacrifices; literally "mother earth" in Aymara
palafitos a stilt village or dwelling erected on bodies of water
panadería pastery shop, bakery
papagayo wild green parrots, or a northeast wind on the Pacific Coast of Costa Rica and Nicaragua
paraíso paradise
pareja a pair or a couple (often romantic)
pasa come in
peluqería haircutting shop, barber, beauty parlor
pensión accommodation for travelers; usually a rented room in someone's house
perro dog
pipas fresh young coconuts
pirarara giant catfish of the Amazon of which there are over 500 species
pirarcu the second largest fish in the world; native to the Amazon with large hard scales and growing up to ten feet long and 400 pounds
pisote also known as coatimundi or coati; masked, long-snouted, ring-tailed small mammals sharing similar markings as a raccoon
preservantes preservatives
preservativos condoms
pocas a few; a little bit
pueblitos tiny towns, villages

Quechua traditional indigenous culture and language in Andean
    regions in Bolivia, Peru and Ecuador
quiero I want

ranas frogs
rancho a hut constructed for basic living, often made from palm
    fronds
refugio refuge; often a shelter from the elements such as a ranger's
    station in a national park

salsa sauce; also, music with complicated percussion rhythms
    ranging from slow to fast within one song; danced with three
    steps during each of four beats, with the one beat being
    skipped used to shift weight from one foot to the other
salto waterfall
sencillo single bed
siesta nap, usually after lunch
sola alone (for a woman)

tamale corn meal stuffed with meat, wrapped in a corn husk and
    steamed
Tico, Tica a Costa Rican
Tierra del Fuego Land of Fire
Tío uncle
tortuga turtle
tranquilla calm, or as imperative to someone to calm down or
    relax
trucha trout

valiente brave or valiant
vamos let's go
verano summer
vino tinto red wine
vizcacha long-tailed rodent related to chinchillas (but to me, it
    looks like a green rabbit)
vicuña wild relative of the domestic llama and alpaca, found in
high altitudes
volcán volcano

womyn preferred feminist spelling of woman (without the "-man")

yerba mate strong tea drunk hot or cold in Paraguay and Argentina; water is poured over tea leaves in a special gourd and drunk from a metal straw; one gourd is often passed around a circle of friends

zampoña musical instrument, Andean pan flute made of reeds

A TRAVELER'S READING LIST

A Natural History of the Senses, Diane Ackerman
Eva Luna, Isabelle Allende
I Know Why the Caged Bird Sings, Maya Angelou
Illusions: Adventures of a Reluctant Messiah, Richard Bach
The Teaching of Don Juan: A Yaqui Way of Knowledge, Carlos
    Castanado
In Patagonia, Bruce Chatwin
By the River Piedra, I Sat Down and Wept, Paulo Coelho
Travels, Michael Crichton
Correlli's Mandolin, Louis De Bernieres
The Prophet, Kahlil Gibran
Kite Strings of the Southern Cross, Laurie Gough
The World According to Garp, John Irving
The Unbearable Lightness of Being, Milan Kundera
Marching Powder: A True Story of South America's Strangest
    Jail, Thomas McFadden
Zen & The Art of Motorcycle Maintenance, Robert M. Pirsig
Celestine Prophesy, James Redfield
Letters to a Young Poet, Rainier Maria Rilke
Fierce Invalids Home From Hot Climates, Tom Robbins
Jitterbug Perfume, Tom Robbins
Still Life with Woodpecker, Tom Robbins
Succulent Wild Woman, Sark
Nine Kinds of Naked, Tony Vigorito
The Color Purple, Alice Walker
In Search of Captain Zero, Allan C. Weisbecker

Proof

44614306R10179

Made in the USA
Charleston, SC
29 July 2015